WHERE AMERICA'S DAY BEGINS

WHERE AMERICA'S DAY BEGINS

A Reporter in Guam and Micronesia

(second edition)

Janet G. Go

Copyright © 2001 by Janet G. Go.

Library of Congress Number: 2002091315
ISBN #: Hardcover 1-4010-3369-5
         Softcover 1-4010-3368-7

All rights reserved. No part of this book may be reproduced or transmitted in any form or by any means, electronic or mechanical, including photocopying, recording, or by any information storage and retrieval system, without permission in writing from the copyright owner.

This book was printed in the United States of America.

To order additional copies of this book, contact:
Xlibris Corporation
1-888-7-XLIBRIS
www.Xlibris.com
Orders@Xlibris.com

CONTENTS

Acknowledgments 11
Foreword 15

Chapter One
    Hafa Adai 21
Chapter Two
    Jungle Journalism 35
Chapter Three
    Accidental Guests 70
Chapter Four
    Disasters, Natural and Man-Made 95
Chapter Five
    Lifestyle 127
Chapter Six
    Up, Up, and Away 151
Chapter Seven
    Celebrity Stopovers 179
Chapter Eight
    Hams and Gams 201
Chapter Nine
    Sailing Through Micronesia 211
Chapter Ten
    Island Hopping 244

Afterword 264
Appendix
    Information For Travelers 274

In Fond Memory of
Dorothy Karberg Fritzen

Dorothy Karberg was working for the *San Francisco Chronicle* when she met real estate editor Claus Alfred Fritzen. They were married in February 1936. While Claus served in the military, Dorothy worked as a reporter for the *San Mateo Times*. In 1967, the Fritzens retired to Guam, where Claus opened a real estate office. Dorothy took over business editorship of the *Guam Daily News* and, later, the *Pacific Daily News*. Seven years later, the Fritzens moved back to the U.S. mainland, wintering in Las Vegas and summering in Emeryville, California. Dorothy died of lung cancer in 1991.

Also by Janet G. Go

Non-fiction

Micronesia Visitor Guide
Where America's Day Begins, Confessions of a Jungle Journalist First edition copyrighted in 1998 by Janet G. Go

Novels

Dance of Desire
Waltzing on the QE2

ACKNOWLEDGMENTS

Many thanks to friends who shared their Guam experiences in this book: Dorothy Horn, Roy Anderberg, Hilda Netzley, Sheila Stevens, Priscilla Gaison, Betty Bennett-Lyon, Phyllis Rice, Dick Marsh, Sheila Mawhood, Jodell Rabe, Guam Reunion members, and the late Tere Rios-Versace and George Roberts.

Thanks also to the following individuals, who contributed vital information: Al Neuharth, Lee Webber, Madeleine Z. Bordallo, Robert Underwood, Pierre Salinger, Dirk Anthony Ballendorf, Suzanne Hendricks, and Alice Dean.

I salute my editors, who taught me the pearls, and perils, of jungle journalism: Joe Murphy, Carol McMurrough Green, Red Garrison, and Glenda Moore.

The following agencies provided invaluable assistance: Guam Visitors Bureau; Grand County Libraries at Fraser and Granby, Colorado; Micronesian Area Research Center, University of Guam; and Library of Congress, Reference and Bibliography Section, Washington, D.C.

Without the histories of Guam journalism written by Jackie Teare and the late Montie Protasio, many of these incidents would have been forgotten.

Si yu'us ma'ase' to the generous, friendly people of Guam who let me share their lifestyle.

Janet G. Go
Grand Junction, Colorado
August 2001

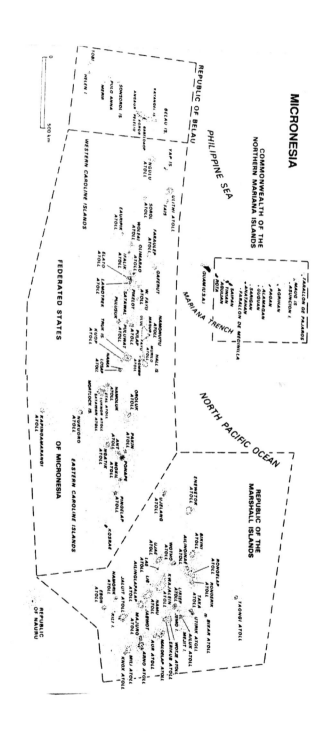

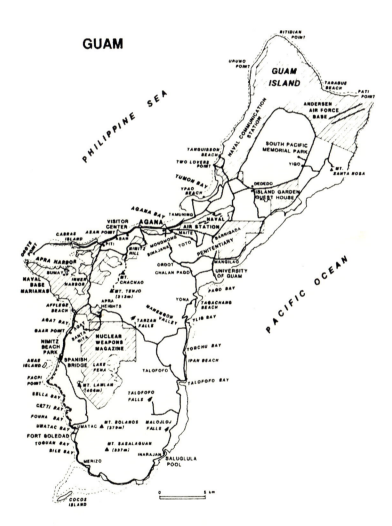

FOREWORD

Whenever Guam and Micronesia are mentioned, Americans smile enigmatically and change the subject.

Most Americans are unaware of this vast colony of their forgotten cousins, perched on islands like microchips in the Western Pacific Ocean, the world's biggest saltwater pond.

The U.S. Government, which has been sitting on Micronesia since 1945, considered the area to be of great strategic importance and the less the public knew the better.

In 1962, President John F. Kennedy issued National Security Action Memorandum 145 setting forth as policy "the movement of Micronesia into a permanent relationship with the United States." An American-oriented curriculum was used in the schools and many of the brightest students studied in the United States mainland. Large numbers of Peace Corps volunteers began arriving after 1966 to teach English, spread American attitudes, and speed social change. Beginning in 1974, color television, an important part of the Americanization program, was introduced throughout Micronesia.

This cultural region includes thousands of tropical islands scattered between Hawaii and the Philippines. Micronesia consists of four large archipelagos: the Marshalls, Carolines, Marianas, and Gilberts. The islands are scattered over 11,649,000 square kilometers of the central Pacific, north of the equator. Some 125 islands are inhabited.

Every island is different. The largest volcanic islands are Guam and Babeldaop, while Agrihan is the highest. Kwalajein is the world's largest atoll. Some are "high" islands with volcanic peaks, others are "low" islands of sand and coral. All of the Marshalls are coral atolls or islands. Micronesia's only active volcanoes are located in the Northern Marianas. The Caroline Islands include both coral and volcanic types. Kosrae, Pohnpei, and Chuuk are high volcanic islands. Guam and Belau are exposed peaks of an undersea ridge stretching between Japan and New Guinea, volcanic in origin but partly capped with limestone. Yap is an uplifted section of the Asian continental shelf.

Micronesia is one of the last frontiers on Earth. The mysterious ruins of Pohnpei and Kosrae rival those of Easter Island; "star wars" technology develops in the Marshalls; tradition-oriented Yap revolves around stone money; Belau and Chuuk rank among the world's premier scuba locales; and Japanese tourists cavort on Guam and Saipan.

When the first Congress of Micronesia met on Saipan in 1965, American officials were surprised by the political sophistication and solidarity displayed by the Micronesian legislators. In 1966 this congress asked President Johnson to appoint a status commission to expedite the transfer of political control from the American officials on Saipan to elected Micronesian leaders. Negotiations toward a new status began in 1969.

In 1972, the Micronesians rejected an offer of commonwealth status, which would have allowed the U.S. Government to exercise eminent domain over the areas it needed for military use. After that, Micronesia was fragmented into four separate entities: the Northern Marianas became the Commonwealth of the Northern Marianas, a permanent American possession with tracts of land assigned to the military; the four central districts–Yap, Pohnpei, Chuuk, Kosrae— banded together, proclaiming the Federated States of Micronesia in May 1979; and the compacts of free association included the Republics of the Belau and Marshall Islands. The United States is obliged by treaty to protect these islands and retains the right to use them for military purposes.

In 1998, Guam marked a century as a possession and an unincorporated territory of the United States. Two years later, Guam celebrated fifty years of U.S. citizenship, with the passage of the Organic Act. During ceremonies in 2000, the first civilian governor, Carlton Skinner, and former speaker of the Guam Legislature, Carlos P. Taitano, were honored.

This book is an account of my two years in Saipan working for the Trust Territory of the Pacific Islands, thirteen years on Guam working for the daily newspaper and the U. S. Navy, and travels by sea and air throughout Micronesia.

My reporter's view is told through news stories and Fourth-Estate humor, culled from my years as a journalist and U.S. civil servant. In 1998, I published the first edition of this book, which sold out. Due to popular demand, I decided to issue a second edition, which corrects the many errors that appeared in the original book. I've updated facts and rewritten sections, where possible.

Though some of my stories are thirty years old, they're still pertinent and, often, humorous. This is the story of people who made Guam and Micronesia what it is today, for better or worse.

Tourists, searching for remote, unspoiled islands in which to fish, snorkel, dive, and kick back, see Guam and Micronesia as tropical paradises. Reporters, as well as sociologists and economists, see something less. This book is not a handbook for travelers to the Pacific; it's a personal account of interest to anyone who wants to know more about the area.

Readers will notice I use two versions of Micronesian place names, which in the past decade have reverted to historical spellings. Early on in the book, I use the names I learned when I first stepped off an airplane in Saipan in 1964. In later chapters, I use "new" and "old" names, interchangeably.

For instance, the name of Guam's capital city, Agaña, has reverted to the early spelling, Hagåtña. The Guam Federation of Teachers now encourages the use of Chamorro, and there are no penalties in the public schools for speaking Chamorro, or Chamoru, as it's now spelled.

Although written fifteen years ago, the following musical parody from the Guam Press Club's 1986 Gridiron Show, "Paradise on Parade," continues to reflect the island's lifestyle.

G-U-A-M, Guam!

(Tune: "There Is Nothing Like A Dame")

We got beaches in the sun
We got hotels on the beach
We got miles and miles of roads
Fourteen holes in every mile
Garbage cans along the highway
Dogs and chickens eat in style
What have we got? A new rat race!

There are lots of things like mail and phones and traffic lights we haven't got—but, oh brother! We got sun and wind and clean fresh air in this place that is positively like no other!

There is nothing quite like Guam
Nowhere in the world
There is no place, cold or warm
That is anything like our Guam!

Nothing looks quite like Guam
No one cooks like on Guam
No place grows quite like Guam
No wind blows like on Guam
There's no rain like on Guam

No campaigns like on Guam
With all her problems, big and small,
There's just no place that is anything at all like
G-U-A-M, Guam!

CHAPTER ONE

Hafa Adai

"You've moved WHERE?"

"Guam. Micronesia," I answered.

"Where?" my friend repeated.

"MIC-RO-NEEES-I-A!"

"Mike WHO? Are you near Marlon Brando's island in the South Pacific?"

"No," I said. "Guam is in the western Pacific, north of the Equator."

The word Micronesia, derived from the Greek words *mikos* (small) and *nesos* (island), means many islands. Some 2,100 atolls and volcanic isles, representing 1,045.3 square miles of dry land, dangle like beads in a necklace across three million square miles of Pacific Ocean.

Anchored in the northwest corner of Micronesia, the Mariana Islands are tips of a submerged mountain range stretching 1,400 miles from Indonesia northeastward across the Philippine Sea to the Marianas and north to Japan's Bonin Islands.

Guam, the southernmost of the Mariana Islands, floats at 13 degrees North Latitude and 144 degrees East Longitude. The island is approximately 30 miles long and 4 to 12 miles wide, totaling 212 square miles. Its 78-mile coastline stretches 22 miles from Ritidian Point in the north to the village of Merizo in the south.

The island is surrounded by a 20-to 700-yard-wide fringing coral reef, broken only where harbors and streams flow into the ocean.

From the air, Guam looks like a pousse-café: layers of lapis lazuli sea, pink coral reef, turquoise lagoon, verdant palms, ironwood trees, and patina-green mountain jungles. Its shape resembles a giant human footprint or a fish diving into the sea: southern Guam is the head, northern Guam its tail, and Apra Harbor its back fin.

Millenniums ago, two volcanoes sank beneath the ocean to form Guam. Later, the chunks of land above water joined at a narrow waist, dividing the island in two. The northern end is a rolling limestone plateau, edged by cliffs rising 600 feet above sea level. Here, 828-foot-high Mount Santa Rosa provides a panoramic view of Puntan, a legendary giant whose body formed Guam.

As the legend goes, the mythical Puntan willed his magical powers to his sister, Fuuna. When Puntan died, she tossed her brother's body towards heaven: his breast became the sky, his eyes made the sun and moon, his eyebrows turned into rainbows, and his back became the earth. Fuuna turned Puntan's body over on its stomach, placed it in the water, and created Guam. Local names have been given to the giant's anatomy: Barrigada (side), Tiyan (belly) Hill, Hilaan (tongue) Point, and Achae (chin) Point.

Southern Guam comprises mountains and valleys, with open fields, jungles, waterfalls, rivers, and bays. A ridge of volcanic hills rises from 700 to the highest point on the island, 1,334-foot Mount Lamlam, meaning lightning in the native language of Chamorro.

Mount Lamlam could be considered the tallest mountain in the world, if measured from the top to its submarine base in the Marianas Trench, also called the Challenger Deep. Some 200 miles south of Guam, this deepest place on earth plunges 11 kilometers (35,800 feet), 9 kilometers lower than the Grand Canyon.

Archaeological evidence confirms that the ancient Chamorros were of Indo-Malayan descent. Linguistic and cultural similarities tie the Chamorro race to Malaysia, Indonesia, and the Philippines.

Geologically, Guam appears much as it did some 3,000 years

ago when Malayo-Polynesians, or Austronesians, crossed the Philippine Sea in hand-carved log outrigger canoes, called proas, with single, woven-fiber, triangular lateen sails. About 100,000 of these stalwart people settled in the Marianas and brought with them bananas, taro, breadfruit, yams, rice, coconuts, and betel nuts.

Chamorros were an advanced fishing, horticultural, and hunting society. They were expert seamen, who navigated by stars, winds, and ocean currents. Skilled craftsmen, they built unique houses, carved canoes, wove palm fronds, crafted pottery, and they liked to sing, dance, and spin legends.

They erected carved stone pillars, called lattes, in double rows. Upon the tops rested half-globe stones that supported wooden beams. Ruins of latte stones, dating from 1527 B.C., can be found in jungles throughout the Marianas and in Latte Stone Park in Agaña, Guam's capital. Some say you can smell a latte site a mile away due to the lingering odors of coconuts, bananas, and rice once stored in the structures.

Guam had a strong matriarchal society. It was the power and prestige of women that preserved the essence of Chamorro culture: the language, music, dance, and traditions.

In 1999, cave paintings were discovered in Guam that appear to have been made before the first Spanish ships arrived in the region centuries ago. The paintings were found in a cave on Guam's north coast. The cave was apparently used as an ancient burial site, and some fragments of human bones remained in the cave's dirt floor. The paintings, which have been confirmed as authentic ancient Chamorro art, show people gazing at specific constellations of stars and at what may be the image of a unique 16-month calendar used by early Micronesian navigators.

The island's first-known contact with the western world was on March 6, 1521, when Portuguese explorer Ferdinand Magellan, who circumnavigated the globe on behalf of the Spanish Crown, reached the Mariana Islands with a semi-starved, scurvy-ridden crew. His flotilla–the *Concepcion*, *Victoria*, and flagship *Trinidad*– put into port to refurbish supplies. During their three days on

Guam, they received fresh fruit, vegetables, and water and offered iron in exchange.

Magellan was impressed by the natives' sailing canoes and called Guam the Island of Lateen Sails. He described the islanders: "The men were handsome and powerfully built, and the women were usually opulent, busted, and graceful."

However, after experiencing the natives' sticky fingers and accusing them of stealing one of his skiffs, Magellan changed the name to the Isle de los Ladrones (thieves). Before he left Guam on March 9, Magellan and a landing party of 40 armed men went ashore, killed 7 men, and burned 40 or 50 houses and boats.

Exactly where Magellan landed has long been disputed. The popular Chamorro notion is that his three ships anchored in sheltered, reef-free Umatac Bay.

Present-day historians, however, conclude that Magellan probably dropped anchor at either Tumon or Agaña Bays, the two largest and calmest inlets on Guam's northwest coast, where boats could row safely over the top of the reef during medium to high tides.

Today at horseshoe-shaped Umatac Bay, fishermen sit mending their nets on the white sand beach in front of Magellan's monument. The original plaque, attached by the Guam Teachers Association, is believed to have been sold for scrap iron during World War II. In 1962 a granite plaque, donated by the Circulo Cervantino de Guam, was placed on the obelisk.

Disputed or not, Magellan Day, March 6, is celebrated annually in Umatac. Renamed Discovery Day by the 11th Guam Legislature in 1971, the festivities include a village fiesta and a reenactment of Magellan's landing: school kids and teachers, portraying Magellan and his crew, come to shore in motorboats, and Navy SEALS parachute into the bay.

The Discovery Day celebration in March 2001 spread over two weekends and attracted hundreds of onlookers to watch the re-enactment of the Portuguese sailor's legendary landing in Umatac.

This re-enactment involved more narration and more participation of younger people than in previous years. Nearly twenty children and adults, dressed in traditional Chamorro clothing, greeted a handful of men, who were portraying Spanish explorers arriving by sea. After a mock fight ensued between the Chamorro and Spanish men, three huts made of coconut leaves and wood were set on fire.

Carabao rides, a merry-go-round, and food stands selling shish-kabobs and fiesta plates were scattered around Umatac's village center during the event.

Since the 16th century, waves of conquerors, merchants, and adventurers swept across Guam like the constant ebb and flow of tides. The Marianas were meccas for explorers, pirates, whalers, and conquerors. Guam was a provisioning port of call for galleons sailing from Acapulco, carrying passengers, cargo, and Mexican silver to buy silks and spices in Manila.

Later, Spanish galleons and Miguel Lopez de Legazpi's three ships moored in Umatac Bay to lighter supplies between ship and shore. Legazpi, who claimed Guam for Spain in 1565, dubbed the native people Chamorros, the Spanish word for bald or shorn, meaning men who wore a topknot on the crown of their shaven heads.

In 1662 Father Diego Luis de Sanvitores, a Jesuit, arrived in Guam, where he became the chief missionary. He named the islands the Marianas in honor of Mariana of Austria, Queen Regent of Spain, who provided funds to establish a Catholic mission. He brought a measure of European civilization, including Christianity and trade.

The Chamorro chiefs on Guam, Rota, Tinian, and Saipan were impressed by the white man's possessions and inclined to welcome a new religion apparently associated with such things. But the chiefs would receive religious instruction only if common men did not. They feared that brotherhood in Christ would blur the rigid caste distinctions of Chamorro culture.

That same issue appeared in Micronesian islands. Religious

wars on Ponape were due to puritanical teaching of Boston missionaries who preached equality of all men before God. This idea disrupted the relationship between subjects and their feudal lords.

The second bloody foray on Guam happened when Spanish Jesuit missionaries accompanied Spanish secular powers to occupy the islands in 1668. The islanders rose in open rebellion against the Spaniards in the 1670s. During the Chamorros' battles against the missions, many were killed by the Spaniards.

After a brief peace, violence returned to the island. When Father Sanvitores baptized the infant daughter of Tumon's Chamorro chief, Mata'-pang, against the man's wishes, the chief killed the Jesuit. Ironically, Father Sanvitores himself had baptized Mata'-pang.

Among the Spaniards, the Gospel and sword were always coupled. This legacy of no separation of church and state can be seen in Guam today.

For the next 100 years, the Jesuits Christianized the Chamorros. The Spanish taught the Chamorros how to cultivate maize, raise cattle, and tan hides. Christians wanted Chamorros to adopt western-style clothing, learn the catechism, and give up their myths and gods. Both the population and language became creolized. Once Christianity was firmly established, the Catholic Church became the focal point for village activities.

By royal decree, the Fathers were expelled from the Marianas in 1769. Their work was continued by Augustinian friars from 1769 to 1899, when they, too, were expelled from Guam, this time by the American authorities after the Spanish-American War. The last two Spanish Augustinian friars left the Northern Marianas in 1908, during the German administration. Capuchin fathers replaced the Augustianians on Guam.

British raiders also contributed to the exploration of the Pacific. Baron George Anson, British admiral, sailed around the world to attack Spanish possessions. As first lord of the admiralty, he sailed from England with five ships in 1740. With only his flagship left and barely enough survivors of all the ships to work her,

Anson stopped at Tinian, north of Guam, for badly needed supplies.

In the 1870s, a British yachtsman was annoyed to find natives of Ponape talking English full of Americanisms, such as "I guess" and "fixing" things. The cause was simple: of 56 whaling vessels calling there a few years earlier, 49 had been American.

A quarter of a century later, in June 1898, Captain Henry Glass, USN, commander of the cruiser *USS Charleston*, captured Guam for the United States.

Guam and Puerto Rico were ceded to the United States in the Treaty of Paris, following the Spanish-American War. Today, Guam remains a possession and an unincorporated U.S. territory.

Reminders of Spanish colonial rule remain in the Plaza de España in Agaña. The Plaza contains ruins of the 1736 Spanish Governor's palacio, a white wooden bandstand, a stone wall covered by flame-red hibiscus, a stucco kiosk with a red tile roof where Spanish ladies served chocolate to guests, and the old Guam Museum, the former servants' quarters.

By 1909, Americans officially designated the island's name as Guam, American currency became the sole medium of financial exchange, and the United States Congress authorized duty-free importation of Guam products into the U.S. At the same time, Naval Governor Edward J. Dorn stressed observance of U.S. federal holidays and prohibited aliens from purchasing or leasing Guam land for more than five years at a time.

Guam fell to Japanese military forces the day after Pearl Harbor was attacked. Until 1944, Guam was occupied by enemy forces.

During the occupation, Japanese soldiers marched many Chamorros to concentration camps, where they were forced into heavy, back-breaking labor, abused, or beheaded. The soldiers searched local households looking for spies, destroyed homes, and held adults at bayonet point. Those years were extremely hard on Guamanians, and, today, older Guamanians' memories of the war years remain vivid.

In 1945, Guam was retaken by American forces in bloody

campaigns of World War II. Liberation Day, July 21, is the island's largest celebration.

On July 30, 1945, the *USS Indianapolis* was torpedoed by a Japanese submarine after delivering to Tinian key components of the Hiroshima atomic bomb. Only 316 of the 1,196 men survived the sinking in shark-infested water. Soon thereafter, the Japanese surrendered.

When the U.S. Naval Government was reinstated in Guam, ancient latte stone sites were bulldozed into oblivion, and Tumon Beach became an Air Corps recreational area. An officer's club was built on Two Lovers Point, where legendary Chamorro lovers leapt to their death rather than be separated by disapproving parents.

The northern plateau, from Pati Point to Ritidian Point, was turned into a military complex, including Northwest Field and naval communications facilities. Many ifil trees in primeval forests were razed. The best beaches—Tarague in the north and Sumay in the south—were incorporated into military bases behind barbed-wire fences and declared off-limits to Chamorros.

Before World War II, Agaña was a slow-moving town of low, traditional houses, home to half the population. Transportation was by carts pulled by carabaos along rutted, flooded roads.

Agaña, leveled during the recapture of Guam, was totally rebuilt and transformed into an American city with concrete roads, a gas station, a supermarket, and apartments.

After the war, an increase in American servicemen and their dependents swelled Guam's prewar population from 22,000 to 100,000. The civilian economy burst forth, initially due to war surplus sales, then to military construction.

A number of U.S. servicemen and civilians stationed on Guam teamed up with Guamanians to form successful businesses that thrive today. For example, Kenneth T. Jones, Jr., a former Seabee, and Segundo P. Leon Guerrero became partners in Jones and Guerrero (J&G) Enterprises, a multi-million-dollar empire. Eduardo T. Calvo, working his way from messenger to assistant cashier at the pre-war Bank of Guam, started Calvo Enterprises and opened the first insurance agency. Pedro Ada became Guam's first millionaire, and Mark Pangilinan, an 18-year-old sailor in the Philippine merchant marine, began an import business.

New Chamorro-American families were formed. Marcelo Sgambelluri, a musician in the Navy band, married Joaquina D. Camacho. A schoolteacher and former Marine, Corporal James H. Underwood, married Ana Martinez. Another Marine, First Sergeant John F. McDonald married Dolores Mariano. These families are prominent in present-day business and social circles.

President Harry Truman signed the Guam Organic Act in 1950, granting Guamanians U.S. citizenship and establishing the civilian government. Guam's economy was assisted under this act by designating it as a duty-free port.

In these post-war years, the Chamorro culture began to change. Although saints' day fiestas continued to be held in villages, traditional activities and the *paré* system were still important. Young people were becoming Americanized, and family ties and the traditional retention of land were threatened.

In the 1960s, English began to replace Chamorro as the main language in most homes. Elders forbade children to speak the native language because they wanted them to assimilate to American culture. Children were beaten with a stick or a rope if they spoke Chamorro.

The down side of liberation was the American acculturation. Towns were turned into suburbs with single-family homes, contrasting with the Chamorro style of married children living with parents in multi-family dwellings in village centers. The new homes were concrete and typhoon-proof, insured and financed by mortgage companies

In 1962, President John F. Kennedy lifted security requirements, including the ban on commercial air traffic, photography, and tourism, that had hung over the strategic islands since World War II ended.

All Micronesian islands, except Guam, were transferred from the Navy to the U.S. Department of the Interior and governed under a United Nations mandate. However, military commands, still bent on obscuring the islands' locations, continued to dateline press releases, "Somewhere in the Western Pacific."

In 1964, I was one of a hundred U.S. civil servants—teachers, nurses, draftsmen, secretaries, and administrators—recruited to work at the headquarters of the Trust Territory of the Pacific Islands (TTPI) in Saipan. We were there to train indigenous citizens to be self-sufficient and to govern themselves.

While I was in Saipan, I married a Chinese-Filipino sea captain and, after a sojourn on his freighter in the South China Sea, we moved to Guam to set up housekeeping.

Guam's main thoroughfare is Marine Drive, named for either the ocean it skirts or the U.S. Marines who liberated the island. The road, which stretches from Andersen Air Force Base south to Apra Harbor, is now called Route 1.

The Agaña-Tamuning corridor became a sprawling community of medical clinics, a hospital, shopping centers, restaurants, and residences. Streets soon became bumper-to-bumper with rental Toyotas and tour buses crammed with Japanese honeymooners.

North of Tamuning, Ipao Beach and Tumon Bay, which curve around a limeade-dyed lagoon and coral reef, were transformed into Japan's mini-Waikiki. In this scenic playground, children and grandchildren of Kamikazi fighter pilots and crews descended with snorkels, cameras, and golf clubs in hand.

In 1966, civilian housing was scarce in Guam. Islanders lived in villages of wooden houses, painted in Crayola colors, with corrugated tin roofs. Newcomers rented surplus Quonsets, those prefabricated, arched-roofed metal huts built to house World War II forces. In 1941, the U.S. Navy bought 160,000 Quonsets to ship to bases in Africa, Newfoundland, and Guam.

In Tamuning, I rented half a Quonset, one of four perched on a square block owned by a Stateside waitress. The other half of the Quonset was rented by an Airman and his 18-year-old wife, who spent her long, lonely days blasting music around the compound and entertaining sailors.

My Quonset was furnished in surplus military style: rattan dinette and livingroom sets, with seat cushions covered in sunfaded material of red and yellow hibiscus as big as beach balls. The sofa looked like a dead carabao. Shrews—those six-inch-long rodents with pointed snouts and squinty eyes that attack when cornered—had tunneled underneath the sofa to build a birthing nest.

These critters also burrowed in hot lockers (clothes closets in which low-wattage bulbs burned constantly to prevent mildew in the days before air-conditioning).

Six feet from my dining room window stood another Quonset owned by a middle-aged Filipino couple. When the husband lost money at cockfights or Catholic church bingo games, his wife would yell at him, "You're nothing but a lazy old carabao!"

The carabao, a water buffalo imported to Guam from the Philippines by Jesuit missionaries in the early 1700s, is a fast-fading native. In the past, these beasts of burden pulled plows through rice paddies, turned millstones, hauled people in bull carts, and provided meat and milk. Today, they are brought out from farms to race and play carabao baseball at fiestas. Some 300 domestic and 1,000 wild carabaos wallow in water holes on 9,000 acres at the Naval Magazine in central Guam.

I learned to live in harmony with wildlife, two-stepping along window ledges and skittering up and down pipes. Besides shrews, there were snails, toads, ants, mosquitos, termites, chirping geckos, and flying cockroaches big enough to play polo with Pele.

In those days, trips to the lone civilian market were adventurous, and food was as scant as Lenten fare. I was lucky to find Spam® or Australian corned beef, cold-storage eggs, cabbage, potatoes, and canned fruit and vegetables. Bread was so old I held it up to the light to pluck out bugs before toasting it.

In late summer of 1966, my husband arrived home from sea for the first time since I settled on Guam. During his week's stay, the U.S. Immigration and Naturalization Service issued him a Green

Card, which allowed him to work in the U.S. territory. He was hired immediately as skipper of the *Gunners Knot*, a copra freighter operated by the Micronesia Interocean Line. He bought me a used Toyota and shipped out to sea.

My husband had no sooner sailed out of Apra Harbor than a Chamorro neighbor called to ask me to go with him to a movie that evening. I was shocked. I recalled that the man, who worked at the commercial port, had visited our house when my husband was home. I knew the man had a wife and four or five children. Some nerve, I thought. I bawled him out for thinking I'd go out with him while my husband was at sea. (For more on this propensity, see Chapter Five.)

When my landlady's Australian Silky Terrier gave birth to seven puppies, I bought a female, the largest of the litter. I named her Chichi after one of the Bonin Islands in the North Pacific. She turned out to be a first-class shrewer, as well as my best friend.

I tolerated my clammy, noisy, insect-ridden Quonset for a year. When the temperatures changed, the Quonset pinged and popped, like a motor cooling down. If I battened down the wooden shutters over the unscreened windows to keep out daily horizontal showers, the hut became a Miwok sweat lodge.

After scouring the real estate For Sale ads, I bought a long narrow compound with three houses a block off Marine Drive in Tamuning. There were one Quonset and two frame houses, whose paint was peeling in layers like a bad sunburn. Along the rear of the lot sat a Quonset, occupied by a bachelor PanAm pilot, and an air-conditioned, one-bedroom house that I moved into.

Belle, and her Doberman Pinscher, rented the front wooden house built on stilts. It had a red-curtained porch, living room, kitchen, bath, and three bedrooms.

One night I was awakened by a car braking on the gravel driveway. I peeked out the window to see a taxicab parked by Belle's house. A man climbed out of the taxi, stepped up to the porch, dimly lit by a shaft of rosy light, and disappeared inside the house.

The taxi sped away. Again the next night a taxi woke me when another man arrived at Belle's.

The former property owner told me that Belle was one of the women who had come to Guam as taxi dancers after World War II. These women worked in dance halls and earned a percentage of tickets sold to men they danced with. When the dance halls began to die out, some women who couldn't afford to return to the mainland became prostitutes.

The island of eternal summer grew on me. I welcomed the dawn serenades of roosters crowing and boonie dogs barking. I quickly learned to greet people with "Hafa Adai," Chamorro for "hello." The islanders' lack of concern for the tyrannies of time was frustrating. When friends invited me to their homes, I always arrived punctually. However, after arriving a few times before the hosts were dressed for company, I adjusted to island time and showed up half an hour to an hour late.

Meanwhile, I applied for a job at the Civilian Industrial Relations Office on the Naval Station. As a former U.S. Government employee in Honolulu, I was eligible for reinstatement. I accepted a job as a secretary at the U.S. Naval Supply Depot's Fuel Farm, located on Marine Drive between Naval Station and Agaña. During my eleven months at the Fuel Farm, I had the office running as smoothly as a destroyer at 28 knots. However, the job was boring, and I was no longer amused by fuel operators saying, "Pump me a cup of coffee, will you Jan?"

In November 1966, I answered an ad for a proofreader and women's page editor at the *Guam Daily News* (GDN).

A few days later, I was called for an interview with GDN Publisher Joseph C. Flores in the executive office of his new Guam Savings and Loan office in Agaña. Flores' bushy moustache twitched as he squinted through thick eyeglasses at my published newspaper and magazines articles.

Flores was impressed by my résumé, but wondered why I would give up a permanent civil service job to work for his newspaper. I explained that I had been interested in writing since I was a young girl in Maryland, and I had majored in journalism at the University of Colorado, Boulder.

When Flores hired me, I gave the Navy two weeks' notice and resigned. During the next twelve years, Guam was my beat.

CHAPTER TWO

Jungle Journalism

For centuries, triton shells heralded typhoons approaching Guam, and priests traveling from village to village carried news to the islanders.

When the Guam-Manila and San Francisco-Guam telegraphic cables were laid in 1903, wire service items arrived daily. Although news was censored, newspapers then became an integral part of Guamanians' lives.

Today's *Pacific Daily News* (PDN), the only English-language daily newspaper covering the Western Pacific, evolved from a Navy paper.

Three newspapers were published before World War II: the *Guam News Letter*, published in English and Spanish; the *Guam Recorder*; and the *Guam Eagle*, its title alluding to the island's flying cockroaches.

When the Japanese bombed and occupied Guam, radios and newspapers were banned. However, Jose Gutierrez, Anatacio Blas, and Frank Terlaje secretly operated a Silvertone radio in Agaña Heights, a stone's throw from enemy headquarters.

George R. Tweed, a Navy radioman who escaped into a cave in the boondocks when Japan invaded Guam, also owned an illegal radio. One day Paul Muña, a Guamanian working in the Navy Commandant's office, brought a typewriter and paper to the cave.

Tweed revived the *Guam Eagle,* recapping U.S. and world news for locals.

Several Guamanians, including a priest, were tortured or killed by Japanese for aiding the American, who stayed under cover for two and a half years. Tweed was rescued when the Americans recaptured the island. Then the Secretary of the Navy pinned a medal on him, and Tweed published his memoirs: "Robinson Crusoe, U.S.N."

In the mid-1940s, the Vicarate Apostolic of Guam began publishing the weekly tabloid, *Umatuna Si Yuus* (Blessed Be God) to serve the Catholic community. The paper was edited by Bishop A. W. Baumgartner, OFM Cap., who had a master's degree in journalism, and assisted by Monsignor Felixberto C. Flores. The *Umatuna* was the first bi-lingual—Chamorro and English—newspaper in Guam. Presently, it's called *Pacific Voice.*

The daily *Navy News* was published from 1945 to 1950, and when Guam's nonmilitary government was established in 1950, the *Navy News* plant was put up for bid.

Joseph C. Flores, the only Guamanian with journalism experience at that time, bid for the Navy paper. Flores was one of a handful of Chamorro men allowed to enlist in the Navy in 1917. He had served five years, become an American citizen, and then, as a civilian, published a weekly shopper in San Francisco. Flores returned to Guam to start an export business. When Flores won the Navy's bid, he dissolved his firm and purchased the Navy's presses, Quonset offices in Agaña Heights, and two elephant Quonsets full of newsprint.

The Good *Guam Daily News*

The first issue of Flores' *Guam Daily News* (GDN) came out June 15, 1950. The eight-page morning tabloid sold for five cents a copy, with a circulation of 12,000. Its Sunday edition was called *The Territorial Sun.*

Flores built a new plant on a square block, the site of the former Naval Hospital in Agaña. The GDN was an easy walk to the Government of Guam's administrative buildings, the Legislature, post office, police department, Dulce Nombre de Maria Cathedral, and Latte Stone Park. Across the street, Skinner Plaza honors Guam's first American civilian governor, Carlton F. Skinner. Statues of General Douglas MacArthur and other war heroes also stand there.

The GDN plant faced Martyr Street. On the opposite side on the ground floor along O'Hara Street, Flores opened his Guam Savings and Loan Association and Marianas Finance. "Money-lending is a community service," he said. "It's much easier than newspaper work and more peaceful."

Flores hired Antonio (Tony) Palomo, who had a degree in journalism from Marquette University, Milwaukee, and worked three years on the *Milwaukee Sentinel*. Flores sent Palomo a ticket to Guam, then deducted the fare from his salary.

Next to be hired were Elaine Cruz, society writer and, later, business editor; Eddie Calvo, sports editor; and Josephine Concepcion, advertising salesperson.

In 1960 President Dwight D. Eisenhower tapped Flores to be the first Guamanian governor. While in public office, Flores monitored the paper's activities and acquired a Goss press, converting the GDN from hot-type to offset. As governor, he also upgraded the two-year college to the accredited four-year University of Guam.

Typhoon Karen ripped across Guam on November 11, 1962, lifting the roof off the *News* building, soaking newsprint, and freezing the new press with instant rust. Flores chopped salaries, borrowed a mimeograph machine, and printed a daily information sheet. The plant was rebuilt, more newsprint ordered, and rust was sanded off the presses.

In 1965, Joseph C. Murphy of San Jose, California, answered a help-wanted ad for "an adventuresome soul to be a newspaperman in a frontier community." Thirty-nine-year-old Murphy, a 1951 graduate of the University of Wisconsin with a degree in journalism, had edited newspapers in Wisconsin and Oregon. Flores hired Murphy and paid his plane fare to Guam, but refused to finance the trip for Murphy's wife and seven children.

When Murphy arrived at the GDN, the editorial staff comprised Elaine Cruz; Dick Williams, a Statesider married to a Chamorro; and two other Statesiders, one of whom was an alcoholic sports writer.

During Murphy's first week, Williams and Cruz quit to join the *Pacific Journal,* a new afternoon paper. One day Williams came to the GDN to recruit reporters, and Murphy kicked him down the stairs from the second-floor newsroom. The two didn't speak to each other for three years.

When the remainder of the staff left, Murphy became a one-man newspaper. He hooked paragraphs on AP copy, wrote headlines, dummied in photos mailed from Hawaii, answered telephones, dealt with the problems of a multi-lingual society, and wrote a daily column, "Pipe Dreams."

Murphy didn't have time to cover the scandalous Gold Room trial, during which several senators were accused of consorting with prostitutes at a strip joint. The senators were caught when they wrote personal checks to pay for the girls' services. None was convicted.

My first day at the GDN was in early December 1966.

The newsroom resembled the set of a summer theater production of "The Front Page." Desks were scattered in the center of the second floor of the building, and in one corner of the spacious room three young women huddled over typesetting machines. The front wall was lined with drafting tables below a row of high windows, and a teletype clicked-clacked from a cubbyhole on the opposite side.

Editor Joe Murphy sat in a cubicle at a desk stacked with newspapers and magazines. His shirt sleeves were rolled up to his elbows, and he clenched a pipe between his teeth as he typed with two fingers on an old upright Underwood.

When I introduced myself, Murphy shifted his pipe to the

other side of his mouth, ran his fingers through his black hair, and stretched his lanky frame to six feet tall.

Murphy led me to a woman seated at a desk in the center of the newsroom. When he introduced us, the woman looked up from piles of galleys, layout sheets, and boilerplate dress patterns, recipes, and how-to-home projects. She stood up, grabbed her purse, and ran down the steps.

Murphy shrugged and sucked on his pipe. "You have to proofread these galleys and put out two women's pages." He tossed a copy of the Honolulu-oriented Associated Press (AP) Style Book on my desk.

My heart sank. I had counted on learning the job from the previous editor.

Soon a pretty young woman clogged up the steps and sank onto a chair at her desk. She turned towards me and smiled, "I'm Carol McMurrough. You must be the new women's editor."

"Yes. The former editor just ran out mad."

Carol smiled and tossed her long blonde hair behind her neck. "She almost knocked me down at the bottom of the steps. Have you done this before?"

I admitted I hadn't. The only paper I had laid out was the hand-printed weekly newsheet I delivered to neighbors for five cents when I was ten years old.

Carol, a Texas journalism school graduate and an Air Force wife, was the GDN's sole reporter. She taught me how to lay out and paste up the women's pages.

"Mainland and international wire stories come over the teletype," she explained. "The antenna on the roof catches those radio signals. Photos come in a mail pouch."

Around noon, our hunger was appeased by a Guamanian teenager, tagged the Empañada Kid, who toted a box slung on a frayed string around his neck. Inside were a dozen crispy empañadas stuffed with spicy red-orange meat, hot off his mother's griddle.

In the afternoon, a short man with slicked-back brown hair breezed in. He spilled the cup of coffee in his hand and groaned as he plopped into a chair at his desk to my right. When he saw me, he said, "Hi. I'm George, sports editor. Welcome to the zoo."

A few minutes later, George said, "Hey, Janet," and handed me his reporter's pad. His Beefeater's breath almost knocked me off my chair. "Would you rewrite my notes from last night's game? I've got so much to do for tomorrow's paper, I'll never get it done by deadline."

"Well, I don't know anything about baseball." I looked at his notes and groaned. Though I didn't know a two-base hit from a bull pen, I rewrote the high school baseball game story the best I could. George never asked me to rewrite his stories again.

On my second day, Montie Protasio, a tall Stateside woman wearing a long Hawaiian muumuu and zoris, brought me a news release for the Guam Women's Club's Christmas tea.

Montie wrote features and a column for the *Guam Times Weekly*, owned by Filipino businessman Manuel L. José. He personally edited the 20-page crusader and cranked out anti-GovGuam editorials. I was familiar with Montie's stories because when I lived in Saipan, I sold travel stories about Micronesia to the news magazine.

Before she left, Montie gave me a copy of her Guam recipe calendar, the first of its kind, and a mimeographed copy of her "History of Guam Journalism."

The dimly lit newsroom was a sweat shop. Fresh air came from slits of windows that opened slightly, not enough to capture breezes but enough to let in Guam's horizontal rains. The roof leaked and rain dripped on our desks.

The unisex bathroom was similar to WCs in European youth hostels, except GDN's stalls had piles of newsprint in lieu of toilet tissue.

One day, photographer Jesus Manilisay, carrying an open umbrella over his head, charged up the steps and into Murphy's office. "The toilets are dripping into my soup again!" The bathroom was directly above the first-floor darkroom.

"How can I make good photos with sloppy soup? It's been like this for years."

"I know, 'Sus, I know. I'll ask Flores to get the leaks fixed," Murphy grumbled as 'Sus stormed downstairs.

Guam's blue skies and warm trade winds gave no indication that Christmas was approaching. The season was heralded by the word GUAM spelled out in colorful lights on the hill above Agaña. Santas descended, like red-suited commandos, by helicopters and parachutes, or came ashore by motorboat. They traveled to shopping centers on golf carts, fire trucks, and carabaos.

On the Friday before Christmas, a potluck lunch was held in the PDN's business office on the first floor. Desks had been pushed aside, and in the center three tables were laden with fiesta food. Employees had prepared the dishes at home, and, grudgingly, Publisher Flores had supplied the turkey and soft drinks.

We were still eating when Flores handed out Christmas cards containing bonuses. Then he said, "Time to get back to work."

The business manager received $3. Murphy, Carol, and George each got a $1 bill. Flores thought he was being generous by giving employees a dollar for each year they had worked for the paper. I didn't even rate a card.

During the dogwatch on January 27, 1967, the newsroom was stuffy and, as usual, the water cooler was empty. I was checking AP copy on the teletype that clattered from 8 a.m. to 8 p.m.

Suddenly bells started ringing, and the ticker repeated "FLASH! FLASH!" When I read the headline, I gasped, ripped off the story, and gave it to Murphy.

Jumping up from his desk, Murphy shouted, "Stop the press!" Then he grinned. "I've always wanted to say that."

Sadly, he redid GDN's front page to tell the tragic news: astronauts Virgil I. "Gus" Grissom, Edward H. White, and Roger B. Chaffee had been killed in a flash fire during a test aboard their Apollo 1 spacecraft.

Murphy was plagued by understaffing and constant turnover. Between 1966 and 1969, he hired 36 reporters: Statesiders, derelicts, alcoholics, military dependents and moonlighters, Peace

Corps dropouts, college students, housewives, and any good-looking doll he could find.

Flores believed he employed "sufficient staff to put out a daily paper." However, there were never more than 4 full-time employees who worked 13 hours a day, 7 days a week, for minimum wages.

Because I was married, I didn't depend on the miniscule pay. I pitied the business manager who couldn't afford housing, and, for a while, slept under the Addressograph in his office.

Despite the antique plant and chaotic newsroom, Murphy told his wife, Marianne, in California to sell their house and cars, pack their furniture and six kids, and come to Guam.

Flores, who hawked ads on street corners and kept notes in his coat pocket, once said, "I'm not the best newspaperman, but I always manage to turn a profit."

A former GDN editor described Flores as "the cheapest bastard going." Flores kept a tight reign on the PDN staff by controlling supplies. We had to sign our names to get new pencils, pens, and paper. Editors were not allowed to call off-island, even to verify facts.

Flores was convinced that air-conditioning was superfluous. The newsroom was so hot that young typesetters often fainted after lunch. The afternoon heat affected pregnant typesetters more than others. Someone once quipped that one of the girls was always "sex weeks pregnant." It was rumored that some girls spent their lunch hours in the boonies having abortions performed by unlicensed herb doctors, called *suruhana*. (Read more about this in Chapter Five.)

On one unusually hot afternoon, a typesetter swooned out of her chair and onto the floor.

Murphy drove her home, and then stormed to Flores' cool office. "Please get us some air-conditioning."

Poker-faced Flores answered, "Joe, we've just got to get stronger girls."

Late one evening as we were putting the paper to bed, Father Canice, a Capuchin priest who wrote for the parish paper and was a member of the Guam Press Association, skipped up the stairs to Murphy's office.

Suddenly the wooden building began to shake. The one escape route from the newsroom—the stairwell—swayed like a rope bridge. Layout sheets slipped off composing tables and pencils dropped to the undulating floor.

I ran to Murphy's office and stood with my arms on both sides of the door, supposedly the safest place to be during an earthquake.

Inside, Father Canice had gathered up his long brown robe, dropped to his knees, and prayed. When the shaking stopped, Murphy hugged the priest. "Thank God you were here, Father."

The GDN's morgue, a collection of cross-reference files, was the eight-foot-high stacks of newspapers leaning against Murphy's office walls. Rats and mice nested in the papers, and the office cat used the papers for a litter box.

One morning loud meowing announced that momma cat had given birth to five kittens. When they were a few weeks old, three were taken home by staff members, but two remained to keep the mother cat company and hold down the newsroom's rodent population.

The Fourth Estate and whiskey have been cozy bedfellows since the advent of newspapering. Two-fisted, twisted, profane editors and printers, in green eyeshades, habitually ran to pubs as soon as papers hit the streets.

Murphy was no exception. Most editors in his predicament would have turned white-haired and developed ulcers within a week under the drudgery of putting out the GDN with unskilled help and great distances from supply sources. He collected tickets for speeding and driving while under the influence of alcohol and, like candy wrappers, threw them in the glove compartment of his car.

He took solace in local watering holes. After work, Murphy stopped in bars, ended up in brawls, and got arrested for drunken misconduct. Many a morning, his wife brought a clean shirt to Murphy's office after he had spent the night in jail.

Typographical errors were like cockroaches: they crept in no matter what we did and no matter how many we had already squished. Murphy blamed GDN's numerous typos on the languages spoken by employees. Guamanian typesetters spoke Chamorro to each other while they set stories in English. A Filipina read galley proofs and a Palauan made corrections. Guam's languages were a chop suey of Chamorro, Spanish, Filipino, American, Japanese, a dozen Micronesian dialects, and Navy jargon.

Mechanical errors cropped up too. Rushing to meet a deadline, a pressman accidentally flipped over a half-page negative, which made a reverse image on the plate. No one noticed the mistake until the next day. Readers had to hold the page up to a mirror to read it.

The Micronesian Christmas Drop began in 1967 and continues to this day. This tradition started when crewmembers of the 54th Weather Squadron were tracking a December typhoon near the isolated atolls of Kapingamarangi and Nukuoro, near Ponape. The crew put candy and cigarettes in a plastic bag and dropped it to islanders, who had gathered on the beach to wave when they heard the drone of the turbo-prop craft.

The next Christmas, families of the Weather Squadron donated pencils, pencil sharpeners, crayons, coloring books, food, clothing, and toys for the drop. The aircraft first made low passes over atolls to alert the people, then, on the last pass, dropped presents by parachute. Islanders eagerly waded into the lagoon to retrieve the gifts.

My GDN gig lasted only one year and two months. Long hours and poverty wages prompted me to quit in January 1967.

The Passing *Journal*

In 1966, Guam's prominent businessmen—Bordallo, Jones, Calvo, and Martinez–agreed the island needed a second paper to provide better local coverage than the GDN. The *Journal*'s first issue hit the streets in the afternoon of July 17, 1966.

Madeleine Zeien Bordallo, who was then the wife of *Journal* board chairman Ricardo "Ricky" Bordallo, went to Washington, D.C., to find an editor. There she met Milton E. "Red" Garrison. Madeleine convinced the former *Washington Star* copy boy, who later worked on a variety of newspapers, to move to Guam.

Editor Garrison hired former GDN reporters Dick Williams, Carol McMurrough, and Glenda Moore. Williams soon grew to dislike Garrison's derring-do style and quit after he and Garrison got into a fist fight.

I was hired as a reporter in March 1967.

The plant was located in a huge metal warehouse on Marine Drive in Tamuning. We reporters wrote on state-of-the-art electric typewriters at teak desks, while AP and UPI teletypes clacked away around the clock. A Fairchild press and Photo Fax equipment produced a good-looking newspaper.

Garrison, who was endowed with carrot-colored hair, a boyish smile, and Irish charm and temper, edited as much copy as time permitted. His headlines were printed equivalents of punches in the face, and he could write catchy ads in seconds.

I felt somewhat akin to Garrison because I, too, worked for the *Washington Star* when I was a teenager. I wrote features about happenings in Hyattsville High School, Maryland, for the *Sunday Star's* youth page.

Carol assigned my beats: GovGuam, courthouse, police and feature stories. Then she added, "I want you to cover the Legislature. It's a full-time job, but it's a reporter's heaven. You don't have to run around town to get stories, and you'll get plenty of human interest pictures."

On the opening afternoon of the session, I drove to the Legislature building in Agaña. Inside the hall, a clerk directed me to the press box at the front, to the right of the speaker's bench.

The 1950 Organic Act of Guam gave Guamanians U.S. citizenship and a constitution. The Act called for a unicameral legislature to be elected by popular vote and a governor to be appointed by the President.

Citizens depended on senators the way they used to depend on ancient chiefs to solve their problems. Traditionally, Chamorros respected a person of authority, such as a bishop, governor, benefactor, or senator. Well aware of their grass-roots aura, senators remained reachable.

The senators subscribed to Cicero's words, "*Cum dignitate otium.*" They met, with dignity, leisurely, late each day, after putting in a full day's work at their respective businesses: funeral parlors, car dealerships, department stores, food markets, insurance companies, pharmacies, jewelry stores, real-estate offices, or law firms.

At that opening session, the senators, bedecked in flower leis, greeted each other like kids returning to school in September. They hugged and slapped each other on the back, "Paré, hafa?" (How're you, buddy?)

Then the chaplain opened the session with a prayer. There is no such thing as separation of church and state in Guam. Government functions mingle with religious aspects, a legacy to centuries of Catholic domination under Spain. The archbishop is consulted on government protocol. In fact, one archbishop threatened to excommunicate senators who didn't vote as he suggested. GovGuam shuts down on religious holidays, and prayer breakfasts are popular with GovGuam officials and senators. It's said they first pray for themselves, then for the taxpayers.

The church and state correlation was accidentally exposed in a 1996 Guam phone book published by Holmes Management Company. The Archdiocese of Agaña was listed, erroneously, among Government of Guam agencies.

Symbols of Catholicism are everywhere: in government offices, grocery stores, and on cars, such as a row of red Jesus statuettes with blinking eyes staring out of rear windows.

The crime of the century was when thieves stole the 250-year-old, two-foot-high wooden statue of Santa Maria del Camarin from its niche in the Agaña Cathedral. Retrieved unharmed, the icon leads the procession of the Most Holy Name of Mary fiesta each December.

Once I quoted a nun who became irate when the Legislature refused to fund the hospital budget. "They don't deserve the title senator," she said.

When my story came out, the nun called me because the bishop had jumped on her neck. I reminded her that those were her exact words. She answered, "Nevertheless, you shouldn't have printed them."

"Guess you'll have to forgive me, sister," I said. She hung up.

At the opening session, House Speaker Florencio Torres Ramirez told a few dull jokes, then some senators gave even duller oratories with meaningless statistics about the upcoming budget.

Revenue, in part, comes into the Treasury of Guam by keeping on island U.S. federal income taxes paid by residents, non-resident federal employees, and military personnel on active duty or retired, as well as fees from customs, passports, and immigration. This fund, which runs GovGuam, is like holy water: everyone helps themselves to it.

After their first brief session, the Legislature adjourned early to eat and drink a-plenty at the opening-day fiesta.

During the next afternoon session, I surveyed the floor and recognized Senator Richard F. Taitano, whom I met in Saipan when he was deputy high commissioner for the Trust Territory of the Pacific Islands. One of the most conscientious Chamorro leaders, Taitano had also been the Interior Department's first Chamorro director of territories. He was elected senator in the 12th to the 15th Guam Legislatures.

When one senator said, "I'm filled with humidity," he wasn't far wrong. Though air-conditioned, the Legislature hall was warm and humid, perhaps due to the hot air wafting from the floor as senators rolled out riders on bills, never feared vetoes, and put the governor on the run.

While Speaker Ramirez or another senator was bloviating for

the record, others were doing their own things. One senator was always zipping up his fly, another was scratching his "little soldier," one was picking his nose, and some were chewing betel nut. I used to think one member was always bowing, but someone said his suspenders were pinching him.

Some were pothole politicians: unflamboyant officials who maintained their popularity by concentrating on voter priorities, such as street repair, sanitation, and public utilities. Of course, the senators had nothing on GovGuam employees.

During a 1990s gubernatorial campaign, a private gathering for Department of Administration (DOA) employees turned into a campaign gimmick. Flyers were circulated within DOA inviting employees to come to the Anigua pavilion for a party called, "Tequila Sunset by the Sea." Gubernatorial candidates claimed it was an accident that the DOA and campaign parties were scheduled for the same place at the same time.

The commissioner of the Bureau of Internal Revenue ordered a crackdown on corruption. She once said that if she removed all of the department's corrupt officials and employees, nobody would be left working there.

GovGuam employees had to fit in. For years, Sister Jean Marie Menke, Guam Memorial Hospital administrator and member of the Press Association, had battled with GovGuam over hospital funding. When she resigned, she thanked the hospital board of trustees for their support and added, "I trust you will recruit an administrator who fits into the island's political machinery."

The number of bills introduced in the Legislature were staggering. Many didn't stand a snowball's chance in Guam, while others were passed after lively debates.

Fridays had already been designated Island Day, or Hafa Adai Day, when everyone was encouraged to wear floral shirts and dresses.

During one session, a bill was entertained to make Fridays also "Official Flower Lei Day." The senator introducing the bill thought it would encourage the growing and wearing of floral leis, enhancing Guam's island paradise image.

A hot discussion ensued, in which most senators agreed the use of plastic flowers wasn't appropriate on a tropical island. Senator Carl Gutierrez, now Governor, put in his two cents: "I've never heard of statutory lei."

Another bill was introduced to name an official flower. For weeks, flower-power lobbyists leaned over the railing of the second-floor gallery in the Legislative Hall. They roared or booed and waved bunches of their favorite flowers: plumeria, hibiscus, and orchid. Some joker even suggested tangan-tangan.

Finally, senators voted to name the bougainvillea, or *Puti tai nobio,* as the official flower. In Chamorro this means, "it hurts to lose a lover." Or, as one senator remarked, "There are thorns in my lover's hand."

During my Legislative beat, Senator Al Ysrael introduced a bill to set up a swimsuit-optional zone to allow sunbathers to legally bare it all. Ysrael's bill was prompted by Hawaiian entrepreneur Larry Beck, who wanted to establish a nudist camp on Guam. Lieutenant Governor Kurt Moylan told Ysrael that GovGuam had better use for land.

"My bill," Ysrael said, "might increase tourism and the sale of binoculars. You women's libbers are always talking about equality. Well, men are topless on the beach so now you women will have the opportunity." He offered use of his Tamuning beach property for sunbathing.

One senator remarked that bill had a "bare chance of passing."

The bill didn't get anywhere. Today, only boonie dogs are allowed to run around Guam's beaches in their birthday suits.

Gambling, a way of life on Guam, has always been a hot issue. It permeates all age, social, and economic layers. Guamanians don't have to fly to Las Vegas to gamble. They lose their assets at cockfights, dog races, bingo games, pachinko parlors, and other vices there on the rock. Gaming is legal. Businessmen pay taxes, buy annual licenses, and contribute regularly to fund-raisers. At one time there were gambling ships offshore Guam, but they were deemed illegal.

Every few years, the Legislature introduces a casino gambling bill. Most senators favor gambling because they think it would be good for their businesses, but governors always veto the bills and the Bishop stages anti-gambling campaigns.

When Guamanians and Filipinos refer to "chicken every Sunday," they're not talking about Auntie Rosa's Sunday dinner. They mean Guam's goriest diversion: cockfighting, aka gang-pluck. Small fortunes are won and lost at almost every cockfight derby.

Guam and Puerto Rico are the only places on American soil where cockfighting is legal, although in some States, like Louisiana, cock-fighting goes on despite laws forbidding it.

In three Guam cockpits, entry fees for bettors range from $500 to $800 and prizes soar to $10,000 as bettors lay odds on which armed rooster will end up on the dinner platter. The fights are two sneezes long, then dead clucker.

Most people think of August as the dog days of summer, but Guam has year-round dog days and nights. The Greyhound Park, founded by Australian Norm Smith in 1977, is another popular betting spot. Some 700 purebred racers, imported from rabies-free Australia, live in the track's kennels.

Guam's Super Bowl is bingo, the most popular form of low-priced gambling in the world. Super jackpots range from $7,000 prices to $25,000 with bonuses $1,000 a game, not to mention door prizes. The Catholic Church sponsors bingo games, once supervised by Father Canice. Organizations such as the Guahan Donation and Scholarship Foundation, Chamorro Women Association, Pangasinan Association, and the Agaña Elks Lodge 1281 conduct weekly bingo games to raise money for charity.

The first Huegon Chansa Powerball Bingo took place on July 13, 2000. Money raised supported Team Guam at the Sydney Olympics and other Guam National Olympic Committee endeavors.

There are also infrequent gamblers who only place bets when the annual Liberation Day carnival gives them the opportunity to play casino games, or beto beto.

Journal Editor Red Garrison enjoyed rocking the government's and advertisers' collective boats.

In an investigative piece, Carol McMurrough exposed squalid conditions in Filipino Quonset labor camps, particularly those maintained by the newspaper's principal backer Ken Jones of J & G Construction.

After World War II, thousands of Filipinos were brought to rehabilitate Guam because there weren't enough skilled cement workers, carpenters, and heavy equipment operators on island. The Guam Department of Labor imported some 14,000 construction workers for large projects, such as Navy housing, a southern high school, airport expansion, power plants, and hotels.

During her investigation, Carol was appalled when she saw workers eating food with their fingers. The headline on her story read "Filipino laborers deprived of knives and forks." Carol, who had come straight to Guam from Texas, had never traveled to rural barrios where Filipinos customarily ate with their fingers.

Irate, Ken Jones pulled his ads from the *Journal* and put them in the GDN.

When a typhoon struck Saipan in April 1968, I asked to cover the story. Carol, however, had never been to Saipan and she wanted to go.

I went AWOL and sailed to Saipan on my husband's ship. The cargo contained Quonsets to replace houses, as well as food and medical supplies for field kitchens and medical clinics to be set up in tents in the devastated capital of Chalan Kanoa.

When I returned to Guam, I knew I was in hot water and I resigned. It really didn't matter—the *Journal* was gasping its last breath.

Editor Red Garrison had inherited a mountain of accounts receivable, accounts payable, and bank loans. With no money in the bank, Garrison had been cajoling friends into releasing supplies and newsprint rolls from the port without first receiving payment. One employee even stole supplies from the GDN.

Guam's business community couldn't support two daily newspapers. The fifteen *Journal* investors competed in enterprises, such as automobile and insurance sales, and they fought for editorial control of the newspaper. Bankrupt, the *Pacific Journal* ceased publication on July 21, 1968.

In his farewell editorial Garrison wrote, "This is the final edition of the *Pacific Journal*. . . . We sell twice the number of newspapers as does the Good, Gray *Guam Daily News*. In spite of a boycott by the principal advertisers on the island, we sell just about the same number of ads, day in and day out. Yet . . . we owe more money than we collect. . . .

"The *Pacific Journal's* editorial staff has rushed into a lot of places where angels fear to tread: the Filipino contract labor camps; the question of military holdings in Guamanian land and its effect on our economy; the anomaly of extraterritoriality for servicemen committing crimes in Guam; Guam's agricultural problems; Guam's crime and police problems—any matter of interest or importance and never mind whose toes are stepped on."

PDN Publisher Joseph Flores bought the *Journal's* press for $50,000, probably to keep it out of someone else's hands.

With the demise of the Journal, I returned to writing freelance magazine articles and producing news releases for the Micronesian Interocean Lines, Guam Chamber of Commerce, and Guam Visitors Bureau.

One morning in late 1968 Joe Murphy called to ask if I was interested in writing Micronesia's *first* visitor's guidebook. Is the Bishop Catholic?

The editor of the Hawaii Business Publishing Company offered me a contract to write the Micronesia counterpart of the company's Tahiti guide. I agreed and rushed out to buy an electric typewriter for $95.00.

I spent a year working on the Guam/Micronesia book. After publication, I distributed the books to hotels, tourist shops, military exchanges, and grocery stores on Guam and Saipan. The next year I revised the guidebook, but other publications eventually superseded it.

My story about Guam's Chamorro governor, Carlos G. Camacho, appeared in the March 1970 issue of the dental magazine, *Cal*. It was subtitled, "In Guam politics and dentistry go hand in hand."

Camacho, born in Agana in 1924, was the 108th governor of Guam, the 7th American civilian governor, 3rd governor of native ancestry, and the last appointed governor.

Graduating in 1952 from the Marquette University School of Dentistry, Camacho worked for the GovGuam Public Health Service. In 1955 he began practicing at the Catholic Medical Center.

In 1964, Camacho and twelve other candidates of the defunct Territorial Party were elected members of the Eighth Guam Legislature. He wasn't reelected senator in 1966, but he formed the Republican Party of Guam.

In the *Cal* story, Camacho compared his careers. "Both dentistry and government require the skill of good public relations. In both professions you have to hurt people, but you try to ease the pain by making them think it is for their own good.... You cannot please everyone, but you try to please whenever you can."

Governor Camacho and Kurt Scott Moylan, secretary of Guam, served a year and nine months as the last appointed executives. After the elective governorship bill passed, Camacho and Moylan were elected governor and lieutenant governor for a four-year term.

In his inaugural address, Camacho stressed, with foresight, "This is the end of federal paternalism, the beginning of a greater measure of home rule, the culmination of 72 years' effort to mold a closer kinship with the American nation.... Guam today is the communication and transportation center of the Western Pacific.... I envision Guam as the primary economic chain linking the continental U.S. with Pacific and Asian countries."

In January 1971, the inauguration of Guam's first elected chief executives was celebrated at a ball. Held at the Continental Travelodge, champagne flowed like Federal money. Arthur Lyman and his band from Hawaii played music for dancing, and Lyman presented maile leis to Camacho and Moylan, a Hawaiian.

At Guam's big bashes, it was customary to throw dignitaries into swimming pools: wigs, purses, eyeglasses, and bits of clothing floated while owners paddled to dry land. At Camacho's inaugural ball, Montie Protasio unsuccessfully tried to guide Governor Camacho near the pool, but Mrs. Camacho was hanging on to him too tightly.

The Powerful *Pacific Daily News*

In late 1969, Publisher Joseph Flores put the *Guam Daily News* up for sale, including a quarter-million dollars in accounts receivable.

Hawaiian millionaire businessman Chinn Ho, co-owner of the *Honolulu Star-Bulletin* with Alexander S. "Pug" Atherton and James Cooey, offered $1.2 million for the GDN. Flores accepted.

When Ho came to Guam to negotiate the sale for Capital Investment of Hawaii, he checked into Flores' Casa de Flores hotel for $22 a night. He was asked to pay in advance.

Ho named Robert E. Udick president and publisher. Udick had covered the Korean war for UPI and, in 1954, served as UPI bureau chief in Hong Kong. Joe Murphy continued as editor, and Glenda Moore returned as managing editor. Lee P. Webber, hired to take over the circulation department, soon doubled the paper's sales.

Udick and Cooey bought stock in Guam Publications, Inc. Ho offered newspaper stock to Guamanians, and Josephine Concepcion of the advertising department bought in. Ho loaned Murphy $10,000 to buy stock, then sent him and his family on an expense-paid trip to Honolulu.

The first edition of the newly christened *Pacific Daily News* (PDN) came out February 2, 1970.

When I went to work there in April, I met Ho. "Hello Mr. Ho, I'm Go."

First, Ho boosted salaries. Then he had the newsroom air-conditioned, the bathroom divided into his and her compartments, and the plumbing repaired so it didn't drip below to the darkroom. Surplus military equipment was replaced with electric typewriters and Justowriters. AP wire service was increased and UP added.

In those days, Joe Murphy would do anything for a story. He dove in an atomic sub, flew through typhoons' eyes, rode in Phantom fight planes, soared with Navy's Blue Angels, and broke a leg during his first parachute jump.

Among my beats at the PDN were GovGuam and the Legislature. I continued writing weekly maritime columns, "Through the Porthole," that I had written for the *Pacific Journal*. PDN renamed it "The Log."

When Publisher Udick decided to print the police blotter, I was assigned to stop by the police station every afternoon. The police log was popular. I converted dull police language to folksy stories, especially when they concerned carabaos or iguanas snarling Marine Drive traffic or snakes slithering up from commodes.

One afternoon in the summer of 1970, PDN Business Editor, Dorothy Fritzen, and I were pounding typewriters in the newsroom. She lit a cigarette and looked over at me. "It's about time we had a tourism column. You could write it."

Thus, my "On the Go" column was launched. I filled weekly columns with news of tourism and tourists, where-to-go items, and openings of restaurants, hotels, nightclub shows, a brewery, oil refinery, and roller rink.

Frequently, when one of the PDN's photographers wasn't available or the city editor didn't think the story was hot enough to send him, I took photos. However, I could never compete with the professionals: 'Sus Manilisay, 'Sus Manibusan, Tommy Thompson, and Manuel Perez.

Being a photojournalist could be hazardous. One day I drove

to the Glass Breakwater to shoot pictures of a passenger liner making her maiden voyage to Guam. While aiming my Minolta's long lens at the sleek ship in the harbor, I didn't hear someone shout "Halt!" After the third shout, I noticed a Marine aiming his rifle at me.

The Marine, who was about 19 years old, ordered me to turn over my camera and film. I refused. He insisted. I told him to call the admiral. He called Commander Naval Forces Marianas from the sentry booth, and the admiral vouched for me. I drove away with my camera and film intact.

My photo of the cruise ship appeared the next morning on PDN's front page. That same photo has been published many times since, without giving me photo credit.

Glenda Moore also took pictures, but instead of the usual "Say cheese," she told her subjects to "Think sex." Everyone smiled broadly in her pictures.

Reporter Margy Clapp was the PDN's comic relief. Her husband was an Air Force doctor. (Imagine how airmen felt being treated by Dr. Clapp.) Readers thought it was a bad joke when Margy's byline appeared on a series of articles about venereal diseases.

In late 1971, Ho's Hawaii corporation exchanged stock with the Gannett Co., Inc., newspaper chain. Thus, the PDN joined an empire of 50 papers in 15 states.

Gannett's Allen Neuharth came to Guam to look over his acquisition. He gathered the PDN staff in the conference room and grilled us about our backgrounds and what we did on the paper, but he didn't fire any of us.

Udick, Murphy, Webber, and Moore were asked to stay. Their presence helped minimize negative effects from the acquisition of the local newspaper by a giant, off-island corporation.

Most of PDN's editors and reporters, mainly women, were transplanted mainlanders, or temporary residents on military, government, or business assignments.

Gannett also recruited reporters and editors from its mainland stables. Although it was hard to find anyone to live on the rock, some wet-behind-the-ears journalists did fly straight from Syracuse University's Journalism School to Guam. These newcomers didn't know a carabao from cumshaw. They had no desire to learn Chamorro, and they thought everyone born around the Pacific looked alike.

Guamanians were unhappy with these brash newcomers. One senator complained. "We have an island society being interpreted by media managers from outside the island. They emphasize what must seem strange to them. Frequently, and sometimes inadvertently, their reports come across patronizingly."

John Walter, from the *Rochester Times-Union*, was recruited as city editor. Five weeks later, Managing Editor Glenda Moore left for England to join her husband and Walter was promoted to her job.

Walter didn't believe that cleanliness was next to Godliness: his BO permeated the newsroom. One day when Walter was out to lunch, someone put a can of Ban on his desk. When he returned, he held it up. "Who put this here?" We shrugged.

The next day, and from then on, Walter was a new man. His hair was shampooed, combed, and blow-dried. Every day Walter wore a clean shirt and trousers and polished shoes, and he smelled of after-shave lotion. Never underestimate the power of the press.

Local men and women were usually hired as printers, operators, business managers, typists, clerks, and photographers.

Guamanian Martha Ruth became business editor after Dorothy Fritzen retired.

Another local, Fina Concepcion, hired in 1959 as an accountant, became PDN's top ad sales person. She had a reputation for being strictly business, as political candidates knew who tried to get ads on goodwill. "Don't you trust me?" harried candidates asked. "Hell no," Fina replied. "Not until I see cash in my hand. Then we're talking business."

Early in 1972, a modern printing plant was ordered and ground was broken for a new building. Dillingham Construction Company (DILCO) began clearing Quonsets from the site.

Governor Camacho and Joe Murphy spoke at the pile-driving ceremony. When the first pile was driven, oil gushed into the air. A practical joker had hidden a barrel of oil beneath the first pile.

Murphy shouted, "To hell with the building, we'll all get rich." DILCO personnel stopped the gusher before it ruined the Governor's orange and purple shirt.

During months of pile-driving, the ground shook so much I thought the old building would collapse. It was like working during a continuous 7.0 earthquake. While writing, I wore a hard hat, given to me by the Officer in Charge of Construction at the groundbreaking ceremony for the new Commercial Port.

PDN's new 10-story building was the tallest one in Agaña. It was designed to withstand natural disasters with a built-in subsurface suspension that allows it to sway during earthquakes. It has reinforced, typhoon-proof walls and windows. The PDN also has its own water supply and a generator to run the press and newsroom equipment when island utilities fail.

Publishing a paper on a Pacific island is maddening—there's no place to borrow a roll of newsprint! More than once, PDN had to reduce its pages because the supply of newsprint from Canada and the States was running low. Once we thought the paper might have to be printed on toilet paper—if we could find any of that commodity. Five days before the paper supply ran out, 80 tons of newsprint were found on a dock in Japan and shipped to Guam.

Publisher Udick hired an assistant city editor from Rochester. The editor was like a cock who thought the sun rose to hear him crow. I nicknamed him Smoky because he chain-smoked cigars in the newly carpeted newsroom.

No one else in the newsroom smoked. When we politely asked Smoky to refrain, he laughed. "I'll do whatever I want, you stupid old fogeys." The more we protested, the more pleasure he got from blowing smoke under our noses.

Because of Smoky's arrogance and cigar smoke, I quit the PDN for the second time in November 1972.

Glenda Moore had been managing editor of the PDN until

December 1973, when George Blake was hired from Gannett to take over. Moore was then appointed managing editor of the Sunday paper.

I was regaining strength after a nephrectomy at St. Francis Hospital, Honolulu, when Glenda Moore called. She asked me to join the *Sunday News*, a full-sized edition, separate from the PDN. I eagerly accepted.

While working four days a week and the Saturday night dog shift, I continued writing two columns, features, and news stories. Moore and I were a great team: I wrote articles from notes she took during interviews with her secret sources, who gave us scoops instead of giving the items to PDN reporters.

After Glenda interviewed Hyundai's president and officers, we broke the story of how the South Korean company had brought their cement knowhow to Guam to build typhoon-and earthquake-proof houses in Santa Rita. We dubbed Hyundai the "Can Do" company.

Founded by Chung Ju Yung in 1947, the company cashed in on cement factories left by American forces after World War II. Hyundai operated in South Korea until 1965, when it initiated a road building project in Thailand. It grew into a multinational conglomerate in the fields of construction, shipbuilding, locomotives, industrial equipment, and consumer goods, as well as automobiles.

In late 1974, Ricky Bordallo summoned me to Ricky's Auto in Anigua. Although Ricky had been one of the owners of the *Pacific Journal*, I had never met him. Ricky, who attended University of San Francisco, dabbled in finance, publishing, housing, real estate, insurance, tourism, and car sales, service, and parts.

Ricky spent fourteen years in the Guam Legislature. He was chairman of the Popular Party in 1958 and first chairman of the Democratic Party in 1960. He was again elected chairman of the Democratic Party of Guam from 1971 to 1973 and became a member of the Democratic National Committee. He was president of the Marianas Lions Club from 1956 to 1957, and a member of the Guam Tourist Commission, Chamber of Commerce, American Red Cross, Navy League, and Air Force Association of Guam.

Pacing up and down the narrow think tank on the second floor of his car dealership, Ricky gave me a scoop: he and Rudolph "Rudy" Guerrero Sablan were going to campaign to be Guam's first Democratic elected governor and lieutenant governor.

. Ricky began his 1974 campaign by helicopter, cruising above the island from Yoña south to Talofofo. On ground tours, he waved campaign signs and blasted horns and music as he drove along Marine Drive, escorted by taxpayer-paid police.

Later, Ricky asked me to join his campaign public relations staff. If he won, this would mean a job for me in the Governor's Office. I thought writing press releases for Ricky and Rudy would be easier than reporting, and the salary was double what I was making at the newspaper. Unfortunately, my husband didn't want me working for politicians.

PDN's circulation was decreasing by March 1974, and the *Sunday News* was made a part of the regular daily newspaper. Moore was offered the assistant managing editor's job for features (a downgrade) and she quit in March 1974. When I was ordered to return to the smoky newsroom of the daily PDN, I quit too.

I think jealousy had something to do with our demise. PDN's male publisher and editors got their noses out of joint when we females scooped them. The bliss of working for the *Sunday News* lasted seven months.

Gannett's Al Neuharth, who gave birth to a new nationwide daily called *USA Today*, retired in 1989. In his book, "Confessions of an S.O.B.," he wrote,

"The best job in our company right now is publisher of our Guam paper. . . . The farther removed from company headquarters (Washington, D.C.), the more independence you have, the more fun you have. . . . I had . . . staffs to look after my care and feeding in Gannett locations from the Virgin Islands in the Atlantic to Guam in the Pacific. . . ."

TV Tales

In mid-1974, Lee Holmes, owner of Guam Cable TV System, asked me to write for his weekly *TV Guam* magazine. Unemployed at the time, I agreed to write "On the Go" columns for the magazine. Soon I was working full-time writing feature stories. The staff was small: a managing editor, an accountant, an ad saleswoman, and myself.

Off-island publication was troublesome. The TV magazine was printed in Manila, which led to atrocious English grammar and spelling, as well as shipping delays.

Another example was author-painter-TV host, Betty Bennett-Lyon, who sent the manuscript and layout of her "Children's Color Book" to a print shop in Taipei. When 5,000 copies of her book were returned, they were printed backwards: the first page said, "Adios," and the last page said "Hafa Adai."

Holmes hired writer Tere Rios Versace to help me produce feature stories for the magazine.

As a young girl in Puerto Rico, Tere wrote a book, "The Fifteenth Pelican," which inspired the television series, "The Flying Nun." Unfortunately, her book wasn't copyrighted, and she never received a penny from the subsequent movie and TV series.

Tere came to Guam to edit the Catholic paper, *Umatuna Si Yuus*. When she arrived, the lay editor left for Hong Kong. He "willed" her his apartment and a newspaper with debts of $7,000 a week. Tere tried to balance *Umatuna*'s books by collecting debts. When she asked for $3,000 owed by one advertiser, he said, "I consider that my contribution to the church." The Bishop agreed.

Tere resigned and was fired on the same day. "My Puerto Rican burro personality clashes with the Bishop's oriental psyche," she said.

Around 1 a.m., on election night in November 1974, Ricky

Bordallo and his blond, pretty, mannequin-thin wife, Madeleine, arrived at Democratic campaign headquarters. When word was received that Bordallo had won the election, someone yelled, "Praise the Lord and pass the Oly." Their victory party, which moved to Rudy's house, broke up at 7:30 a.m.

About 11 p.m. on election day, Glenda Moore, her husband, and I learned that Ricky was winning, and we held our own celebration. We hightailed it to the swimming pool of the Continental Hotel, where we romped in the water for about an hour. We slurped beer from six-packs that we floated in a Styrofoam cooler in the pool. A hotel security guard told us to be quiet and not disturb the guests, but he could see we were just having fun and didn't tell us to leave.

On January 6, 1975, Ricky and Rudy were inaugurated as the first Democratic governor and lieutenant governor. After Mass at the Agaña Cathedral, the swearing-in ceremonies and speeches took place at the Kiosk in the Plaza de España. This was the first time that newly elected officials had invited the public to an inauguration celebration: a fiesta to end all fiestas. The Plaza grounds next to the cathedral were jammed with food and beverage *palapalas* (booths), a dance floor, press booth, and cable TV tower.

The First Family couldn't move into Government House immediately because it was in disrepair. After three months and $90,000 in renovations, the house was officially opened April 17.

My *TV Guam* story about the reopening of Government House included a brief history of the house and its occupants.

Casa Gobierno, a palace built on the south side of the Plaza de España, had been home to Spanish governors. Damaged by typhoons and earthquakes, the palace was rebuilt in 1887.

In 1899 the governor's residence was ready for occupancy. The building had the first corrugated tin roof on Guam and was painted white with green typhoon shutters hinged to doors and windows. Governor Leary moved in with a band, Japanese house servants, a pair of white stallions from Manila, and Filipino coachman to drive them. Leary had a fine array of table linen, silver, porcelain, and glassware. American governors used the home until World War II, when Agaña was flattened by bombs.

After the war, naval governors lived in military quarters outside Agaña's ruins. Under naval governors' supervision, war ruins were cleared and the new towns of Agaña and Agat were built.

In 1949, President Harry S. Truman signed Executive Order No. 10077, transferring Guam from the Navy to the Secretary of the Interior.

Guam's first civilian governor, Carlton Skinner, organized postwar GovGuam. In a 10-year plan, he improved public buildings, utilities, highways, agriculture, housing, commercial port, and the boat harbor. Under his leadership, the two-year Territorial College of Guam was established.

At first Governor Skinner lived in military housing on Nimitz Hill, then moved closer to Agaña, again in military housing. He ordered an ifil dining room set as well as china, silver, and crystal etched with the Guam seal. He chose the site for a new Government House on the hill overlooking Agaña. Construction began on the new home in 1952 and, in 1954, Governor and Mrs. Ford Q. Elvidge, Guam's second appointed governor, moved in.

Next to occupy the house was Governor Richard Barrett Lowe, former governor of American Samoa. When Lowe resigned in 1959, the territory was considered to be in such fine shape that appointment of a Guamanian governor was possible.

Then, the Kennedy administration sent to Guam Governor Bill Daniel, who seemed to have no qualification other than his brother had once governed Texas.

When Governor Daniel moved into the house, he changed its name to the "Governor's Palace." Calling himself a western actor, after appearing in a bit part in a John Wayne movie, Daniel wore fancy cowboy clothes and rode a white horse named Alamo. He had longhorns mounted on the walls of the house and hooks installed to hold his ten-gallon hat collection.

He imported prize bulls and stallions, milk goats, boars, peacocks, and armadillos. Peacocks added color to the palace grounds, and armadillos were supposed to rid the island of African snails. When the armadillos multiplied faster than snails, the armadillos mysteriously disappeared into the ocean. The bulls were imported to upgrade island livestock. When the Governor brought a pair of bulls into the palace for a photo opportunity, GDN captioned the photograph: "The one in the middle is the Governor."

Under Governor Flores in 1960, Pan Am inaugurated eastward jet airline service across the Pacific via Guam in Boeing 707s, and the Bank of Hawaii was licensed in 1961 to operate in competition with Bank of America.

After the Korean War, former Governor Daniel persuaded President John F. Kennedy to discontinue the Navy security clearance for Guam in August 1962.

In November 1962, Typhoon Karen swept across Guam and destroyed windows, doors, and furnishings of Government House. The Guam Women's Club helped redecorate the house after typhoon damage was repaired, and Governor and Mrs. Manuel Flores Leon Guerrero moved in. This second appointed Guamanian governor changed the name back to Government House. Only five months later, before reconstruction was completed, Typhoon Olive undid the work.

In 1969, the third appointed Guamanian Governor was Dr. Carlos Garcia Camacho. When he and his family moved into Government House, it was redecorated: blue carpeting was laid, ceiling fans were removed, air-conditioning was installed, and furniture and appliances were replaced. In October 1970, little Camacho became the first baby born to a family residing there. Later that year, Camacho became Guam's first chief executive to be elected by the people.

Madeleine Bordallo supervised the renovation of Government House in 1975. She decorated it with Chamorro and Spanish accents to reflect Guam's heritage. The house had four bedrooms, four baths, three offices, and two pianos in the music room. The livingroom was converted into a "local room," with island-style rattan furniture and red and white hibiscus-patterned cushion covers. Walls were painted white and set off by green, red, and gold furnishings. In the family's quarters, bedrooms were refurbished, and a study, kitchenette, and winter clothes locker were added. One wall was devoted to a revolving art exhibit, featuring local artists and scenes and sponsored by the Guam Women's Club. The window walls were enlarged to take in the panorama of Agaña Bay.

The Bordallos were the first family in Government House to provide guest rooms. Children of other first families filled the bedrooms, but the Bordallos had only one daughter, Deborah. The Bordallos opened Government House for weekly public tours and also made the house and grounds available to youth events, dances, concerts, and civic receptions.

Bordallo had a red-tiled roof and a second floor added to Government House. At first he was criticized for this extravagance, but when public functions were held free each week, his foresight was applauded.

While Ricky was governor, one senator asked another, "What do they call Government House since Bordallo moved in."

"The tomb of the well-known car salesman."

Though in poor taste, that joke was prophetic. Six years later, Ricky ended his life tragically.

Freebies

Writers, press officers and photographers will eat and drink anything and travel anywhere, as long as someone else pays.

Once, Senator and Mrs. Adrian Sanchez invited the media to a "pour" in their home. Sanchez, a lifetime member of the Guam Press Club, had leased space on the ground floor of his house to Dr. Park–Guam's first acupuncturist. A bar and buffet table had been set up in the reception area of Park's clinic. Fortunately, the doctor was off island, so we didn't have to sample his needle art.

We were always invited to shows given by the military Far East circuit and Hilton Hotel entertainment groups. For instance, I met the Ink Spot's Roland Smith, who sang and played piano at the Cliff Hotel; and Jose Feliciano who performed at the Guam Women's Club's Mardi Gras Ball, held at the Guam Reef Hotel, to benefit the blind centers of Guam and the Cultural Center of the Pacific.

Airlines, businesses, and public relations firms offered journalists free trips called familiarization (fam) tours.

The only freebie I ever declined was a ride in a storm chaser, which entailed flying into the eye of a typhoon to plot the storm's arrival onshore. I pictured myself scared to death and upchucking on the pilot's cap. I said, "Thanks, but no thanks."

I was invited on fam trips to Truk and Palau by Continental Air Mike; a nuclear submarine by the U.S. Navy; Tokyo by Japan Air Lines; and Rio de Janeiro and Johannesburg by Pan Am.

One of my most memorable freebies was a trip to Taiwan.

An immigrant to Guam, businessman Charles L. Corn, affectionately called Charlie, used to invite as many as eighty servicemen who couldn't get home for Christmas to a beach bash at his cabana on a beach in Talofofo.

In 1971, Charlie invited thirty GovGuam officials, University of Guam directors, businessmen, friends, relatives, and myself to accompany him to Taiwan, where he was to receive an Honorary Degree of Doctor of Philosophy.

We left Guam November 25, and a few hours later checked into the posh Grand Hotel on a hill overlooking Taipei. The next day, the degree was conferred on Corn during a ceremony at the China Academy, on the mountain campus of the College of Chinese Culture on Yangming Mountain.

The founder of China Academy, Dr. Chi-yung Chang, spoke in Chinese. "Charles L. Corn, a native of Taishan, Kwangtung province, was born Yao Kung Chan in 1898. ..At first, he worked in a newspaper printing shop and at the same time began to learn English. . . . Shortly after the Sino-Japanese war broke out, he established an aviation school with the help of American friends to train overseas Chinese youths and encourage them to join the Flying Tiger Corps for defense of China.

"When in the Philippines during the war, Corn busied himself with activities in support of U.S. forces and earned praise from Gen. Douglas MacArthur... After V-J Day, he moved from the Philippines to Guam where he established a firm foundation in business, including trading, construction, food, and hotel management.

"He is a devotee of Confucianism and a great lover of Chinese culture. When in the Philippines, he established a Chinese school for the cultivation of overseas Chinese children and propagation of Chinese culture."

Corn, 74, spoke in his native dialect. "I left my fatherland when I was very young and stayed abroad for several decades.... It gives me great joy but with much humility to accept this honor. I remember a saying made by the ancient sage, Confucius, to the effect that when your parents are still alive, do not travel far but if you travel you must have a direction and purpose....

"During the Second World War, following the instructions of General Chiang Kai Shek, president of China, I followed the call to resist the Japanese aggressive action. In the Philippines I tried to help organize the guerilla forces to support the American military forces, and I joined the war effort until the war ended with victory. During the war I was arrested three times and was a prisoner of war. My life was in danger but I was lucky to escape death.

"I have one motto in my life and that is to be loyal to your country and love your country. The real happiness of life is to be able to help others and to make others happy.... From my own observations, China has a tradition and culture of over several thousand years and its own moral standard. This is the foundation of our fatherland and also is what the other democratic countries in the world are trying to achieve.... I have no doubt that friendship between China and the U.S. and cooperation between them will be strengthened.... Guam, the gateway to America's Western Pacific, has strategic value much like Taiwan's...."

At the reception after the ceremony, Charlie, wearing a purple and yellow robe and hat, remarked, "I'm still old Charlie Corn under these robes."

During the last days of the trip, Charlie became ill and was hospitalized in Taipei. Later, he was flown to San Francisco and died shortly thereafter. Charlie was mourned by his Guam family, as well as his early family in mainland China. His children carry on the family businesses in Guam.

While working for *TV Guam* magazine, I was invited to freebies similar to ones I was offered while working on newspapers.

For example, Pan Am's manager, Charlie Nara, called me one Monday in April 1976 and asked if I'd like to fly to Rio and Johannesburg the next day. Of course!

When I told Lee Holmes, my boss at the cable TV station, about the PanAm trip, he was furious. He frowned on freebies and didn't want me to take a week's leave. If I went, he forbade me write one word about the trip in the magazine. Though my job was on the line, the thought of refusing this trip-of-a-lifetime didn't enter my mind.

Tuesday I took the night flight to San Francisco, where I obtained visas for Brazil and South Africa. The next day I hopped on PanAm's 707 flight to New York. On board, I saw Jose, a prominent Guam businessman. We were the only ones invited from Guam. Along with a planeful of travel agents, writers, and friends of PanAm, Jose and I enjoyed a whirlwind trip to Rio de Janeiro, Johannesburg, and back to Rio.

When I returned to Guam, Holmes refused to let me mention the trip in my *TV Guam* column, and he prevented the editors of the *Pacific Daily News* from publishing my Rio story. However, I did get an article about the trip to Rio de Janeiro and Johannesburg published in "Trip 'N Tour" magazine.

Meanwhile, I had left an abusive marriage and moved to a condominium. I found that my *TV Guam* salary was so low I could barely afford to make mortgage payments, get my old Ford Maverick repaired, and buy dog food for Chichi and victuals for myself. I returned to U.S. Civil Service, where I published a monthly newspaper for Navy Public Works Center for two years.

Then I applied for and was accepted for a job as editor of a Navy newspaper in New Orleans. The Navy paid my airfare as well as the shipment of my household goods to the mainland.

I was leaving the island where I had been a big fish in a little pond and moving to the mainland, where I would have to learn to swim in a big pond. Some of my colleagues, I knew, couldn't make it as a little fish in a big pond, so they stayed on Guam until they retired or were so wiped out they couldn't have left if they'd wanted to.

When I left Guam in 1978, Dorothy Horn hosted a farewell lunch for me. Twenty of my friends were on hand to watch as Dorothy presented the Governor's Ancient Order of the Chamorri to me. The certificate, given to loyal friends of Guam, was endorsed by Governor Bordallo.

CHAPTER THREE

Accidental Guests

Pacific Daily News' headlines never rated a 30-second sound bite on the "Huntley-Brinkley Report," the "CBS Evening News" with Walter Cronkite, or the "McNeill-Lehrer Newshour," but Guam was put on the world map by the disappearance of an aviator, discovery of Japanese stragglers, welcoming of refugees, and caring for distressed ships at sea.

Amelia Earhart

The 1937 disappearance of aviator Amelia Earhart and co-pilot/navigator Fred Noonan in Oceania is an unsolved, secrecy-shrouded mystery. Several theories about their journey's end have been proposed in books, and some Americans call it a government cover-up.

Despite conflicting stories about the fate of Earhart and Noonan, it is presumed they were on an American espionage mission when their Lockheed Electra crashed in the Pacific in July 1937.

The couple was supposed to land on Howland Island, but they never reached that Pacific atoll, 1,650 miles southwest of

Honolulu. This 0.6-square-mile island had been colonized from Hawaii in 1935 and placed under the U.S. Department of Interior. The atoll, which had no permanent residents, became a field laboratory for ornithologists and a stopover for planes flying between Hawaii and Oceania.

Some reports say Earhart and Noonan were shot down for violating top-secret air space and landed on Hull Island or Mili Atoll in the Marshalls.

Since 1987, the 50th anniversary of Amelia Earhart's final flight, the Library of Congress has listed more than two dozen books about the aviators.

One author revealed new evidence from three residents of the Marshall Islands. Bilimon Amaron, a merchant on Majuro, was a health aide to a Japanese physician on Jaluit Atoll in 1937. In July, he was summoned to treat a man and a woman who had been picked up on a reef near Mili Atoll. Japanese claimed the pair had run out of fuel and landed near Mili. The man was wounded in the leg and head, and the woman wore pants. The pair, who didn't leave the ship during 24 hours at Jaluit's dock, was flown to Saipan because they were spies, said Amaron.

Majuro residents John and Dwight Heine said they helped unload an airplane, with a wing missing, from a ship at the Taroa dock. The Caucasian flyers stayed aboard the ship, they said. The twin-engine plane was taken off the wharf and rolled into an airplane hangar. Later, when Americans bombed the island, the airplane was placed in an underground hanger in a concrete revetment, which had been built to house Admiral Tomada's two-seated Zero.

Today, the tiny island of Taroa is alive with unexploded bombs and ammunition. The above-ground buildings and underground facilities remain unchanged. Earhart's Lockheed Electra may still contain 6,500 first-day-issue philatelic covers, estimated at more than $25 million in today's market.

The Mariana Islands were occupied in the late 1930s by Japan. Saipan was the headquarters of Nanyo Kohatsu Kaisha (NKK), a civilian organization suspected of covering for Japan's military operations.

Many Saipanese believe they know what happened to Earhart and Noonan. As many as a hundred Saipan residents admitted seeing two Americans matching descriptions of Earhart and Noonan in July and August 1937. Elders assumed that the Japanese thought the pair were spies and held them in the Garapan jail until they were executed by Samurai sword. Other Saipanese say the pair died from dysentery in the jail.

On November 19, 1970, Joe Artero, an employee of the GovGuam Department of Commerce, told his story to me when I was a reporter for PDN.

Twenty-two-year-old Artero and his cousin obtained visas for a three-month visit to Saipan. They had booked passage for July 13, 1937, aboard the Japanese copra schooner, *Mariana Maru*. However, their trip was delayed two days because the Japanese fleet was doing maneuvers around Saipan. Artero thought that officials with the fleet probably went to Saipan to witness Earhart's execution.

The *Mariana Maru* docked at Garapan pier at 5 p.m. on July 16. Artero and his cousin stayed with Mariano Pangelinan, a friend of Artero's father. The boys were restricted to the city, as were the Saipanese.

The following day, a police detective, Jesus Guerrero, told the cousins that Earhart and Noonan had just been executed, but he didn't say where. Guerrero had worked with the Japanese police before and during World War II to keep the Saipanese in line.

Sunday morning, Artero was kneeling in church when someone told him he had to leave Saipan immediately on the *Mariana Maru*. Artero returned to Pangelinan's house to find his packed suitcase at the door.

Artero spent nine days on the 30-foot schooner and arrived in Yokohama in late July. He was taken to Tokyo where he had dental work done before he was ordered back aboard the *Mariana Maru*. After a stormy 10-day trip, Artero arrived in Guam on August 26.

The following Monday, Artero was questioned about his trip to Saipan by a Navy commander, probably Benjamin W. McCandlish, head of the Naval Government of Guam. Artero told the commander he heard that Earhart and Noonan had been executed on Saipan, and that Japanese were fortifying the island, building a submarine base, and preparing to capture Guam.

The commander ridiculed the story because he thought Earhart couldn't have made a 1,000-mile mistake. If the commander had investigated Artero's report, the mystery of Earhart's death might have been solved, Artero believed.

Thomas Blas, a Saipanese police officer, said that he had photographed the Americans in 1937. He saw Earhart, whom he called "Tokyo Rosa," riding in a military auto with Admiral Miamoto, governor of Saipan. Blas, who was working on construction sites at Tanapag Harbor and the Aslito Airfield, was afraid to tell anyone about seeing the strangers.

When American forces invaded Saipan in 1944, they confiscated tons of documents and photos. A G.I. found Earhart's briefcase filled with papers indicating she was a spy. Another envelope was found, postmarked Saipan, that contained a faded photo of a ravaged Earhart, her hands bound in back—evidence that she survived beyond July 2, 1937. These papers were classified Top Secret by the U.S. Chief of Naval Operations.

Japanese Stragglers

In January 1972, Guam became famous when Soichi Yokoi, dubbed the last *Zanryusha* or Japanese straggler, was discovered hiding in the boonies. International journalists flocked to Guam and vied for photo opportunities like Texas blue flies fighting over roadkill.

Of the 8,000 Japanese forces who survived the invasion of American Marines on Guam, July 21, 1944, some committed harakiri, others disappeared into the jungles, and many were taken prisoner by the Guam Combat Patrol. One of the prisoner-of-war camps was located on the present Hilton Hotel site in Tumon.

Fifteen members of Guam's combat patrol were outfitted with American Army uniforms and armed with submachine guns, automatic rifles, carbines, pistols, and hand grenades. Led by police staff sergeant Juan Aguon, the patrol roamed the boonies daily for a year and a half.

One day the patrol bagged five hungry, thirsty Japanese. Clad in loincloths, the men had been picking coconuts, washing clothes, and playing cards when captured.

The patrol killed 117 stragglers, but a Japanese shot one patrolman and another patrolman died falling into a ravine. One wounded Japanese begged a patrol member to shoot him and put him out of his misery. Aguon's report noted, "His request was granted."

Guam's mild temperatures and jungles made it a perfect hideaway for these nature boys. They survived undetected by remaining undercover all day. With utensils, such as bayonets and G.I. kitchen knives, they gathered food, picked fruit, poached deer, and snagged shrimp and crabs. Ashes from cooking fires were either buried or scattered in the sea. They moved in single file; obliterated their tracks; never broke twigs, trampled down patches of grass, or displaced stones; and didn't follow the same route twice. They stole clothes from lines and food from farms and did calisthenics on moonlit beaches.

Few of those modern-day Robinson Crusoes knew the war was over, and those who suspected it hid anyway, fearing death or torture.

In April 1948, a Japanese, thinking the war was over, stepped onto a road and waved a copy of an old American magazine at two military policemen cruising past in a jeep. When the MPs halted, the Japanese bowed deeply, showed them a photo of Emperor Hirohito being escorted around Tokyo by American MPs, and climbed into the vehicle.

Eleven months later, Guamanian hunters spied two Japanese near Yigo. The hunters killed one straggler, but the other got away.

A year later, some American soldiers broke out of a military stockade. When they were returned to custody, they reported that they had seen six Japanese near Tumon Bay. Since they were on the lam themselves, they made no effort to detain them.

At the Navy ammunition magazine, sentries were often rattled when a Japanese straggler slipped up behind them and screeched in their ears. By the time the sentries swung around, the Japanese had vanished into the boonies.

On September 25, 1951, two fishermen on the beach at Anan Point, a couple of miles from Andersen AFB, found four stragglers asleep on the sand. When awakened, three of them fled. The fishermen hauled in the fourth, Taira Koshin, a 38-year-old Okinawan who had come to Guam eight years before as a civilian employee of a Japanese Navy weather outfit.

The next year another straggler, hiding in a cave, thought the war was over and came out into the open. A military bus driver stopped when he saw the Japanese, clad in a loincloth, standing with his arms upraised in the middle of the road. Before he boarded the bus, the Japanese removed his sandals. The driver high-tailed it to the Provost Marshal's office.

That straggler could have been the one seen by Jodell Rabe, an Air Force dependent living at Andersen AFB on Guam in the '50s. She recalls the day that she and other women riding on an Air Force bus were almost scared to death when a Japanese straggler hopped aboard.

The next day, the straggler led a search party to his cliff dwelling. No one was home, but he left a note for his friends. On finding the note, his companions, wearing white mess jackets swiped off a Navy clothesline, walked into the custody of an Air Force sentry.

Mrs. Rabe remembered that there were many stragglers on Guam in the '50s, and when search planes passed overhead, they scurried for cover. She also heard that some civilian picnickers at Talofofo had seen a Japanese brandishing a carbine and another fishing in a cove.

In early 1953, the U.S. government allowed Japan to send a party to collect bones of troops who died on Guam. The bones were taken home for burial.

Also that year, the Navy launched Operation Straggler, during which posters were left in caves or nailed to trees, and planes dropped 15,000 leaflets. When no stragglers came forth, the operation fizzled.

Four years later, off-duty Marines hiking near the Naval Magazine came upon a campsite with cooking gear and hand tools. They reported this to Naval Intelligence, who whipped up an investigation because they were always alarmed when someone nosed around the island's principal cache of ammo.

Later, Marines patrolling the region found ashes of a fire; piles of breadfruit, shrimp, and coconuts; sleeping pads made of logs and palm fronds; and a pair of tabi, chopsticks, and a toothbrush embossed with a Japanese Navy emblem. In a nearby cave, they found hack-saw blades, three files, a saw, two pot holders, three rounds of rifle ammunition, a pestle, jar of oil, cooking pots, a glass bottle etched with Japanese characters and containing salt, and a garrote, a weapon made of two pieces of wood tied together with wire used to strangle and rob.

A few months later, a woman playing in the rough at the Windward Hills Golf and Country Club, a couple of miles east of the Naval Magazine, was distracted in mid-swing by a scrawny, ragged long-haired man who darted away. She flubbed the shot. Later, she told her partner that she had seen a straggler.

Elizabeth Perry, a Guam poet, delighted in spotting Japanese stragglers and bringing them out of the boonies to the Naval Hospital.

In 1956, a 19-year-old airman stationed at Andersen AFB was swimming at Tarague Beach when he met a Japanese. They communicated by sign language and swam together among the coral, fish, and sharks. The lonely straggler invited the airman to share tuba, eggs, and pig and iguana meat cooked over a fire in his cliffside cave. By the time the airman reported the Japanese to his superiors, the straggler had disappeared.

Guam made worldwide headlines again in May 1960 when two stragglers, Masahi Ito and Bunzo Minagawa, were discovered.

Vicente Manibusan and Clemente Santos of Talofofo had risen at dawn to check their coconut crab traps. While walking along a jungle trail, they spied Minagawa carrying a sack containing a stolen chicken.

The fishermen waited until the Japanese had climbed 30 feet up a breadfruit tree and shouted at him. Minagawa fell from the tree. The Guamanians caught him and tied him with his own belt. Pouches on his belt contained a dirty bandage and a small wooden Buddha. A passing motorist drove them to a police station.

Naval Intelligence took Minagawa to the Naval Hospital where he gobbled doughnuts and drank coffee. He was given a shave and haircut and locked in the neuropsychiatric ward. Minagawa thought the bath was a pre-execution cleansing ritual, and when pricked for a blood specimen, thought he was being drugged. He didn't believe the war was over. Not wanting to expose Ito, his companion, Minagawa insisted he was living alone.

However, the Navy learned about Ito and put Minagawa at the head of a search posse. They found Ito waving a piece of white cloth as he came out of hiding into the arms of two agents. At the Naval Hospital, both men were pronounced fit.

After their capture, a U.S. census-taker from Agaña conferred official existence on Ito and Minagawa—something they didn't enjoy in Japan. In the fall of 1944, their names had been stricken from registers in their prefectures because they were presumed to have died in action.

The Navy asked the American Red Cross for help. A volunteer arranged phone calls to the men's families in Japan, but the stragglers thought their relatives' voices were put-up jobs.

When a shipwrecked sailor or other hapless person needs clothing, it is customary to outfit him in hand-me-downs. But American-Japanese relations were strained during the '60s, and the two Japanese stragglers were repatriated looking as natty as possible. The Red Cross found a two-piece tan outfit for Ito at $53 and a brown suit for Minagawa at $39.95. The men wore new white shirts and black Navy-issue shoes.

On May 28, the pair was flown to Tachikawa Air Base, Japan. When they alit, they were surrounded by 12,000 U.S. airmen and 200 Japanese reporters and photographers. Moments later, they embraced teary relatives.

Both men received 40,000 yen (about $100) each in back Army pay, and publishers paid for their stories. A movie was released about them in October 1960 by Toei Motion Picture Company. But "Saigo No Nihon-Hei" (The Last of the Imperial Army) didn't make a splash at the box office.

Other incidents took place in the early '60s. An illegal poacher shot a Japanese straggler, and a fork lift operator trespassing in the Naval Magazine shot another man lurking in the underbrush. By the time these incidents were reported to authorities, the bodies had been devoured by wild pigs.

In the late 1960s, Guam authorities thought there could be no Japanese left in the jungles.

However, on January 24, 1972, Sergeant Shoici Yokoi surrendered to two fishermen, Jesus Duenas and Manuel De Gracia. Yokoi had survived for 28 years in the jungle and outlasted two companions.

At the discovery of Yokoi, the world's paparazzi flocked to Guam. Many visiting journalists, wearing winter clothes, almost suffocated in Guam's humid heat.

A tailor by trade, Yokoi kept his shears when he fled to the jungle and made shorts and jackets from the bark of tangan-tangan. He dug caves in Talofofo and Naval Magazine areas. He rested by day and foraged at night, surviving on coconuts, mangoes, breadfruit, fruit bats, freshwater shrimp, eels, snails, and rats.

Yokoi kept track of the months and years by knife slashes on a tree. He was so frugal that when the two Guamanians who found him offered him a pancake, he took a bite and put the rest in his pocket for a rainy day. He had read leaflets stating that the war was over, but felt he could not surrender.

When Yokoi was brought out of the boonies and taken into custody, PDN editor Joe Murphy and I rode with the police patrol. Murphy welcomed the straggler to Guam, forgetting that Yokoi had been on Guam longer than Murphy had, and quipped that perhaps Yokoi was a tourist trying to beat his hotel bill. A Guamanian who owned the cave in which Yokoi had been hiding joked about charging him back rent.

A modern-day Rip Van Winkle, Yokoi was hiding in the jungle when jets and TVs became part of daily life. When he saw his reflection in the lens of a TV camera, he thought it was a mirror.

The Japanese government sent Yokoi tape recordings of several relatives speaking to him. He listened and, thinking the tape recorder was a new kind of telephone, began talking back.

At the Naval Hospital, Yokoi had his first haircut in 28 years. When he jumped from his wheelchair, pushed aside attendants and grabbed a Marine guard's arm, onlookers were scared. WWII again? No. Yokoi grinned widely and raised his arm in the air—victory!

The PDN used to run a Foremost Ice Cream ad featuring a picture of a smiling Yokoi captioned, "What was the first thing Sgt. Yokoi asked for after spending 30 years in a cave? 'Give me some Foremost Ice Cream!' Well, maybe not his first request . . . in 1972, when Sgt. Yokoi emerged, Foremost was here supplying fresh, great-tasting ice cream in Guam."

Flying back to Japan, Yokoi burst into tears of joy when he saw Mt. Fuji. He was greeted as a hero by 5,000 people at the airport. The following year, Yokoi returned to Guam to help search the jungles after people reported seeing a straggler near the Naval Communications Station. None was found.

At age 58, Yokoi married. He and his 44-year-old bride honeymooned on Guam and frequently followed the Yomiuri Giants baseball team for spring training on Guam.

Yokoi's clothes, made from jungle fiber, his rusty Army rifle, shrimp and fish traps, a knife, and cooking utensils were displayed in the Guam Museum, located in the Plaza de España in Agaña. Artist G. Little donated a portrait of Yokoi to the museum, contents of which have been moved to the hillside behind the Governor's Office at Tiyan and renamed the Guam Museum Adelup Exhibit Facility.

While Yokoi was hiding, his countrymen had returned to Guam to construct the South Pacific Memorial Park at General Obata's last command post near Mataguac Hill, Yigo. The general died after a fight with U.S. forces in August 1944. The park, dedicated in May 1970, honors those of all nationalities who died in World War II. It comprises a chapel, an ossuary with bones of hundreds of Japanese soldiers who died on Guam, and a 15-meter-tall white tower symbolizing praying hands.

In September 1997 Sgt. Yokoi, 82, died of heart failure in a Japanese hospital.

Vietnamese Refugees

Early one morning in April 1975, Henry Kissinger, one of President Richard Nixon's advisers, called Guam Governor Ricardo J. Bordallo to tell him that Guam would become a stopover haven for more than 100,000 refugees fleeing the war in Vietnam. Before the exodus was over, more than 250,000 Vietnamese citizens fled from South Vietnam to Hong Kong, Malaysia, Philippines, Singapore, Thailand, and Guam.

When the first planeload of refugees arrived on Guam on April 23, 1975, "Operation New Life" began. Some 140,000 refugees passed through Guam during the United States' relocation project. The number of Vietnamese on the island at any one time outnumbered Guam's 100,000 residents.

By mid-May, 103,983 people had arrived by ship at Naval Station, or by air at Naval Air Station or Andersen AFB.

Most of Operation New Life ship arrivals had nothing but the shirts on their backs—and some of them didn't even have that. One young boy carried a hunk of opium; an old man toted a crucifix, two pipes, and a pack of opium.

Many evacuees who clambered down the gangway were barefoot. Red Cross and Navy officials gave zoris to people without shoes and provided a tent where they could take showers.

In other tents, they were given medical examinations and identification cards. They were assigned to one of the receiving stations for subsequent permanent settlement. About 1,120 people a day were processed and allowed to leave for the U.S. mainland or other sponsoring countries.

Individuals helped too. A Navy Wave arrived with an armful of diapers, soap, and towels to clean up a mother and her baby.

One sailor, taking an orphaned baby girl home with him, said to authorities, "What's one more when I have ten others?"

Islanders came out in force to minister to the refugees. Many took them into their homes. Others donated toys to the children being housed at the old Navy Hospital in Asan. The Guam Lions Club provided barbers at no cost for the refugees.

Military personnel fed, housed, and clothed these people. Refugees were billeted in Orote Point, construction company barracks, the Tokyu Hotel, Asan Federal Annex, and Andersen AFB.

Orote Point's tent city was temporary quarters for 50,000 refugees. Military personnel cleared 500 acres of land and provided medics and cooks. Some 3,200 tents were erected, and 191 toilets and 300 showers were placed in lavatory buildings. About 20 miles of water pipes, 2 miles electric cable and 9 miles secondary electric lines, 16 miles of phone lines, and 16 miles of PA system wire were laid. Also, 35 transformers were connected, and 20 plywood huts and 8 field kitchens were erected. The camp was supplied with cots, tents, blankets, mess kits, emersion burners, mattresses, field kitchens, G.I. cans, fire extinguishers, water cans, compressors, sleeping bags, ponchos, spoons, towels, pillows, walk-in reefers, hand saws, reefer van, rope, can openers, memo paper and machines, a PA system, 2,500 tons of rice, and 5 carabaos.

My former boss, George Roberts, U.S. Collector of Customs in Honolulu, and three Customs inspectors, came to Guam to clear 65,000 Stateside-bound Vietnamese.

One afternoon Roberts and I walked through Andersen AFB's tent city, a prison-like camp of steel webbing and barbed wire fences guarded by U.S. Marines. People rested on cots or strolled on boardwalks among the tents, and a Vietnamese priest walked from tent to tent giving solace. One tent held orphaned children.

In a hospital tent, we paused near a mother, crooning to the infant cradled in her arms. A medic bent over for a closer look at the tiny girl. "She died during the night," the mother said.

Outside, the stench from outhouses permeated the compound. These people can't stay, one official said, typhoon season is starting.

"There were a lot of people who made it safely out of Vietnam on our planes and ships who didn't deserve it," said Roberts. "While there were hundreds, perhaps thousands, left there who had so committed and identified themselves to our side that they faced a grim future when we pulled out so unorganizedly and left them to their fate.

"Countering that was the spirit of hope that pervaded so many of the refugees at the prospect of a new life after leaving all their possessions and their way of life behind them," said Roberts.

"I was really touched one morning when a shipload of refugees were debarking in Agaña Harbor. Down the gangway came a black U.S. Army sergeant cradling an old crippled Vietnamese woman in his arms like a child. Following them was the woman's son. He wore shorts and a T-shirt but he had no shoes. He carried the only worldly possession they had—a gallon-sized vegetable can containing about two inches of cold cooked oatmeal saved from a shipboard meal as insurance against going hungry. They constituted about as close to a rock-bottom situation as anything could be, yet, the son was cheerful and most attentive to the welfare of his mother.

"It was heartwarming to see such a positive demonstration of the human spirit in the midst of a situation which most people would regard as very bleak," Roberts said.

The people of Guam welcomed the refugees and adopted some of the babies and children and sponsored entire families. Island life was not disrupted by the deluge of refugees, for most refugees stayed in their camps. However, there was a violent scene when hundreds of refugees, who demanded to return to Vietnam, staged protests and burned a building.

Midst the chaos, Roberts found some former colleagues with whom he had worked in Vietnamese Customs during a five-year tour of duty there. He did his best to allay their fears about the future.

One day while clearing passengers at Andersen AFB, Roberts saw former Vietnamese Air Marshal Nguyen Cai Ky, who escaped from Saigon on a U.S. military cargo flight.

Ky sat alone on a box in the cargo shed. What a come-down from the years of privilege, attention, and adulation Ky had garnered as Chief of the Vietnamese Air Force and Prime Minister, Roberts thought.

Introducing himself, Roberts reminded Ky of their meeting ten years earlier, when Ky had awarded Roberts the Vietnamese Medal of Merit.

(Roberts retired as Collector of Customs in Honolulu in February 1997. He died of cardiac arrest in August that year at his Kaneohe, Hawaii, home.)

Writer Tere Rios Versace also ran into Ky during the exodus.

Tere asked Ky where he was going.

"I'm a refugee. I don't know."

Then, she told him, "My son, Rocky, is missing in Vietnam."

"I'm so sorry," Ky answered.

Tere asked if he knew anything about Rocky, or if he could help her get word about him from the Viet Cong who'd captured him.

"I'm so sorry," he said. "So sad. Fortunes of war."

Humbert "Rocky" Versace had wanted to become a priest. He attended West Point Military Academy, then did three tours of duty in Vietnam. The 26-year-old fell into the hands of the Viet Cong in October 1963, soon after he had received a seminary's letter of acceptance.

Captain Rocky Versace's Army unit endured a six-hour firefight with a band of Viet Cong guerillas the unit had been pursuing outside a tiny South Vietnamese village. When it was over, Versace and two soldiers, all wounded in the ambush, were captured. Versace perished in 1965 at the hands of his captors.

Rocky's remains were never found, but his marker stands near his father's grave at Arlington National Cemetery. Tere and her husband accepted Rocky's Silver Star at a Wisconsin high school ceremony five years later.

Two months before Tere died of cancer at her home in Sarasota, Florida, the commander of the John F. Kennedy Special Warfare Center presented Tere with her long-deceased son's newly issued awards. In July 1999, 81-year-old Tere accepted honors on behalf of her son, the oldest of five children. Major General Kenneth R. Bowra gave Tere with her son's newly issued Special Forces patch and certificate. The awards represented official, albeit posthumous, notices of membership in the elite U. S. Army's Green Berets.

The presentation was made in the atrium of the Bayou Assisted Living Facility in Sarasota where Tere lived. A photojournalist, reporter, and editor for several military publications, Tere had moved to Sarasota from her native Puerto Rico six months previously. She succumbed to lung cancer in September 1999.

The book on the massive arrival and departure of refugees closed on October 15, 1975, during the repatriation of more than 1,000 refugees.

Beginning with the first refugee airlift arrival from Saigon, Guam Cable TV System's cameras recorded the massive and historic human drama of evacuation. Their videotape footage of refugee arrivals and living conditions were shown on "NBC Nightly News" and "Today" programs.

Guam Cable TV was commended during the 1976 National Cable Television Association Cable Services Awards competition "for taking the initiative and lead in covering newsworthy events" during the Indochinese refugee movement through Guam.

All the Ships at Sea

Sea and ships have been important to Guam since Malaysians, with dead reckoning and knowledge of winds, sailed thousands of miles across uncharted waters in open boats to settle on the island. With the arrival of Magellan and, later, whalers, commercial and military sea lanes became Guam's life lines.

Guam's shipping was controlled by the U.S. Navy after the Spanish-American War, when the Navy established a coaling and watering station at Apra Harbor.

The Navy restricted commerce and required security clearance for anyone traveling to and from the region. Airfields and Apra Harbor were closed to civilian commerce except for Pan Am flights carrying passengers and airmail and military charters of civilian ships and aircraft.

Three local wholesalers were authorized to import goods by military transport through the Navy Supply Depot: A.T. Bordallo, T.A. Calvo and Sons, and J.M. Torres. In those days, businesses were required to be at least 51 percent owned by Guamanians, and only Guamanians could purchase property or lease it for more than five years.

The Merchant Marine Act of 1920, authored by Wesley H. Jones, regulates shipping to and from Guam. The Jones Act, as it's called, requires that all merchandise moving between U.S. ports be carried on American-owned vessels built in the U.S. and employing mostly U.S. crew. Forty countries besides the U.S. have such cabotage laws to protect their merchant shipping.

Guam businessmen claim the Jones Act drives up shipping

rates by keeping out foreign competition. On the other hand, U.S. carriers say the act guarantees superior service for Guam.

A Jones Act Repeal Coalition was recently formed to get the law overturned or at least to have Guam exempted, as are the Virgin Islands, American Samoa, and the Commonwealth of the Northern Mariana Islands.

Modern "whalers" returned to Guam in 1964 during the Vietnam War. For two decades, Russians kept their eyes on Guam's military activities.

The first B-52 was delivered to the U.S. Air Force in 1955, and the last one came off the production line in 1962. The planes carried conventional and nuclear bombs and missiles. It took Guam-based B-52s twelve hours to complete round trips to Vietnam from Guam, a distance of 6,760 miles. Crews were bone-tired by the time they returned to Guam.

Soviet spy ships lying offshore, just beyond Guam's three-mile limit, monitored B-52 flights from Andersen Air Force Base. They recorded arrivals and departures at Andersen and monitored movements of eight nuclear-powered Polaris submarines based on Apra Harbor.

By 1980, instead of the 165 or so B-52s that flew out of Guam to hit targets in Vietnam, there were only 18. Those few bombers took part in the Indian Ocean as the United States' show of force following the Soviet invasion of Afghanistan.

One Soviet ship disguised as a whaling trawler arrived off the entrance to Apra Harbor, and the next day, the USS *Proteus,* mothership for the Pacific Fleet's Polaris submarines, came to port.

In the early 1980s, seven Poseidon missile submarines based at Apra Harbor were withdrawn, which left attack submarines, with the *Proteus* as tender. Also, Military Sealift Command ships cruised out of the harbor to be logistical backups in the Persian Gulf War.

Hovering in the sanctuary beyond the territorial limit, Russian trawlers, actually electronic workshops, rotated surveillance duty. The crew was ordered to get as much information about U.S. nuclear submarines as possible. By cruising north along the coast, they also observed Strategic Air Command's activities at Andersen AFB.

Life on the ships was the pits and the Russians were dying to talk to people other than their crew members. The Russians were not allowed ashore, but local yachtsmen exchanged greetings with the spy ships' crews.

Some Guam fishermen used to motor within a quarter of a mile of a trawler. They reported that about thirty Russian crewmembers, basking in shorts or swim trunks on deck, waved and held up a fish or two. There was a volleyball court on deck, and the ball was tied to a line attached to a trolley so the balls wouldn't sail overboard.

Editor Joe Murphy and a couple of Italian newspapermen once tried to board the trawler, but they were sent away. "Nyet!"

At night, it was rumored, Russian sailors swam to shore to swap vodka for American cigarettes. They allegedly gave cases of vodka to harbor pilots as bribes to ignore the trawlers anchored outside the breakwater.

Computers at the North American Aerospace Defense Command went berserk when rumors spread that the Third World War would start when Soviet missiles, shot from the trawlers, struck Guam. Fortunately, this never occurred.

When Navy Chief Warrant Officer Roy Anderberg left Guam in October 1967, he willed me his weekly column, "The Spray, Voice of the Waterfront." I took up his legacy in weekly "Through the Porthole" columns, published in the *Pacific Journal*, and then in the *Pacific Daily News* as "The Log."

Anderberg, a public information officer for the submarine tender *USS Proteus* and, later, public affairs officer for Commander

Naval Forces Marianas, edited the Navy's *Crossroads of the Pacific* paper and moonlighted for the *Guam Daily News*.

His biggest scoop occurred on Valentine's Day 1967: while he was snorkling on the Glass Breakwater of Guam's Apra Harbor, he witnessed the grounding of the SS *Guam Bear*.

Before daylight the *Guam Bear*, a Pacific Far East Line (PFEL) cargo ship approaching Apra Harbor with $2,500,000 worth of cargo, 6 passengers, and 46 crewmembers, collided with the *Esso Seattle*, an empty bulb-nosed oil tanker, heading out of Apra Harbor.

The bow of the tanker penetrated the *Bear*'s No. 4 hold, ripping a hole 40 by 50 feet and carrying away the bulkhead of the No. 5 hold. The ship was in danger of sinking, but it still had power and a pilot on board. Assisted by Navy tugs, the *Bear* was grounded near the Glass Breakwater and the crew and passengers were taken off.

Experts battled to keep power up and the engine room and Holds No. 2 and 3 dry, but after a day they gave in to the sea. Three-quarters of the cargo was lost, including military autos and household goods. Rolls of toilet paper and cans of beer floated to shore.

The press unit Publisher Flores had ordered to boost GDN's capacity to 24 pages was aboard the *Bear*. Fortunately, the press was saved.

After salvaging what they could, PFEL and insurance companies abandoned the derelict, and the Navy took possession of the ship to protect classified material in the cargo. The Navy Ship Repair Facility, with the help of Naval Station tugs and fire department personnel, refloated the vessel.

On July 15, 1967, the *Guam Bear* was towed three miles out to sea, where a charge was set off in the engine room. Within 45 seconds, to the sounds of explosions, tug whistles, boat horns, and shouting, the vessel slipped beneath the waves.

The sinking created a local saying, used whenever merchandise was scarce, "It musta gone down on the *Bear*."

Many vessels rest in Davy Jones's locker, deep in watery graves off Guam's reefs. Some of these derelicts have become pleasure palaces for divers.

In 1904, the cable ship, *Scotia*, was heading toward Apra Harbor when it struck Calalan Bank. Engine room compartments flooded, but no lives were lost. Owned by Cunard Lines, the paddle wheel steamer *Scotia* was built in 1861 in Glasgow, Scotland. In 1879, the ship was converted into a twin-screw cable ship. Today, scattered remains lie in 20 to 30 feet of water outside the Glass Breakwater.

Seventy years later, another Cunard ship, *Caribia*, sank a few hundred yards away from the *Scotia*. Both vessels were salvaged by a Japanese wrecking company.

The saga of the SMS *Cormoran* was of continuing interest to maritime buffs. One GovGuam teacher had furnished his Quonset with items he salvaged from the vessel: dishes, silver trays, candlestick holders, glasses, ash trays, toast holders, coffee pots, lanterns, and portholes. Other divers continually snatched souvenirs from the ship.

Shortly after the First World War began in August 1914, President Woodrow Wilson issued a proclamation of neutrality for the U.S. When Guam's Governor Maxwell heard this, he issued a similar proclamation.

At the same time, Japan entered the war. Since Germany owned the Northern Marianas, Japanese and German warships began playing hide-and-seek among the Micronesian islands.

On December 14, 1914, the captain of the *Cormoran* entered Apra Harbor for coal and provisions. The ship's presence violated the neutrality of Guam. The ship, Capt. Zuckschwerdt, officers, and crew were interned as "guests" of the Naval Governor of Guam.

Actually, this was the second *Cormoran*. In August 1914, the original *Kormoran* (with a "K") was a German armored cruiser in need of repair laying alongside a pier at Tsingtao, China.

Meanwhile in the South China Sea, the Russian passenger steamer, *Rjaesan*, was captured and escorted into Tsingtao harbor. No berth was available, so the steamer was put alongside the *Kormoran*.

German authorities wanted to convert the *Kormoran* to a raider, but realized that conversion of the *Rjaesan* could be done quicker. Fitted with the old raider's armament, coal, ammunition, and searchlights, the Russian steamer was changed into a German raider. During commissioning of the new *Cormoran*, the old ship was sunk outside Tsingtao harbor.

In December 1916, *Cormoran* sailed into Apra Harbor, and American naval authorities gave her 24 hours to steam out, in keeping with neutral port regulations. However, the ship's coal supply was exhausted and the ship was interned.

Guam's Governor, Captain Roy C. Smith, sent the Navy commandant's barge, flying a flag of truce, to order surrender of the raider. Meanwhile, Capt. Zuckschwerdt had dispatched a boat to get supplies at Piti. The Navy barge intersected the German cutter and ordered it to stop. When the cutter didn't stop, a marine corporal fired several shots across her bow and ordered it to surrender.

Those were the first shots of World War 1.

Boarding the *Cormoran*, Navy Lt. Bartlett demanded capitulation from Capt. Zuckschwerdt, but the skipper refused to surrender his ship. After the American boarding party left, the captain detonated a bomb in the hold, and he and the crew jumped overboard. Seamen who drowned were buried on Guam. Those rescued were taken as prisoners of war and shipped to the U.S. mainland in April 1917. *Cormoran* sank in 120 feet of water about a half a mile from land.

Scientific research ships often called at Guam during Pacific expeditions. In the '70s, a group exploring the Marianas Trench brought me a paper cup that had been crushed at the sea bottom, where the weight of the water exerts a pressure of 16,000 pounds per square inch.

The pressure in the deep was great enough to compress and crack the five-inch-thick exterior walls of the U.S. bathyscaph, *Trieste*, by a tenth of an inch.

The standing record for depth achieved by a manned probe in the Marianas Trench was measured at 35,810 feet when the *Trieste* explored the deep in 1960.

In 1993, Jules Verne's *Explorer* dove into the Marianas Trench. The following year, the vessel tested hull materials for *Deep Flight II*, a single-passenger underwater "airplane" that explored the deep in 1996.

The Japanese undersea vessel, *Kaiko*, touched the bottom of the Marianas Trench at 36,008 feet or 6.8 miles. From above, operators manipulated a mechanical arm to place an inscribed plaque on the ocean floor on March 24, 1995.

Humorous incidents were common in Guam's maritime world.

Capt. George Fleming of the M/V *Mas Mauleg* transported celebrants from Saipan and Tinian to attend a fiesta on Rota. Roast deer was the dish *du jour*.

A pilot who took the *Ada Gorthon* out of the harbor on a Sunday in November 1970 reported that the skipper asked him to take the ship way out beyond the breakwater because "it's too easy to meet with an accident on a Sunday."

Once, five Trust Territory sea captains checked into Guam Memorial Hospital concurrently. This coincidence aroused the curiosity of the hospital psychiatrist, who stopped to chat with each captain. The doctor surmised that, although each man complained of a variety of aches and pains, they all suffered from reef fever, laced with alcoholism. One of the captains was convinced that treacherous coral reefs had a magnetic attraction, throwing compasses out of whack and luring ships into their jagged snares.

Guam was the landfall for international bottoms laden with

spirits, furniture, and crystal plus bulk cargoes of lumber, sugar, fruit, rice, automobiles, fuel oil, and equipment to build the San Miguel brewery.

A shipment of 500 cases of Dewars White Label Scotch, which arrived on the *Gay Phoenix* from Japan, was weighed while unloading and found to be less than what the manifest stated. It turned out that 37 cases were filled with soy sauce. Evidently during transshipment in Japan, bottles of soy sauce had been placed in Scotch cases and soy sauce had been poured into some Scotch bottles.

Many vessels stopped by Guam to drop off ailing crewmen or to make repairs to hulls, bearings, engines, or power and radio systems. Missions of mercy were also common in Micronesia's waters.

In 1964, field ship skipper Dewey Huffer learned that a 12-year-old girl on an isolated Truk island had been burned and had to reach a hospital quickly. He steered his 560-ton vessel into a reef-ringed lagoon in the middle of a moonless night. He made it without losing his briny maidenhood and saved the girl's life. From then on, he was called the Virgin Captain.

The *Galveston Navigator*, with a cargo of rotten rice, was abandoned in Apra Harbor. The vessel was purchased by United Tankers, Inc. of New York, renamed the MV *Majuro*, and put into service with the Micronesian Interocean Line headquartered in Saipan. Money from the sale of the vessel's rice cargo went to repatriate crewmembers.

While on the PDN's *Sunday News* staff, Glenda Moore and I were invited on a nuke dive. On February 8, 1971, we joined Navy dependents, local officials, and press members for a trip aboard USS *James Monroe,* a Strategic Ballistic Missile Submarine (SSBN-622) stationed in Apra Harbor.

Monroe was a first-generation U.S. Navy nuclear submarine carrying mines, torpedoes and 16 Polaris missiles. These formidable boats of the silent service patrolled at sea for 60 to 70 days, alternating between the Blue and Gold crews.

Glenda and I crossed the gangplank at daybreak. The sub's hull was straight and level: a 33-foot-diameter tube of steel built for high-speed performance.

After all guests were aboard, the boat threaded its way out of the harbor past ocean tugs, oil tankers, destroyers, and fishing boats. Beyond the breakwater, we landlubbers gathered in the brightly lit control room. The Navy can't do anything without a briefing and cups of coffee.

In the control room were two periscopes, the ship control station, Navstar GPS receiver, navigational equipment, automated plotting board, plotting tables, weapons control panel, plotting tool racks, and mission status board. Here, the Deck Watch Station Officer monitored status boards and fire and ship controls.

Maneuvering a 6,900-ton submarine required a delicate touch on the planes and rudders to prevent unwanted noise. While the sub ran underwater, nobody raised their voices, slammed a hatch, or dropped a toilet seat. After a few hours, we guests began to think small and silent.

During the 12-degree-angle dive, old salts took pride in walking and not spilling cups of coffee. However, I set my coffee cup on a desk and clung to a bolted-down chair to keep from plummeting down the length of the boat.

After the boat was trimmed and level, there was no sensation of motion.

We visitors were restricted to the unclassified areas of the boat. A few of us at a time were allowed into the sonar room, where we heard dolphins and whales singing and laughing as they swam beneath or alongside us.

In the bowels of the boat, we watched and listened as a dummy missile was launched from the firing room. My headset didn't shut out the deafening noise, and I felt like my body was being sucked out the tube.

We ate lunch in the enlisted men's mess, the largest open area on board. We sat on benches around six tables, where 48 sailors usually sat, and gobbled Navy chow: hot dogs, beans, cole slaw, and coffee. It seemed impossible to me that one hundred men worked and lived in this confining, seagoing tube without bumping into each other.

After looking through the periscope to be sure there were no vessels around us, the captain gave the order to surface. This procedure was noisy: the rush of compressed air from air flasks into the ballast tanks and the hull popping from the decreased water pressure.

On the surface, the boat rolled drunkenly in mild harbor swells until we sailed inside the breakwater. Like seasoned sailors, we stood on deck as we docked.

Before we left the boat, we guests received the Royal Order of Polaris Submarines: agents of Davey Jones and Neptunus Rex proclaimed each of us an "honorary member of the ship's company for performing feats heretofore not witnessed by my court will be duly recognized as a Polaris Submariner."

CHAPTER FOUR

Disasters, Natural and Man-Made

Asked whether he had been to Guam, a traveler replied, "I went through once but it was closed." The island was probably in the midst of a supertyphoon, a destructive earthquake, or a power outage caused by a snake. Residents have adapted to this stormy lifestyle by stocking emergency shelves with rice, soy sauce, Spam®, canned and powdered milk, bottled water, candles, toilet tissue, paper towels, and portable electric generators.

Salud!

Guamanians have suffered second-class health care ever since explorers discovered this little corner of the Pacific.

Ancient Chamorros practiced a religion based almost entirely on ancestor worship. Though most Guamanians are Roman Catholics, who observe holy days, never miss Sunday Mass, and erect saints' shrines in their backyards, many still have a healthy respect for *makanas* (sorcerers), *taotaomo'na* (ancestral spirits), and *suruhanas* (healers).

Native medicine was practiced by ancient Chamorro makanas. Today, about one-third of Guam's residents, more women than men, use suruhanas. The links in the chain of traditional healing go back at least a century. Suruhanas have their own specialties in medicine and treatment that were passed down to them, usually from relatives, and they, in turn, pass the lore to future generations.

A true suruhana, according to legend, is born breech (feet first). A breech-birth child is said to have magic hands and will become a healer or nurse, adept at removing throat ailments, including fish bones, by rubbing the throat of the afflicted person. Although some healing plants are disappearing, suruhanas still practice massage and herbal medicine.

In 1994 a suruhanu asked the taotaomo'na for permission to use the bark from the hale-nunu tree for medicine. As a child she had followed her suruhana mother through the jungle to collect plants, which she dried and combined with tea to treat fevers, sore throats, teething pains, and mild pneumonia.

Before 1960, Chamorro midwives, *patteras*, usually assisted with the birth of babies. Some fifty Chamorro women were trained to be midwives by the Naval Nurse Training School and received practical experience at the Naval Hospital and in the field.

Nearly every Chamorro family has a taotaomo'na story, whether it's an uncle or auntie who was punished for a lack of respect or a nephew or cousin who was kept safe when lost in the jungle. The spirits of ancient Chamorros often assume a powerful deformed or headless form, which can be benevolent or malevolent, but should always be respected.

The belief is that if you anger taotaomo'na, you can become sick and die. Some say that if you have to urinate in the jungle, you must ask permission of the taotaomo'na. Beaches, bushes, river beds, banyan trees, and graveyards are favorite haunts of these spirits. Their presence has been felt near the Naval Hospital and at the Naval Ship Repair Facility (SRF), site of an old graveyard.

A sailmaker at SRF attests that her sewing machine sometimes ran without her. Her fellow workers blamed it on taotaomo'na. After a coworker died, the same sailmaker felt something pinch her thigh while she was napping at home. Friends said that was the coworker's way of saying goodbye and acknowledging that there is life in the hereafter.

Because of the island's isolation, ancient Chamorros were susceptible to infectious diseases introduced by Europeans, and epidemics of measles, smallpox, and tuberculosis caused many deaths. When white man first burst in on Guam and Micronesia, however, the natives weren't disease-free. The islanders probably suffered from hookworm, yaws, filariasis, boils, ulcers, and numerous fungous diseases of the skin.

Clothing has played a part in increasing the incidents of tuberculosis, pneumonia, and other respiratory and skin diseases among people accustomed to nudity. Micronesians used to swim nude until the missionaries arrived. It isn't unusual today to see the indigenous people swimming in shorts, muumuus, pants, shirts, or any garment they happen to be wearing when they feel the urge to plunge into a lagoon. In fact, many times during beach parties, I couldn't resist wading, fully clothed, into the offshore water to keep cool.

In 1902 there was a leprosarium at Ipao on Tumon Bay, where twenty-five lepers were isolated in thatched huts. The camp closed in 1912, and the remaining patients were shipped to an island south of Manila, where many died.

A disease endemic to Guam is Lytico-Bodig, or Chetnut Humatag, the disease of Umatac. As in Spanish times, Umatac is the epicenter of this deadly malady in which the spinal cord and brain are attacked. Lytico is a progressive paralysis resembling Amyotropic lateral sclerosis (ALS) or motor neuron disease, and Bodig is a condition like Parkinson's, occasionally with dementia.

Some neurologists think the disease is caused by eating fadang, the cycad federico seeds. After harvesting, seeds are dried and ground to make flour tortillas and tamales, cycad chips, and a soup or porridge called atole. These seeds are thought to be poisonous if not well washed. The risk of contracting the disease has somewhat lessened in recent years, and the number of victims of the disease is declining.

Between 1926 and 1959, there was one civilian doctor on Guam, Dr. Marsh. He walked between the villages of Merizo and Inarajan to call on patients. He was assisted by a priest, who had been excommunicated by the church for fathering a child. Dr. Marsh, appalled by the large number of children with worms crawling out of their noses, tried to upgrade sanitary conditions in the villages.

Through the years, the Navy has provided good medical facilities for servicemen and their dependents on Guam, but for civilians in outlying villages, medical care was inadequate.

Governor Skinner separated a civilian hospital at Oka, located in two rusty Butler buildings, from the Naval Hospital and named it Guam Memorial Hospital (GMH). Nurses and doctors were recruited from the Philippines, and many remained on Guam to become U.S. citizens.

In 1955, Catholic leaders opened the Catholic Medical Center in Agaña. A few nurses were Stateside wives of military personnel, but most medical personnel were imported from Manila.

When the Seventh Day Adventist Clinic opened, it hired U.S.-trained doctors, dentists, ophthalmologists, and general practitioners. The clinic also offered evening classes in dieting, exercise, and vegetarian cooking, liberally sprinkled with religious messages.

In 1976, the Catholic Diocese opened the 221-bed Medical Center of the Marianas (MCM) at the site of Mercy Convent near the old GMH. However, MCM went bankrupt and closed shortly thereafter.

One of the projects of Governor Ricky Bordallo was to acquire a new building for GMH because the old Oka hospital had deteriorated since its post-Typhoon Karen renovation. When MCM closed, Bordallo moved GMH into the building. Parts of shabby GMH were turned over to the Department of Mental Health and Substance Abuse.

GMH was a chamber of indignities, almost comparable to

American medical facilities during the Spanish-American War. A hospital administrator admitted to the press that patients' lives were in danger. In 1973, a patient died by electrocution when he touched an air-conditioner, and another was scalded to death in a bath.

With the shortage of nurses, some patients recorded their own temperatures and blood pressures, and brought their own pillows and bedding for lengthy stays in the hospital. A sign at the reception desk warned, "Please don't bring in food because of rats." In June 2000, Guam Memorial Hospital nurses were given a much-deserved raise, up to 35-percent of their pay.

In 1994, the Doctor's Clinic was formed by a group of Guam family practitioners as a subsidy of Straub Clinic and Hospital Inc., in Honolulu. By 1997, the clinic was losing $200,000 a month. An immediate infusion of cash from the Straub Clinic saved it, but this wasn't enough, and the clinic filed for bankruptcy under Chapter 11. A reorganization plan was approved by District Judge John Unpingco, and the clinic's financial condition began to improve. By March 2000, the clinic began to pay its creditors, and by August all of the clinic's pre-bankruptcy secured debt and most of its priority unsecured debt had been satisfied. The Doctor's clinic is now regaining its fiscal robustness after its period of critical financial health.

Another benefit to the people of Guam came about when the Honolulu-based Diagnostic Laboratory Services, Inc., recently set up a permanent branch on Guam.

There is much room for much improvement in Guam's health care. For decades, affluent Guamanians flew off-island for medical care. The Guam Medical Referral Office handles transportation for patients and their families to fly to Hawaii, Manila, or the U. S. mainland. Some 1,200 patients and their families were referred to off-island medical treatment this year.

In March 2001, Joe Murphy's wife was flown to Los Angeles to undergo an operation at the Good Samaritan Hospital, because Guam's hospital couldn't handle such an operation.

There are good doctors, surgeons, and nurses on Guam, but it's been thirty years since Guam had a professional hospital administrator and twenty years since the hospital was accredited.

Recently, three cholera cases were treated by physicians on Guam, and cholera killed nine people in Pohnpei, where 377 others were hospitalized during the outbreak. Food imports from the island were banned from entering Guam.

In the past decade, Guam has added an attraction, unrelated to fun in the tropical sun. The Department of Public Health reports that many Asian tourists, while vacationing on the island, get tested for the HIV virus, something they'd lose face doing at home.

Windy Island

The island's all-too-common typhoons are blamed for everything that can't be blamed on politicians.

Every twelve to fourteen years, a supertyphoon devastates Guam, and the island is declared a national disaster area. Records show that an annual average of nineteen typhoons develop out of thirty-four storms.

These tempests boil up around Pohnpei or the Marshall Islands and move erratically west-northwest through "Typhoon Alley," slowing, speeding, careening across Guam, and swerving toward the Philippines or Japan. The devilish winds and rains uproot trees, overturn boats, suck out windows, splinter utility poles, moan through houses, and cause marital squabbles, migraines, and absenteeism.

Typhoon reconnaissance flights began when U.S. Navy armadas were battered by typhoons during World War II. The U.S. Navy and Air Force Typhoon Warning Center was established in 1959.

Five years later, the Navy's Fleet Weather Central Joint Typhoon Warning Center linked Guam with a communications satellite orbiting the earth every 97.5 minutes, providing early warning capability for the islands. By the late '70s, P-3 Orion weather planes, equipped with recording gear, began flying into storms to predict landfall.

Dorothy Fritzen's 1972 book, "The Spinning Winds," is an encyclopedia of typhoon facts.

"It is always typhoon season somewhere in the Western Pacific region from the equator to 25 degrees North latitude, and from 180 degrees West longitude to the coast of mainland China. This immense area . . . is bedeviled every year by 15 to 25 vicious typhoons that take lives and cause destruction amounting to millions of dollars," Dorothy wrote.

Guam is always in Typhoon Condition Four, meaning a storm could occur within 72 hours. Typhoon Condition Three means a storm can occur within 48 hours; Condition Two, 24 hours; and Condition One means it will hit the island within 12 hours—time to batten down the hatches and stock up on provisions in your shelter or typhoon-proof house.

Guamanians will never forget Typhoon Karen, a howling, shrieking creature born near Truk on November 6, 1962. Karen literally blew Guam apart, killing nine people and destroying 90 percent of island housing.

Feeding on wind and rain over 800 miles of open sea, Karen smashed directly into Guam November 11 at 10 p.m. Anemometers broke after wind velocities surpassed 200 miles an hour. Scarcely anything stood in her path of 180-mph sustained winds, with 207-mph gusts.

My friend Karmee Dolley had arrived on Guam to visit friends in January 1962. She had planned to leave in November, but Typhoon Karen changed her plans.

Dolley recalled, "We had already had about ten storm warnings that year, so that afternoon when we were told about Typhoon Karen, my neighbors and I didn't think much about it. I fell asleep but I awoke when waves began knocking on my front door. I barricaded it. While I was standing in the middle of the living room holding my eight-month-old Dachshund, Kookie, the house was picked up like a Dixie Cup and blown away. I was almost swept out to sea by the waves, but I tied my puppy to my arm and wrapped myself around a telephone pole.

"In the morning, I went to a nearby Quonset where people gave me a muumuu, since my clothes were almost torn off me. I made it to Playland Bowl where I got my bowling shoes—the only things I had left. Then I went to the hospital for first aid. My plans to return to the States went out the window with the typhoon. I had nothing to go back with. The only things I saved from the house were my door keys."

As it happened, Dolley stayed on Guam and opened an H&R Block office in Agaña. When I left the island in 1978, she was operating two additional branches of the tax firm.

After Typhoon Karen, Guam was declared a $60 million disaster, and Federal funds for relief and rehabilitation flowed in. Karen was actually a blessing in disguise, igniting a construction boom in which inferior homes destroyed by the storm were replaced with typhoon-proof structures.

Another disaster, Supertyphoon Pamela, struck Guam head-on fourteen years later.

In mid-May 1976, meteorologists predicted that Pamela's main thrust would hit Guam within days. As Pamela continued toward Guam, winds intensified to a peak of 130 knots with gusts to 160 knots. The storm hit with fury: first came the high winds, then towering waves smashed across the reef with such force that boats were lifted from the harbor onto docks. The barometer fell and the surf outside the reef began to rise.

On May 20, Condition One was set at 1400. People left work to batten down their home hatches. The next day the storm knocked out power at 1410, followed by water, phones, and other communication systems.

Destructive-force winds in excess of 50 knots battered the island for 30 hours. During that period, winds increased to more than 63 knots for 18 hours and to more than 100 knots for 6 hours. All but one of the island's anemometers were blown away. Atmospheric pressure instruments recorded extremely large differences on windward and leeward sides of buildings.

When Pamela struck, Chichi and I were living in a two-bedroom, third-floor unit at San Vitores Condominium, a complex of two concrete 30-unit buildings on a hill across from Tumon Bay.

The typhoon came at the worst possible time: two days before payday. My cupboard was as bare as Mother Hubbard's: I was out of kibbles for Chichi and gasoline for my Ford Maverick.

I cooked the lone chicken in the freezer and made salad, which Chichi and I ate for three days. I turned a bedroom closet into a shelter by placing a twin-bed mattress on the floor. I put a battery-operated lamp and radio, deck of cards, half-gallon of sherry, and Chichi's wicker bed in one corner.

Chichi and I hid in the closet for two nights and three days while wind screamed through the windows, cracked open to stabilize the air pressure. Fierce winds drove rain through the air-conditioning unit on my roof and into my livingroom, creating a four-inch-deep pool.

When the eye of the storm passed overhead, my neighbors and I came out on the balconies. Our views of the beach and bay were usually obstructed by a jungle of palms, ironwood trees, and tangan-tangan. However, Pamela's wind had flattened trees and stripped the beach. Waves in the slate grey bay created seahorses that trotted ashore between roofless shacks with walls leaning like houses of cards.

Except for seagulls screeching as they wheeled overhead, the air in the storm's eye was almost still, quiet. Large palm fronds were strewn around the parking lot, and we watched a piece of corrugated tin surf on a zephyr over the roof of my car and slice off the antenna.

Then the furious backside of the storm passed overhead like a freight train grinding down a grade.

KUAM radio was credited for alleviating listeners' typhoon

jitters by playing soothing music, continually updating weather bulletins, and disseminating public service announcements. I, for one, was grateful to KUAM, which kept me from feeling so alone during the storm.

The station had quite a history. Replacing Armed Forces Radio in March 1954, KUAM was first housed in the boonies in an unair-conditioned corrugated tin shack that transmitted the pittypat of every drop of Guam's six-month-long rainy season into customers' radios. Cows, carabaos, dogs, and chickens competed with news announcers for air time. In 1963, Pacific Broadcasting Corporation bought the station, increased wattage, introduced color TV, and built an air-conditioned studio.

During Typhoon Pamela's early hours, KUAM's tall antenna was destroyed. However, the station remained on the air through the efforts of a technician, who stretched a clothesline from a damaged studio wall to a coconut tree—*voila*, an antenna.

Throughout the storm, McDonald's, in upper Tamuning next to the cable TV station, operated on generator power. The manager donated hamburgers and coffee to emergency crews.

The Alupang Cove Condominiums on Agaña Bay were built of typhoon-resistant concrete and steel. During Typhoon Pamela, Maggie Pier, a long-time Guam resident and member of the Press Club, was sitting in a chair in her condo when a window imploded. She clung to the chair's arms and barely escaped being sucked out the window by the fierce wind.

The uncle of Guam's present Governor Carl Gutierrez died during Pamela. He was trying to prevent a window from blowing out of its frame when the glass shattered, cutting him in the face and stomach. He died on the way to the hospital.

On May 22, the winds died down and the ocean was calm. Recovery wasn't automatic. Somehow, crews got power to the Fena Dam pumping station to get water into the treatment plant. The Navy's Orote and Agaña diesel power plants and GPA's Tamuning diesel plant went on line.

Navy Public Works Center personnel left their own damaged

homes to work on military and civilian facilities. Like a speeded-up movie, power and telephone lines went up, debris was cleared, buildings repaired, roofs went back on, village sewer systems were restored, docks were made usable for ships to unload, and the Governor's family was provided emergency housing.

Like most people, I was devastated after Typhoon Pamela—no power, water, phone, or food. I had $5 in my wallet.

I drove on gas fumes to Ben Franklin's, which at that time was the world's largest branch of the chain. I waited in a long line with others to get inside, where I hoped to buy batteries and dog food. Ahead of me in line was the husband of a woman I worked with at the cable TV station. Bless him, he loaned me $25!

Ben Franklin's emergency generator operated lights and cash registers but not air-conditioning. I sweated in another line to walk up to the second floor on the out-of-commission escalator, which was the first on the island.

I was shocked at prices of emergency supplies. Overnight, prices had doubled and, in some cases, tripled on candles, batteries, flashlights, toilet paper, canned goods, dog food, ice, and building materials.

Lack of electricity closed island gas stations and restaurants that did not have emergency generators. Eateries with their own generators worked round the clock to provide food for customers, as well as public service crews. Every night on the way home from work, I stopped at Kentucky Fried Chicken to wait in an hour-long line in the steamy building to buy two pieces of hot chicken to share with Chichi.

The swimming pool at San Vitores condominium where I lived had been filled just before Pamela's visit. Every day I'd dip two buckets of water from the pool and carry them to my third floor condo to flush the toilet. Some residents bathed in the pool, but the water was quickly polluted with bugs, leaves, and bacteria.

Condo residents gathered outside each evening to share barbecue and whatever food we could round up. People like myself, who usually lived in air-conditioned isolation, came to know their neighbors.

One evening an electric company truck drove up to us. The driver asked, "Want some power?" We shouted with joy.

I ran home to turn on the lights and the air-conditioner. However, my air-conditioner had been frozen by Pamela's torrential rain. My homeowner's insurance didn't cover "acts of God." After sweating for several months, I finally saved the $500 needed to repair the unit.

Well-to-do islanders, GovGuam officials, and senators collected food stamps and Red Cross vouchers. They sent relatives to wait in line and complete necessary paperwork, but I didn't have time to wait in line.

Guam Cable TV was useless: TV lines, equipment and systems were either blown down or water-logged. I thought I'd lost my job on the TV magazine until manager Lee Holmes decided to publish a typhoon issue. He paid me by the hour and let me fill my Maverick's gas tank at the company pump. For two days, I drove around the island taking pictures of damage.

On May 31, 1976, I told a PDN reporter, "Although cable TV broadcasting has not been restored, a special typhoon edition of *TV Guam* will go on sale Thursday. The issue will not contain regular TV schedules, since 25 percent of the cable network will not be restored until the end of June, with 60 percent restored in late July and 90 percent by September.

"The 24-page typhoon issue will have photos and articles of island-wide damage, stories on the typhoon's effects on the cable TV system and recovery operations, and Walt Gerber's story on Pamela from a cable TV weatherman's perspective."

Some 10,000 souvenir copies of *TV Guam* were sold. Later, we published monthly issues containing recaps of soap operas and other programs that people were missing.

Power and water were restored on military bases and to tourist hotels on May 26 but not to most civilian homes. Not until mid-June did 90 percent of the island power generation system come on line and the water system return to normal. Residents of southern villages waited months longer for power, water, and phone service.

Typhoon Pamela did her "dampest" to wipe out every island structure. Few unreinforced structures withstood the intermittent pressure and wrenching effects of the winds and rain. Some 33 inches of rainfall, with 27 inches falling in 24 hours, were recorded by the National Weather Service.

Governor Ricky Bordallo declared martial law, and a curfew was enforced for several days. Schools didn't reopen until fall.

Bordallo saw federal disaster assistance as an opportunity to reconstruct storm-damaged facilities and to improve Guam's infrastructure. He obtained $367 million in 1975-78 for typhoon-related rehabilitation, non-typhoon capital improvements, and GovGuam operations and services. Bordallo's projects included a new air terminal, which began operating in January 1976; the Agaña marina; sewer treatment plant; the Guam Public Market; and the 11-foot bronze statue of Quipuha, the first monument to a traditional Chamorro leader.

In August 1976, I replaced Tere Rios Versace as Public Affairs Officer of PWC. I composed pages, took photographs, and wrote press releases as well as feature stories and a column, "Shop Talk," for PWC's monthly paper. Pages were filled with grip 'n grin photos of employee promotions and awards, double-truck photo spreads whenever a change-of-command ceremony took place on Naval Station. During my watch, PWC celebrated its 17th birthday.

While working there, I learned that PWC was the Navy's official fixer-upper. It cleaned, patched, painted, repaired, furnished quarters, caught snakes, dispensed millions of dollars of supplies, and auctioned government rattan furniture, surplus equipment, and jeeps. It managed the island-wide power, water, and telephone systems and Department of Defense family housing units.

Navy Public Works Center (PWC) was Guam's largest civilian employer, with a core of engineers, accountants, technicians, and equipment operators. The Center chose the cream of island youth for apprenticeship programs in mechanics, carpentry, electronics, shipfitting, boilermaking, and printing.

PWC Guam was officially established in December 26, 1949, but public works activities began in 1900. A colonel in command of the marine garrison became head of the public works department, which consisted of a captain, a lieutenant, warrant machinist, a Guamanian, and a former Spanish secretary who inspected roads and sanitation.

When the U.S. Secretary of the Navy was designated to administer Guam, Fleet Admiral Chester Nimitz established a command post atop the hill that later bore his name. He wore two hats: Commander Naval Forces Marianas and Commander in Chief U.S. Pacific Fleet for Area Coordination, Search and Rescue, Disaster Control and Special Operations of Naval Elements in Guam and the Trust Territory of the Pacific Islands.

During the Navy administration, highways, utilities, and the hospital were improved. Apra Harbor developed from one of limited usefulness into one of the deepest, most sheltered ports in the Pacific.

The 103rd Naval Construction Battalion operated the Navy school bus system and earth-moving equipment; installed and maintained island-wide telephone and highway systems; and maintained security.

After Typhoon Pamela, twelve PWC crews made a clean sweep, funded with $2.5 million in Federal Disaster Assistance Authority funds. They replaced a marina at Naval Station, the Mess at Naval Magazine, Publications and Printing Service Facilities, a Ship Repair Facility building, and a transit shed at Naval Supply Depot. They repaired damage to the harbor and Glass Breakwater, the bachelor enlisteds' quarters, support facilities, vehicle maintenance shop, warehouses, chapel, child care center, and hardened military telephone and electric power systems.

Unusual tasks became usual: crews replaced louvered windows and frames in Navy family housing, dried out hundreds of soggy carpets and mattresses, X-ray equipment, transformers, and motors; provided portable toilets to the civilian community; cleared and lit airport runways; brought power to Naval Station galleys; and built a new cooling tower for the Naval supply Depot.

Quonsets, wooden houses, roofs, trees, and an inestimable number of corrugated tin sheets were demolished by end loaders, which had dozens of flat tires from nails dropped on the ground during demolition. Some homeowners wanted all debris removed except a bathroom or kitchen, so they could rebuild around those rooms. A number of rat snakes were snared from caved-in cesspools.

In 1983, Typhoon Olive destroyed much of the reconstruction work in progress after Typhoon Karen. Both Karen and Olive turned out to be the means for more than a decade of capital improvements in Guam. Then along came Typhoon Russ in December 1990 and Typhoon Yuri in November 1991.

On August 28, 1992, Typhoon Omar ravaged Guam's tourist facilities to the tune of $25 million. The storm had winds of 150 mph, with gusts to175 mph.

Japanese tourists who had come to fish returned home because there was no ice for reefers. Japan Travel Bureau canceled tours, and 5,000 tourists, on island during the typhoon, left.

Jon Anderson, a former Honolulu newsman, was hosting a talk show on K-Z Radio Inc. throughout Typhoon Omar. He described the storm as "a train roaring by, rocking the building." He noticed the change in air pressure when the eye of the storm came over. At the storm's height, Anderson saw huge pieces of corrugated tin roofing flying down the streets and toppling utility poles.

The eye of the storm passed over the Guam Hilton Hotel. The hotel's air-conditioning equipment blew off the roof, windows popped out, and the lobby was destroyed.

Hotel Nikko Guam was closed after storm-driven waves battered the pool area and walls of water washed through the lobby. The Sotetsu Tropicala Hotel on Tumon Bay was closed for weeks after Omar destroyed offices and the restaurant.

The Palace Hotel Guam closed while its 11-story atrium was

repaired. Despite that, the 400-room hotel housed 100 workers from the American Red Cross, Army Corps of Engineers, and Federal Emergency Management Agency.

The roof of the discotheque SandCastle was ripped from the building, and a huge metal stage door was peeled away like a banana.

Hotel maids dipped buckets into swimming pools for water to do laundry and to flush toilets. Safe drinking water was scarce, but GovGuam and military tank trucks provided water to villages. Family-sized tents were supplied to residents whose houses were destroyed. Schools closed until water and power were restored.

Eighty percent of the island was without power, TV stations didn't broadcast, and water and phone systems couldn't operate without electricity.

A mayoral primary election was put on hold while incumbents helped with storm cleanup instead of campaigning.

Two years later, 110 families were selected to buy a $1 house from the Federal Emergency Management Agency (FEMA) because Typhoon Omar had destroyed their homes. FEMA homes are concrete, with power, water, sewer, and telephone hookups provided by GovGuam. Residents must paint houses, buy appliances, and install certain fixtures. Ninety-six of those families will pay GovGuam $2,500 in 10-year installments for their lots.

Guam's power line repair experts, experienced in restoring power after storms, have been helping the Virgin Islands with similar problems for years. During the National Governors' Association meeting in February 1996, Virgin Islands Governor Roy Schneider praised the generosity of Guamanians and presented Guam's Governor Carl Gutierrez with a plaque officially thanking Guam for helping restore power after Hurricane Marilyn in late 1995. Gutierrez answered, "Guam couldn't stand idly by—we have our own problems with typhoons."

The 1997 typhoon season began in April when a storm, formed near the Marshall Islands, passed over Guam. The storm's high winds and torrential rains almost caused the PGA Tour's Guam Open to be canceled.

The year ended with a bang in December when Supertyphoon Paka ravaged Guam, causing more than $200 million in property damage. President Clinton declared parts of the island as disaster areas, and the American Red Cross spent more than $2.5 million on relief for Guam and neighboring Rota.

Paka began November 28 as a tropical depression 3,500 miles east of Guam and intensified as it tracked westward across the Pacific. On December 16, the National Weather Service clocked Paka's winds from 145 to 160 miles per hour, with gusts to 195 mph. Andersen Air Force Base reported one gust as high as 236 mph. Some 1,200 residents fled to emergency shelters in schools.

At 6:30 p.m. that day, the island lost power. The eye of the storm passed over Andersen and Dededo beginning at 8 p.m. Paka had two concentric eyes: an outer eye wall cloud 40 miles in diameter and a fragmentary inner eye 20 miles in diameter. Residents hunkered down for the second half of Paka. The Joint Typhoon Warning Center later confirmed what islanders believed–Paka's second winds were more damaging than its first.

The supertyphoon raged through the night, and residents awoke to mass ruin. Boats had been tossed ashore, dozens of cars and other vehicles had been overturned or damaged, thousands of homes had been flattened, tin roof sheets were wrapped around downed power poles, hotel rooms were rain-soaked, and much of the island's vegetation had been stripped and minced.

The Joint Typhoon Warning Center reported that good planning had kept people from being killed. However, there was one casualty. Rodolfo Palacios, a 57-year-old Santa Rita man, fell to the ground while repairing the roof of his house. He died January 3 at Guam Memorial Hospital.

More than 3,000 families were left homeless, and half the island's residences sustained major damage. The Air Force allowed storm victims to use the Andersen South housing area. The Navy made additional housing available, and field kitchens were set up to feed these temporary residents.

Water was restored to most of the island by December 18, but power remained down. Paka's winds had spared only one power plant, and its electricity was routed to the hospital.

Three days after the storm, port operations resumed and planes began flying in and out of the airport. However, Paka struck hard at Guam's tourism industry. Japan Airlines temporarily halted its flights to Guam, citing malfunctioning airport equipment. Japan Travel Bureau, one of Japan's largest tour operators, canceled package trips to Guam and, instead, offered flights to the neighboring island of Saipan, which Paka had spared.

On December 19, people still remained in shelters set up in schools. Residents who couldn't cook at home without power formed 20-car lines at McDonald's drive-in window. Without air-conditioning, residents fought off mildew and pests driven indoors by the lack of vegetation. People were advised to boil water and to get tetanus shots.

Guam's stores, including the world's largest Kmart, ran low on emergency supplies, and complaints were made against retailers who raised prices on ice, candles, bottled water, batteries, butane, generators, and gasoline. Many service stations ran out of gas before Christmas, and those that remained open were jammed with long lines of cars.

Generators that normally sold for $900 were going for $1,500 or more. Saipanese sent portable generators to their friends and relatives on Guam. People gladly put up with the noisy generators to have the comfort of hot water and air-conditioning.

Two weeks after Paka, more than 8,500 residents formed mile-long lines to apply for food stamps being dispersed for emergency aid at the University of Guam field house.

On December 22, landscapers worked to save trees toppled by the storm's winds, and farmers reported wind-damaged crop losses of $470,056. While raking typhoon debris from their yards and gardens, some residents found World War II bombs. Volunteers picked up wood, glass, trash, and 300 pieces of tin tossed along the beach and into West Agaña Bay by Paka.

On Christmas Eve, church services took place by candlelight

as crews worked to bring light to neighborhoods. More than 1,000 people, many of them homeless storm victims, spent Christmas Day together at a special Mass and fiesta held in Skinner Plaza. Islanders shared meals, and 2,500 toys were donated for the children.

Red Cross workers, who distributed clothing, bedding, and other necessities to villagers, reported that 900 homes had been destroyed or severely damaged by the storm.

Mercy flights carrying emergency crews and supplies arrived, and more than 30 tons of supplies were delivered a week after the typhoon hit. A military C-5 cargo plane landed December 23 at Andersen Air Force to deliver water, tents, and other supplies. Members of the Air Force National Guard from Ohio and Pennsylvania arrived to help Coast Guard personnel clean up the island. Guam National Guard members directed traffic on Marine Drive at intersections where traffic lights were not working.

Utility workers from Honolulu and Los Angeles arrived to join the Guam Power Authority crews restore power. GPA estimated damage to the island's electricity system at more than $19 million.

Some 8,800 typhoon victims registered for help with FEMA. By December 29, FEMA had issued and mailed 171 checks totaling $727,000 to residents for food, clothing, and other essentials.

The 45-year-old tradition of the Air Force's annual Christmas Drop, postponed as Paka moved in, took place in early January.

By January 11, 30 percent of the island remained without power, but about 60 percent of the island's water wells had power. Damage to Guam's port buildings, equipment, and property was estimated at $6.2 million.

A month after Typhoon Paka, 77 percent of the island had power, 31 schools were reopened, and stores sold out of shirts that boasted in bright letters, "I Survived Supertyphoon Paka."

One Guamanian said Paka "was hell on Earth." When folks on Guam say that about a typhoon, you know it was bad.

Rock 'n Roll

Earthquakes are also a fact of life under the tropical sun. Guam has two seasons: wet and dry, or typhoon and sunstroke, both punctuated by earthquakes.

Guam and its sister islands perch near the boundary where two slabs of the earth's crust, the Pacific and Philippine plates, come together. The Mariana Trench, the deepest place in the world, lies off Guam's eastern coast, and earthquakes and tremors are daily occurrences. Before a seismograph was installed in Agaña in 1914, violent earthquakes occurred but were unrecorded.

In 1902, a tremor destroyed the Agaña cathedral's bell tower and one wall collapsed. Bridges on the Agaña-Piti road caved in, and the Umatac Church of San Dionisio was left as a pile of wooden rubble, as it had been after an 1849 quake.

A month after Typhoon Pamela struck Guam, a 6.5-quake shook, rattled, rocked, and rolled chandeliers, doors, dishes and shell collections. Power was out for several days.

Guamanians won't quickly forget the strongest earthquake of the century: 8.1 on the Richter scale on August 8, 1993. Damage was minor and no deaths were reported, but 60 people were injured. A 4.5 aftershock rattled the island too.

The earthquake ruined the Guam Hilton's cooling system. The hotel closed for repairs but reopened 430 of its 694 rooms in March 1994. The remainder of the hotel opened in October. Its $70 million, 11-story Magalahi Tower suffered little damage in the quake.

The Hyatt Regency Guam, under construction at the time of the quake, opened in October as planned. The Guam Reef Hotel's 120,000-pound cement canopy fell during the earthquake and crushed several cars. It was replaced by a lightweight metal structure.

The $60 million Royal Palm Resort was so badly damaged by the earthquake, only twenty-one days after its grand opening, that it was declared structurally unsound and was destroyed by implosion in December. The quake caused the hotel's second floor to collapse, causing irreparable damage. In the end, the Department of Public Works determined that the building should be demolished. In twelve seconds, the entire complex was a heap of concrete.

Out of that rubble, would come the largest and most high-tech courthouse Guam has ever seen. The courthouse was constructed in the Harmon office building at no expense to taxpayers.

The bill for the courthouse was paid by a consortium of off-island companies entangled in a legal battle of epic proportions, which began within weeks of the 1993 earthquake. The Royal Palm Resort's owners and commercial tenants sued the contractors and engineers of the project. A second suit was filed by six members of a family, who were staying in the hotel at the time of the quake and sued for medical expenses incurred due to personal injuries suffered during the earthquake, lost wages, and emotional distress. A third suit filed by a corporation alleged that an adjoining two-story building that housed the restaurant wasn't severely damaged and did not need to be demolished.

The trial was to be held on Guam but no courtroom was big enough to hold all participants–lawyers, paralegals, secretaries, technicians. So a courthouse and office spaces were constructed in the Ixora Industrial Complex in Harmon.

Dorothy Horn had invited guests for dinner the evening of the 1993 quake. As she rose to greet her guests, the quake struck and she fell onto the couch. China and crystal crashed all over the dining room and the power went out. Dorothy's sewing machine was broken along with many ornamental masks that fell off the walls. With flashlights in hand, guests picked up broken glass and didn't get around to eating dinner that evening.

Phyllis Rice, a long-time resident of Santa Rita, returned from a mainland trip just after the quake hit. Her wedding china and crystal were destroyed, the hot water heater was torn from its connections, there was a leak in the roof, and the record cabinet had fallen and blocked the library door.

Phyllis said, "Many of the hotel workers lost their jobs, but the new Hyatt Hotel has opened and it's beautiful. The island will pick itself up again.... The people will survive, as they always have done despite war and natural disasters."

In April 1997, a 6.3-magnitude earthquake, centered in the Pacific 46 miles north of Guam and 44 miles west of Rota, struck Guam in early morning, knocking out power to the island and causing four minor injuries.

Guamanians rallied to help India when a 7.7-magnitude earthquake struck that country in January 2001. Guam's Andersen Air Force Base played a major role in the U. S. Air Force's first humanitarian airlift to earthquake victims.

A few days after the Indian quake struck, supplies, equipment, and personnel were flown to Andersen AFB from Travis Air Force Base in California and Dover Air Force Base in Delaware. This cargo was loaded at Andersen onto four C-17 aircraft from McCord Air Force Base in Washington. The cargo was transferred to the C-17s, which are capable of landing on short, remote runways. Relief supplies included sleeping bags, blankets, trucks, forklifts, water trailers, and tents, all of which were donated to the Indian government.

The Indian community on Guam solicited monetary donations for victims of India's worst earthquake in fifty years. Chita Blaise, chief executive officer of the American Red Cross chapter on Guam, said the organization provided an initial $25,000 to the Indian Red Cross to help relief efforts, and an additional $20,000 was given to purchase plastic sheeting and blankets.

In February 2001, the historic San Dionisio Church in Umatac was restored and rededicated at last. The church was originally founded in the late seventeenth century and was renovated in 1939. Over the years, earthquakes, typhoons, and other natural disasters had damaged the building. New doors, tiles, and windows were installed, and cracks on the walls from earthquakes were repaired.

Residents of Umatac and nearby villages held a procession and Mass to celebrate the long-awaited reopening of San Dionisio.

Light A Candle

Power outages are so common on Guam that people don't curse the darkness, they light candles. The power goes off so often, people are used to eating cold Spam® and rice. I never left home without carrying a flashlight. I can't remember how often I had to walk up and down six flights in the dark to my apartment in the Nimitz Towers complex.

After World War II, Navy Public Works Center (PWC) was the sole producer of electric power. The Agaña Power Plant and two diesel plants at Marbo and Harmon met island needs. The first two 11.5-megawatt steam turbines at PWC's Piti Power Plant were built in 1950 and 1951. At the same time, 6-megawatt diesel plants were built at Orote and Agaña.

In 1950, the Public Utility Agency of Guam (PUAG) was established to assume responsibility for civilian power needs. Four years later, a third 11.5-megawatt turbine was added to the Piti Power Plant, and, a decade later, two 22-megawatt units at Piti were completed.

When the Guam Power Authority (GPA) was created by the Legislature, it took over power production from PUAG. Soon, two steam power plants were built at Tanguisson Point, and GPA's Cabras Island Plant had a 66-megawatt capacity.

Finally, the Navy and GPA agreed to jointly generate, operate, and maintain the island-wide power system. The Navy invested $43 million and GPA $61 million in joint-use facilities. The Navy's goal was to phase out its power operations, except for military distribution systems and emergency generating units. The GPA-Navy power pool ended around 1980.

GPA and PUAG lost money steadily. Miles of cable were destroyed by power burns, snakes shorting out circuits, and rain leaking into termite-ridden cables. The agency put a 40-megawatt Cabras 3 generator on line in 1995, and, with legislative approval, a second 40-megawatt Cabras unit should be operating now.

Over the years, Guam has become sophisticated. Today, notices appear daily on TV and in the PDN listing power outages with hours and areas affected. It's rare when the notice reads: "There will be no power outages today."

One recent outage was blamed on two brown tree snakes that grounded a high-voltage transmission line serving Apra Heights to Orote. GPA said the Navy's battery-operated power switch was turned off, thus knocking out the island's power system. However, citizens said the outage was caused by an Unidentified Flying Object because they heard a loud rumble and saw a blue glow in the sky just before the power went out. The high voltage grounded by snakes could cause a loud explosion and a bright flash, GPA said.

In February 2001, an islandwide power outage was blamed on a snake crawling into a power transformer, and a similar outage ravaged the island in March. One Guam resident, in a letter to the editor of the *Pacific Daily News*, believed the second outage must have been caused by the bereaved and heartbroken husband of the snake that died in the first outage. The second snake couldn't accept life without his true love and made the ultimate gesture by slithering into a transformer in the hopes of meeting his dear, departed mate on the other side, the writer concluded.

Then, a big blackout in March 2001 caused the Guam International Airport to shut down because runway lights were knocked out. Aircraft were diverted to Andersen Air Force Base. It's fortunate that Andersen is there as a backup, but why doesn't Guam's civilian airport have backup generators and lights?

Reminds me of the days gone by when planes were often diverted to Saipan when Guam's power system failed.

During frequent power surges and outages, Guam's telephone system shuts down like a circuit breaker in a fuse box. The system is often compared to a carrier pigeon with a broken wing and no sense of direction. In years past, firms lost thousands of dollars because they couldn't call customers or receive calls from them. Businesses hired bicyclists to deliver messages.

In addition to the high cost of freightage across the Pacific Ocean, the high cost of doing business on Guam was attributed to the telephone system, a relic of the Navy's postwar rehabilitation projects.

"Trouble on the line," was the usual excuse for inoperative telephones. However, many phones were bugged—by ants and termites.

It used to take months to get a phone on Guam. A newly opened hotel asked for 50 incoming phone lines for its 250 rooms—it was lucky to get 5.

Old problems still raise their ugly heads. For instance, toxic waste contamination plagues sites, such as the former Naval Air Station (NAS), Dededo's municipal golf course, and the Southern High School in Santa Rita, which was built despite insufficient water and sewage pipes.

Tourists were holding their noses on Tumon Beach in March 2001 when raw sewage gurgled out of manholes and filled a pump station. Guam Waterworks Authority crews and private companies worked around the clock to fix the overflow at the Fujita Pump Station in Tumon.

Unstable World War II bombs are still being found near Yigo.

In 2001, the fate of thousands of pounds of mustard gas brought to Guam in 1945 remains a mystery. World War II records have been found indicating that enough mustard gas bombs arrived in Guam in 1945 to supply fifty B-29 raids. The weapons were stored in case U. S. military leaders decided to launch an invasion of Japan. Some officials fear the mustard gas bombs may have been buried in the Agaña Swamp, which was used as a military dumpsite after World War II.

Though no records documenting the final fate of the mustard gas have been found, Army Corps officials said the weapons were probably dumped at sea, a common disposal method then. Chemical weapon test kits containing diluted amounts of chemical agents have been discovered in Mongmong, which borders the swamp's northern edge. The dense swamp also has been contaminated by chemicals from an old Navy power plant and other sources.

The Agency for Toxic Substances and Disease Registry (ATSDR) is tracing the disposal of chemical weapons, and the study continues.

Still, technology of the '90s has arrived in Guam: Super Bowls can be seen live on CNN, and current issues of the *New York Times* are sold in Pay-Less supermarket. Cellular telephones are being offered by seven companies, even before they get the bugs out of the present phone system.

Guamanians have adapted easily to "fishing the Internet." IT&E's Talaya 2000, a worldwide computer system, makes gathering information from the sea of communications as easy as *talaya*, a fisherman's term meaning "throwing net" in Chamorro.

Snakes Alive

Before World War II, Guam was a snake-free paradise. Today, it's a snakepit.

Deep in Guam's steamy boonies lurks a rapacious reptile: the 2-to 13-foot-long brown tree snake (*Boiga irregularis*), whose reproductive powers are as mighty as its gargantuan appetite.

GovGuam officials estimate there are 3 million snakes on the island: about 13,000 snakes per square mile.

Few people ever see snakes. The only snakes I saw were dead ones that had fried themselves on power lines. While working at

PWC, I took pictures of employees holding stiff snakes by their tails—good front-page photos for the *PWC Journal.*

The story of the ecological balance of Guam's hospitable jungles reads like a tale of Irish blarney.

First, foreign ships brought rats to the island. To kill the rats, the Spanish imported monitor lizards. When the lizards multiplied, poisonous tree toads were imported to kill the lizards. One female toad can produce 40,000 offspring each year, and toads have overrun the island since.

Then after World War II, brown tree snakes stowed away on cargo ships in the Solomon Islands, New Guinea, and Northern Australia and offloaded in Guam.

The explosion of snakes spread in the '50s from the southern savannahs to the northern forests, correlating with bird extinction.

For decades, these rear-fanged snakes, content to devour birds and lizards, went unnoticed. With no natural enemies to prey on them, these serpents killed off nine of the island's twelve native bird species. The Guamanians' favorite food—the *fanihi* or Mariana fruit bat—became scarce.

Having consumed all the birds, the slithering serpents consumed skinks, geckos, snails, rats, shrews, and toads. When those became scarce, snakes dined on eggs, chickens, small house pets, and have been known to nibble on humans.

The problem drew public attention when snakes shorted out the power system, as well as home and commercial electric appliances. Snakes had uncanny talents to trip out part if not all of the power system, interrupting favorite TV shows, and leaving customers without air-conditioning. Blackouts, brownouts, and power surges were common.

Reptiles (snakes and iguanas) crawled over power lines and electrocuted themselves, knocking out power in the process and causing millions of dollars worth of damage.

Between 1978 and 1990, an estimated 680 outages were caused by snakes crawling up supporting guy wires to utility poles. One short-circuit caused by a 3-foot snake blacked out the island for 12 hours—including the former Strategic Air Command at Andersen AFB.

A GPA spokesman said, "You can't build generators that are completely pest-proof."

There are millions of stories about snakes seen in toilet bowls, cribs, shoes, pillow cases, and cuddled around lamps and people.

When two snakes peeked through the commode in a senator's house, she threw boiling water at them. Some people put screens over their sewer vents to keep snakes from entering via toilets. Everyone who lives on Guam learns to keep their toilet seats down when not in use, and tourists are so advised.

While herpetologists relish field days in this living laboratory, GovGuam has venomously declared war on these rampaging reptiles. Drastic efforts have been taken to control snakes, but building better snake traps hasn't worked.

Officials considered importing mongooses, but mongooses hunt by day and sleep by night.

Brown tree snakes wrap themselves around tangan-tangan in the jungle by day. At night, they climb utility poles to dine on rats or roosting birds. Snakes stretch themselves from branch to pole to house, hanging like brown strands of cooked spaghetti. They seek out dark corners and stretch across hot rain-soaked roads.

The reptile problem became more serious when snakes, looking for food, began crawling into homes and attacking children. Snakes have been found coiled around screaming infants or with their mouths locked onto tiny hands in vain attempts to swallow the babies.

PDN Editor Joe Murphy recalled that his wife, Marianne, found a snake in bed and was bitten on her thumb. His daughter-in-law had a snake bite on her eye, and, in 1996, Murphy killed a snake that was wrapped around his TV set.

Doctors treat about 50 bite victims each year, and some 53 emergency snakebite cases were reported in Guam Memorial Hospital between 1986 and 1989.

In 1991, the U.S. Government, armed with $1.5 million from

Congress, mounted a counterattack to control and eradicate this pest. The Navy designed steel arm bands and traps for snakes' demise, and scientists devised electronic fences and sterilization programs.

Snake patrols were formed to catch the culprits before they slithered up power poles, climbed out on the crossarms, bridged lines, ground the wires, blew transformers, and snuffed out island power.

In 1992, a snake census was conducted. Surveyers, wearing gloves, grabbed snakes behind the head and measured, weighed, sexed, recorded, and placed them in cloth bags. Some snakes' stomachs contained spare ribs, chicken bones, dog food, and tampons.

Wildlife biologists have tried zapping snakes in electric corrals, luring them into traps and testing fuminants. And GPA has spent thousands of dollars on guy-wire guards and other clever contraptions designed to keep creepy crawlers off power lines.

A snake-killing virus was one idea, but no one knew which virus would do the trick. Another possibility was using sex hormones to attract snakes into designated poison stations, where they could be killed off. No one knew for sure how sexy snakes were.

Trapping snakes didn't work, so experts proposed to sterilize male snakes and drop them from helicopters onto the island, where they would mate with females, who wouldn't reproduce. This was abandoned because GovGuam was concerned that the reptiles would put a fatal bite in the billion-dollar tourist industry: the vision of neutered snakes crashing onto hotel balconies wasn't acceptable.

Hotels and restaurants armed security personnel with machetes to kill noctural serpents crawling in and around dumpsters and buildings.

In April 1994, a two-foot-long tree snake crawled through the Agaña power substation and caused six power generating units to trip into emergency shutdown condition, leaving 70 percent of customers in the dark.

That year, Norbert Perez of Micropacific Laboratories claimed he was close to finding a repellent for brown tree snakes. In pre-World War II Guam, Puting and Pacao plants were used to repel monitor lizards from chicken roosts. Micropacific researchers, tapping elders' memories, discovered that these plants were mixed with lime and breadfruit sap to make a repelling potion to be spread over the area to be protected. Results of experiments by the company are pending.

What do mainland zoos have that Guam doesn't? Two species of island birds.

Before the entire population of native birds became extinct, officials captured Guam rails (*Rallus owstoni*) and Guam kingfishers (*Halcyon cinnamomina cinnamomina*) to place in captive-breeding programs at the San Diego, Philadelphia, Washington, D.C., and Bronx zoos.

The Guam rail, a small brown flightless bird, once was so abundant it was hunted for food. In the late 1960s the population of Guam rails was 80,000; by 1984, there were only 20 or 30 birds. That year, the remaining 19 Guam rails, known as *ko'ko,*' were captured in the breeding program of the Department of Agriculture's Division of Aquatic and Wildlife Resources in Mangilao. There are about 180 Guam rails in captivity, with 90 on Guam, 200 on Rota, and the remaining distributed among 18 U.S. zoos.

Guam Kingfishers, which have stubby blue, rust and white bodies, short powerful wings and tiny, weak feet, are some of the most endangered birds on Earth. In the mid-1980s, 29 kingfishers were captured for a breeding project; the last wild kingfisher was seen on Guam in 1989. They are extinct in the wild, but 50 birds exist in 15 U.S. zoos.

Another problem reared its head: how to keep snakes from slithering off-island in ships and airplanes bound for other islands.

A two-foot-long female brown tree snake caught at the Saipan airport threw a scare into that snake-free island. The person who picked up this snake on the terminal fence was bitten on the finger. In early 1999, brown tree snakes were sighted numerous times on Saipan and eight were captured there during the decade. Research biologists say there are indications that the island now has a small population of snakes.

Live and dead snakes have traveled to Hawaii in airplanes and ships. Animal Damage Control unit of the Hawaii State Department of Agriculture has specially trained dogs to sniff out snakes in warehouses, airline baggage compartments, and holds of ships.

A few years ago, Gibson's supermarket in Tamuning sponsored a "Sweep Snakes" contest, with prizes offered to sharpshooters who brought in the most dead snakes. Hundreds of wanna-be Saint Patricks combed palms and poles to capture 1,200 snakes, which didn't take much of a bite out of the snake population.

The contest culminated in a madcap fiesta, during which island cooks created delicious recipes. They deep-fried brown tree snake meat, which some said tasted like chicken, or dished it up with coconut milk, sweet-sour sauce, or finadeni, a Chamorro hot sauce.

Guam's Division of Aquatic and Wildlife Resources pushed recipes for snake meat, such as fajitas. Snake tartare isn't *hafa* bad sauced with finadeni.

If the Guam Press Club ever writes a Gridiron Show skit about the snake problem, it could be called "Fangs for the Memories."

After Supertyphoon Paka hit Guam, island biologists kept a sharp eye on the brown tree snake population. With much of the vegetation shredded, they were concerned that snakes would head for urban areas.

The Department of Interior's Office of Insular Affairs delivered $325,000 in late 2000 to control Guam's brown tree snake population. Regardless of efforts to eradicate them, serpents in the garden of Guam will be a continuing problem.

Here's one solution I offer to Guam's ecological murder mystery.

Everyone knows about Saint Patrick's famous exploit of luring the vermin from Ireland. The legend goes that Saint Pat, carrying a drum, arrived on a hill to banish the reptiles. When people gathered to watch, his drum broke. A huge black snake slithering down the hill laughed at the powerless saint. Suddenly, an angel appeared and mended the drum. Then, Saint Pat beat the drum and preached the sermon that drove all the snakes into the sea.

GovGuam should offer Saint Pat a staff job, point him toward the Marianas Trench, and let nature take its course.

CHAPTER FIVE

Lifestyle

"Here with a loaf of Bread beneath the Bough,
A Flask of Wine, a Book of Verse–and Thou
Beside me singing in the Wilderness–
And Wilderness is Paradise enow."

Omar Khayyam

Some people think of Guam and Micronesia as a tropical paradise. At times these islands appear to be just that. Let's explore a few of the qualities that comprise paradise: hospitality, fiestas, and steamy passions, all adding up to a deliciously laid-back lifestyle.

Fiestas

Pierre Salinger, journalist and press secretary to Presidents John F. Kennedy and Lyndon Johnson, was no stranger to Micronesia. At 19, Salinger skippered a World War II minesweeper that cruised in the top-secret waters of Palau and the Mariana Islands.

During a Far East trip in the early '70s, Salinger stopped on Guam and spoke at a Press Club luncheon. Commenting on one of his favorite subjects—food—he said, "You are *where* you eat."

Salinger was certainly right about Guam. Fiestas are gustatory delights, the *raison d'etre* of Guam's lifestyle. Chamorros don't think its unusual to spend entire paychecks to stage fiestas. This Press Club Gridiron Show parody sums up fiestas.

From the 1986 Gridiron Show, "Paradise on Parade," and 1997 Gridiron Show, "The Merry Old Land of OOG." (Tune: "Hava Nagila")

> Hava banana, hava papaya, hava some breadfruit—welcome to our hut.
> Hava Budweiser, hava cold Oly, hava Pepsi Cola—hava coconut.
> Hava helping of red rice. Kelaguen is very nice.
> Meet my auntie and her kids—have some ribs.
> Lumpia—try one or two; hava dish of fruit bat stew.
> There is lots to try—have some pie.
>
> Eat—Eat—Drink—Drink
> It's fiesta time, you're all invited. Fill your plate, you'll be delighted.
> Sit right down, don't think of going. Just relax, the tuba's flowing.
> Hava some steak. . . . Eat some cake. . . .
> Fiesta has the very best for you.
>
> Hava tortilla, hava cucumber, hava banana, hava some betel nut.
> Hava Budweiser, hava cold Oly, hava indigestion, hava coconut.
> Eat until the food is gone. We've been cooking since the dawn.
> Hava helping nice and big—hava some pig.
> If your spirits start to droop, hava cup of corn soup.
> Finadene, nice and hot, hits the spot.

Fiestas were born in the early 1900s, when relatives and guests traveled miles by foot or carabao cart to attend celebrations of village saints' days. For a day and a night, Chamorro, Spanish, and Filipino foods were prepared and set out in private homes or at public centers. On feast day, a Mass was held in the village church, followed by a procession. Then travelers ate hearty meals to sustain them on their long journeys home.

From those early days, the custom of fiestas spread to other occasions, such as weddings, christenings, funerals, luaus for one-year-old babies, birthdays, political rallies, housewarmings, and blessings of new houses, boats, and pets.

Three ingredients are vital to a successful fiesta: plenty of food and beverages and a yard full of people. Someone roasts a pig and guests bring their favorite dishes. The hostess spends days making red rice, finadeni, and shrimp kelaguen.

The day before the fiesta in urban and rural areas, carports and patios are cleaned up; galvanized drums are filled with ice, beer, and soft drinks; bars are set up; and Japanese lanterns are strung around the yard. Long tables are covered with lush greenery, fragrant plumerias, gardenias, or hibiscus, with a centerpiece of red flame tree blossoms.

Traditionally at the head of the table sits a mountain of rice, dyed red-orange from the juice and seeds of the achote. Then come dishes of taro, tapioca, tortillas, lumpia, and pancit.

Next are platters piled high with barbecued pig (roasted over an open fire and stuffed with fried potatoes, celery, onions, and spices), a side of roast beef, baked ham, fried and barbecued chicken, barbecued spareribs, chicken kelaguen, and fritada (intestines, heart, liver, and pancreas of either a pig, cow, chicken, or deer). Fish may be barbecued, served raw as sashimi, or in dishes such as escabeche and kelaguen.

Between the main dishes sit bowls of finadeni, Chamorros' thermonuclear sauce. This spice-of-life may be mild or hot, depending on how many red peppers are used. These thumb-sized red, green, or yellow peppers, pretty as Christmas tree ornaments, grow profusely in Guam's backyards. Finadeni is ladled on all food, from eggs and rice to barbecued meat, fish, kelaguen, and escabeche.

Interspersed among the delicacies are dishes of relishes and salads, often served in large shell or woven coconut leaf dishes lined with green breadfruit leaves. At the end of the table sit tureens of creamed chicken or corn soup served in pastry shells.

Desserts include red velvet or carrot cakes; natiya, a pudding atop a slice of yellow cake and sprinkled with cinnamon; and yam or banana doughnuts.

The food is washed down with fruit punch or tuba, a local drink distilled from coconuts. If made properly, tuba, sometimes called Marianas holy water, may be a delightfully sweet drink or something that delivers a clout like Ali's.

In tourism's early days, the Guam Visitors Bureau issued an official menu for hotels and restaurants to follow to prepare authentic fiestas. A few villages, given a week's notice, staged fiestas for tour groups.

Pessimists say fiestas are a fast fading custom. Hotel and restaurant Sunday brunches, they say, have replaced fiestas, which are too expensive and time-consuming for the average family today.

However, the fiesta custom is alive and well, both in homes and villages. For instance, the mayor of Inarajan invites residents and visitors each year to attend the village's St. Joseph fiesta. Held on the beach, festivities include helicopter rides, jet skis, motorcross, volleyball, carabao softball, as well as handicraft concessions.

Today, fiestas are given at the drop of a coconut: New Year's Eve and Day, Chinese New Year's, Filipino Independence Day, Magellan Discovery Day, Fourth of July, Columbus Day, and Boxing Day.

Gubernatorial fiestas are the *creme de la fiestas*.

The public was invited to a fiesta at the Plaza de España to celebrate the inauguration of Ricky Bordallo and Rudy Sablan, Guam's first Democratic governor and lieutenant governor.

Celebrants devoured 20 dishes, prepared in 15 school cafeterias by volunteers: turtle steak; six 25-pound pots of red taro tips; 75 pots of red rice; 400 pounds cooking bananas; 400 pounds boiled white yams; 400 pounds boiled wild yams; 400 pounds tapioca tamales; 400 pounds taro tamales; 3,000 pounds chicken kelaguen; 4,000 pounds beef steak; 2,000 fried chickens; 40 roast suckling pigs; 1,200 corn and flour tortillas; 400 pounds pork fritada; 400 pounds yam doughnuts; 15 pots aho (young coconut) in tapioca starch; 15 pots corn soup; 300 pounds boiled sweet potatoes; 1,500 pounds salad; 1,500 pounds escabeche; 11,000 dinner rolls; five gallons finadeni; 100 pounds dried beef barbecue; and 400 pounds barbequed salted pork.

It's a mortal sin to run out of food on Guam, Madeleine Bordallo, former First Lady and now Lieutenant Governor, learned quickly. Madeleine invited 600 school counselors and parents of Head Start students for dinner at Government House. Everyone showed up, accompanied by assorted relatives who had been specifically invited. Two buffet tables were laden with food, but the goodies ran out before half of the guests filled their plates. The Governor's chauffeur drove to McDonald's and brought back enough rice and fried chicken to feed the rest of the group.

Guam's fiesta dishes have been well publicized worldwide by Dorothy Horn, Guam's happy cooker, hostess, and author of cookbooks and recipe calendars.

Dorothy, who inherited her love of cooking from her Pennsylvania Dutch ancestors, arrived on Guam in 1960. She taught home economics at Inarajan Junior High School, Barrigada High School, and to accelerated six grades at other schools. For ten years, Dorothy collected and tested recipes from school cooks before publishing "Real Guamanian Recipes." In its 14th printing, this cookbook has sold 190,000 copies printed in English and Japanese.

In 1987, Dorothy's husband, Robert "Tweeter" Horn, died. He had been an active Rotarian, and Dorothy became the first female member of the Rotary Club, Japan-Pacific district. Since breaking down barriers in the all-male organization, Dorothy has served as secretary, treasurer, and board member. A few years ago, a legislative resolution appointed Dorothy as Guam's goodwill ambassador.

Dorothy's publications include Filipino, Micronesian, and Christmas cookbooks and recipe calendars, plus a child's coloring book (see Appendix).

Some say that Guamanians' love of hot food begins at birth, when mothers put a dash of Tabasco Pepper Sauce in their babies' bottles. True or not, the manufacturers of Tabasco, McIlhenny Company of Avery Island, Louisiana, report that Guam boasts of the world's highest per capita consumption of Tabasco. Every year, each citizen of Guam consumes 1.7 to 2 bottles of 2-ounce Tabasco Pepper Sauce.

I attended my first fiesta on a *lanca* (farm) in Saipan to celebrate a couple's 65th wedding anniversary. As I piled food on my plate, I imitated locals who poured finadeni over the food. After the first bite of finadeni-soused chicken, the top of my head blew off, my eyes watered, the inside of my mouth caught fire, and my forehead and cheeks erupted in sweat beads. After a few more bites, endorphin numbed the pain and I was addicted.

Recipes

The following recipes were gathered from various old Guam cookbooks.

Finadene

1 cup soy sauce
Juice of 4 lemons or limes
Mashed fresh pepper and salt
6 finely chopped green onions
3 or more crumbled red hot peppers

Coconut milk

Mix chopped onions and lemon juice, add mashed fresh pepper and salt to taste. Add chopped hot peppers and soy sauce. If a thicker sauce is desired, add coconut milk. The heat depends on how many peppers are used.

Chicken Kelaguen

Broil a whole chicken, bone, and chop meat finely. Add 1/2 chopped onion and juice of two lemons, season with salt and pepper, and add 1 cup grated coconut. Garnish with chopped green onion leaves and whole fresh peppers.

Shrimp Kelaguen

1 pound fresh or frozen shrimp, boiled and cleaned, head and tail removed
1 cup grated coconut meat
1 small onion, chopped fine
2 or more small red hot peppers, crushed
Juice of 3 to 4 lemons

Prepare shrimp and cut into small pieces. Add other ingredients, increasing lemon juice or adding salt to taste. For authentic flavor, grind fish heads and add to mixture. Serve well chilled on lettuce or tortillas.

Red Rice

1/2 pound chopped bacon OR
4 tablespoons bacon grease
1 onion, chopped or sliced thin
2 cups raw rice

2 cups achote water*
1 cup water
Salt and pepper to taste

Heat bacon grease or fry bacon. When bacon is almost done, but not crisp, add onion and fry until soft. Add washed, well drained rice to onion and bacon, stirring well until almost dried out, coating rice well with grease. Add prepared achote water, plain water, 1 teaspoon salt, and 1/2 teaspoon black pepper. Bring mixture to boil, stir, cover, and turn heat low to cook slowly about 20 minutes or until rice is well done and has absorbed all the liquid. Stir once quickly and let stand 10 minutes before serving.

To serve, add one package of cooked and drained frozen peas. You may add thinly sliced Chorizos (Spanish sausage) and cook along with the bacon. Rice may be garnished with quartered hard boiled eggs and finely chopped green onions.

*Achote water gives red rice its color. You can purchase achote seeds in ethnic stores. The water is prepared by mixing about 1/2 cup seeds with lukewarm water, stirring well until the water is red, then straining. Achote water has no taste, but you can't make red rice or many Chamorro dishes without it.

SPAM®

After World War II, Guamanians became enamored with SPAM®. Today, Chamorro *bisteak,* aka Spam, is often the main course of island meals.

Spam was created in 1937 when Jay C. Hormel, son of the company's founder, wanted to use up several thousand pounds of surplus pork shoulder. He concocted a blend of ham and pork shoulder spiced with salt, sugar, and sodium nitrite. Kenneth

Daigneau, an actor and brother of a Hormel executive, won $1000 in a contest naming the new meat product.

During World War II, Spam gained popularity as a staple food for American troops overseas and people in war-torn countries. An Army mess sergeant once bragged that he baked, fried, scrambled, breaded, and creamed Spam. It's still basic—Uncle Sam buys more than 3.5 million pounds of Spam a year.

Some 60 million Americans eat Spam, most of which is sold in Hawaii, Alaska, Arkansas, Texas, and Alabama. Spam is also popular in the United Kingdom and South Korea.

Former British Prime Minister Margaret Thatcher recalls Spam as a "wartime delicacy," shared on Boxing Day 1943 with friends and family. "I can quite vividly remember we opened a tin of Spam luncheon meat. We had some lettuce and tomatoes and peaches, so it was Spam and salad."

During World War II, Russia's Nikita Khrushchev remembers, "We had lost our most fertile, food-bearing lands. Without Spam, we wouldn't have been able to feed our army."

Guam jumped on the Spam bandwagon in postwar days. Much of the food then was stale and buggy by the time it was shipped across the sea, so people began eating canned food, such as Australian corned beef and American Spam.

Some Guamanians relish sandwiches of Spam, avocado, and Monterey Jack cheese with mayonnaise, mustard, and dash of Tabasco. Or Spam, cheese, and Ortega canned green chiles.

Spam has been the butt of jokes for years. David Letterman suggested Spam on a rope for snacking in the shower. Paul Theroux joked that former cannibals of Oceania now feast on Spam because it tastes similar to the porky flavor of human flesh.

But Spam is no joke. The Salvation Army distributed Spam to victims of Hurricane Hugo in South Carolina, Puerto Rico, and the Virgin Islands. Spam was given to survivors of the recent San Francisco earthquake and to the people of Valdez after Exxon's oil spill.

In January 1998, Hormel Foods donated and shipped 5,500

cases of Spam and other products to victims of Supertyphoon Paka in Guam.

This canned luncheon meat has "spammed" the decades from World War II to the present. The Spamnet buzzes with S'pam S'mores, and the Smithsonian Institute has a Spam display.

Hormel's mail-order business exceeds all expectations. Spam giftware includes Spam-logo T-shirts, watches, sweat suits, hats, boxer shorts, fanny packs, mugs, golf balls, magnets, sunshades, and windsocks.

Guam's first Spam Speciality Competition was held at Gibson's Department Store in Tamuning. Dorothy Horn was among the judges who rated 34 cooks' dishes on visual presentation, originality, and taste. Dorothy dedicated her popular cookbook, "Great Classic Spam Recipes of the World from Dorothy's Kitchen," to "all those gallant survivors who fought the great battles of World War II and to all those folks around the world who have also taken Spam to their hearts." The 292-page cookbook contains 500 recipes, including Provencal Spam Stew, Spam Tempura, or Spam Stroganoff.

In the 21st Century, Hormel introduced Smoked Spam and Turkey Spam. A Riesling or Gewurztraminer goes well with Spam, I'm told.

Celebrations

Food plays an important part in many island celebrations, from funerals to religious holidays to civic celebrations.

For many cultures, the passing of a loved one is a personal event, confined to family and close friends. But on Guam, people have a different way of dealing with death. The Chamorro culture, steeped in customs and traditions, places a high value on family, ancestors, and respect heavily laden with religious rituals. Perhaps no event weaves all that together more than when someone dies.

The first thing a grieving family does is the praying of the rosary twice a day at noon and in the evening. This lasts for nine days. Friends, extended family, and co-workers attend. The *techa*, or prayer leader, quiets the murmuring crowd and, in unison, they recite prayers, finishing with the sign of the cross. Afterward, everyone mingles, passing on condolences and catching up on news with those who come from off-island to pay their respects. Some novenas and final viewings are commonly held in the village churches instead of the family's home.

The ceremony culminates in an all-night wake, or bela. On the day of the funeral, a final viewing of the body, the final rosary, and Mass are held. Then the convoy of mourners follows the hearse to the cemetery and burial.

In the midst of all this there are multiple family meetings to discuss who's going to take care of food on which night. Corn soup, sandwiches, or even full dinners are served.

Guam funerals usually cost more than burials elsewhere because of the traditions involved, such as the nine-day rosary and the food served daily at the novena and on the day of the funeral. Caterers often provide food on the final day, freeing families from the burden of preparing and serving food and cleaning up.

Many burials take place in the vaults at Pigo Cemetery. When I was a reporter for the *Pacific Daily News*, I covered the first "high-rise" burial vault erected in the cemetery. It was a joke at the time, but since my day, additional vaults have been built, and they are decorated with inscriptions and flowers by relatives of the deceased.

Another occasion is All Souls' Day, which is often celebrated in villages, such as the Togcha Cemetery in Yona and in the village of Agat. All Souls' Day, designated by the Roman Catholic Church to commemorate deceased members whose souls were believed to be suffering in purgatory, seems to be the only religious practice that resembles ancient Chamorro beliefs. It is more widely celebrated and understood by the people of Guam than Columbus

Day, Labor Day, or Veterans Day, according to some scholars, and has more local significance than even Discovery Day.

The ancient Chamorros believed in the immortality of the soul, which was a sacred subject of worship. This veneration was shown by keeping the skull of one's ancestors in high places in the house and was celebrated daily with prayers and petitions. When fishing and hunting, people call upon their ancestors to bring good fortune.

The most nostalgic and sad celebration on All Souls' Day was a recent one in the old village of Sumay, on the shore of San Luis d'Apra harbor. Sumay was once a thriving port town that traded with Spanish galleons from Mexico. Later it traded with whaling ships from around the world and with pirates who plied the Pacific Ocean. By 1941, Sumay was the second largest town and Guam's center of commerce, with hotels, restaurants, shops, bars, a school, and a church. It was also Pan American's landing base for passenger planes en route to Shanghai.

Sumay village is no more. Residents were evicted from their homes by the Japanese invaders and, later, were resettled into a new village called Santa Rita. The only remaining evidence of Sumay is its cemetery, where grave markers are inscribed in Chamorro, Spanish, and English.

The few remaining former residents of Sumay visit the cemetery to honor the dead on All Souls' Day each November. As the years go by, fewer and fewer former residents of Sumay remain. When the last one passes away, Guam will lose its link to prewar Sumay, where the people were happy, the vegetation lush, the weather balmy, and the fish plentiful.

On this Catholic island, it's quite remarkable that the Protestant Centennial committee organized a week-long observance in November 2000 to commemorate the centennial anniversary of the arrival of the first formal Protestant mission. Today there seems to be cooperation between the Catholics and the Protestants on Guam, as befitting the 21st century.

One of the island's largest religious celebrations is Christmas, or Noche Buena. For nine days, daily novenas of prayers and hymns are held in homes. On the ninth day, families attend Midnight Mass, then gather to eat escabeche and bonuelos dago, yam doughnuts.

In the old days, children used to gather moss, ferns, pandanus, and betelnut to make a belen, a manger. Then kids delivered baskets of taro, bananas, sweet potatoes, yam fritters, tuba syrup, escabeche, crabs, and lobsters to family and neighbors. Coconut and land crabs, taro, breadfruit, and fruit bat were eaten on Christmas Day.

Today Guamanians send Christmas cards and buy gifts in stores. Christmas trees, often artificial, have replaced mangers in some homes, but many homes have both.

One custom on Christmas Day is to send a boy and a girl, who carries a plastic doll swathed in rags, to visit neighborhood homes. The children ask families to kiss the doll, which represents the baby Jesus. Of course, each household also gives the youngsters a few dollar bills, which I presume goes into the Catholic Church's coffer. I always refused to kiss the "dirty doll," as I called it, because it was unsanitary.

Since 1945, Liberation Day, July 21, has been the biggest celebration on Guam.

A Golden Salute took place on Liberation Day 1994 to commemorate the 50th anniversary of Guam's liberation. Silver and gold coins were issued and T-shirts were designed for the event. Fiestas, fireworks, parades, and air shows went round-the-clock.

Veterans returned for Guam's golden celebration: 1,500 Marines, Seabees, soldiers, sailors, wives, and Navajo code talkers.

During the Second World War, U.S. military leaders turned to the Navajo Nation when Japanese military were able to crack almost every U.S. code. Philip Johnson, a World War I veteran, raised by missionaries on the Navajo reservation and who spoke fluent Navajo, suggested to the Marines that they ask for young Navajo men to serve as radio operators.

Navajo is a complicated language with no written alphabet. The first 29 Navajos who volunteered developed a code of about 200 terms to send messages throughout the Pacific Theater. They eventually developed more than 600 terms, and each code talker memorized the entire system. Some 400 young Navajo men left their sacred land to go to war. The Japanese never broke those encrypted messages.

After the war, when each code talker was discharged, his commander advised him not to speak of the work he did. Most code talkers rode buses home and, once they got there, participated in ceremonies to purify their minds from what they saw of war.

In July 2001 the surviving Navajo code talkers were honored in the rotunda of the U.S. capitol, 56 years after World War II ended. Four of the original 29–John Brown Jr., Allen Dale June, Chester Nez, and Lloyd Oliver–were there to receive Congressional Gold Medals from President Bush. Joe Palmer, the last of the five living original 29, was unable to travel to Washington.

The Navajos wore red hats and mustard yellow shirts of the code talkers, and most wore the beads, turquoise and silver jewelry and silver concha belts specific to their culture. After the ceremony, the men exchanged stories about boot camp and code training.

One of the Navajo code talkers, Carl Gorman, died in January 1998 after a lengthy illness. Narciso "Ciso" Platero Abeyta, another code talker, died of a cerebral hemorrhage at age 79 that same year. Abeyta's paintings on Navajo themes are displayed in the National Gallery of Art.

One hundred Japanese veterans also returned to take part in a quiet memorial ceremony July 22.

Official activities of the Golden Salute centered around the War in the Pacific National Historical Park overlooking Asan Bay, where the U.S. Marines Third Division first landed in 1944. This park, created by an act of Congress in 1978, honors those heroes who fought in World War II in the Pacific. The park maintains five battlefield sites in Asan, Piti, Mount Tenhu, Mount Chauchau, and Agat, covering 1,882 acres of land and water. A collection of war relics and photographs are displayed in the visitors center.

A memorial was erected at Asan Beach where U.S. forces landed on July 21, 1944. The memorial is a 10-by 15-foot cube of polished gray marble that rises six feet above the broad, four-tiered octagonal base. An engraved wreath in raised relief, bearing the legend "50th Anniversary," adorns the front panel. Side and rear panels show engraved insignia of U.S. military units. A commemorative message in English and Chamorro wraps the memorial in a ribbon of 10-inch letters: "A grateful Chamorro remembers: *Libra para I tano Chamorro.* Honor to heroic and gallant effort of U.S. Armed Forces: *Onra I mane'luta.*"

Unfortunately, the late Ben Munoz's desire to place the bomber Enola Gay in Guam's War in the Pacific National Historical Park did not come to pass. The display of World War II's most famous artifact opened in May 1995 at the Smithsonian Institute's National Air and Space Museum, Washington, D.C. Called "The Last Act," the exhibit centers around the fuselage of the Enola Gay B-29 bomber, the Tinian-based aircraft that dropped the atomic weapon upon Hiroshima on August 6, 1945, helping to end the terrible war and save American and Japanese lives.

In Guam's centennial year, 1998, activities included a Liberation Day parade; the decommissioning of the *USS Guam* and retrieval of the bell and plaque from North Fort, Virginia, in September; the unveiling of the Centennial Mural on Paseo Loop on October 1; and, in December, the Mr. and Mrs. Centennial Pageant.

In 2001, about 19 million war veterans are living in this country, and some 550,000 World War II veterans die each year. In the near future, there may be a Liberation Day parade where no veteran is alive to salute the American flag.

The Big Summer Festival was first launched in 1997 as a way to promote tourism on Guam. This celebration takes place along Tumon's San Vitores Road between the arches of Pleasure Island, which opened in 1999.

Pleasure Island, a $52.9 million Tumon Redevelopment Program transformed Guam's tourism district by adding cobblestone walkways, underground power lines, and landscaped medians.

As part of the project, two 25-foot-tall arches were built over Pale San Vitores Boulevard in Tumon bearing the words "Pleasure Island." The concrete and metal arches, which each cost about $500,000, are located at the intersection near SandCastle and at another intersection near the northern end of the Duty Free Shop Galleria. The structures identify that area of Tumon as an entertainment zone.

A street carnival is held the day after the opening of the Big Summer Festival, which continues with a beach party July 4. The street party features food booths, a Mardi Gras parade, bands, fireworks, and specials at GameWorks and UnderWater World. The illumination program lights up six main areas of Tumon Bay and Airport Road. Hotels, and retailers help light up the night with their own displays.

During 1999's Big Summer Festival, a lottery gave away about $3.6 million in prizes to hotel guests, and a children's arts and crafts program was staged.

Soon, people will be able to stroll from the Plaza shopping center to the SandCastle entertainment complex via buildings' connections. SandCastle's front lawn now features a tiger habitat, where cubs and their mothers are on display to camera-toting tourists. Let's hope the big cats don't find out about the fish in the aquarium next door.

UnderWaterWorld is where visitors come close to a shark without getting wet. It is a 400-foot-long underwater tunnel, winding back and forth, where viewers see the myriad of sea life that surrounds Guam. GameWorks is the place where visitors can snowboard, hangglide, and bobsled under the same roof.

A Loaf of Bread

Guam hasn't always offered gourmands the variety of international restaurants it does today. But nowadays, as PDN Editor Joe Murphy once said, "Guam . . . is a regular eating machine."

In the mid-'60s, there were few restaurants, the most popular of which were Talk of the Town, Hong Kong Garden's Panciteria, and the Bamboo Room.

The beachside Surf Club in Asan was the home stage for a Hawaiian combo, Liz Kaleikoa and the Kane Leos. The club was the hangout for Hawaiian contract junkies: men and women who had come to Guam in the '40s and '50s to fill Navy jobs. They became hooked on overseas tax breaks and cost-of-living pay raises, and most stayed until they retired and returned home to Hawaii.

Other dining spots popped up: Sleepy Lagoon, Earl's Hut, and Pirate's Cove were joined by Kinney's, where windows were propped open with sticks and gecko's joined you at the table; The Office, where businessmen and women took coffee breaks, lunches and sweethearts; Sourgoses' for Italian dishes; Joe and Flo's and Nina's Papagaya for Mexican food; and the Cliff Hotel's Red Carpet, where Ted Kennedy once breakfasted with GovGuam officials.

Today, Guam is a haven of the culinary arts. Despite the island's relatively small population, many fine restaurants offer scrumptious delicacies to tempt any palate. A variety of fresh fish, octopus, and lobster is served either grilled or baked with vegetables or fruit, sashimi, and in other imaginative ways unique to the Pacific.

These days you can get international indigestion by reading restaurant menus: jambalaya, blackened mahi mahi, Chamorru sushi, miso soup, buffalo wings, grilled Spam roll, Portuguese sausage roll, shrimp tempura, papaya enchiladas, lumpia Shanghai, and Vermont curry.

Some of the best Chinese, Japanese, and Indonesian food outside of Asia can be found in Guam. There are also Chamorro, Korean, Thai, Vietnamese, Filipino, Mexican, and European eating establishments, each with its distinct ambiance. Filipino dishes have slipped into Guam's daily diet: pancit (noodles), lechon (roast suckling pig), daing na bangus (fried milkfish), pinakbet (vegetables), shrimp paste called bagoong, and flan (pudding).

Major hotels and restaurants serve high-quality Continental meals; many offer exotic ethnic dishes, as well. Of course, American fast food chains have become standard fare.

I was shocked to learn that some people in Guam eat dog meat. When our Doberman Pinscher mix gave birth to nine puppies, my husband and I doled them out to friends. A month or two later, I'd ask how the pups were doing. I'd get identical answers: "It was run over by a truck." None of the pups lived to be a year old–they ended up in adobo, or Filipino stew.

Adobo is usually made with chicken, beef, or pork, but some Filipinos' prefer dog. The chopped-up animal is marinated in Seven-Up or Sprite for an hour or so to remove the doggy odor. Then the meat is drained and marinated in soy sauce and lemon for an hour. It is drained again, then fried with garlic, onion, and potato. Tomato sauce and pineapple chunks are added and the whole mess is stewed for an hour or more. It's often served with cheese and crackers.

On my 1990 visit to Guam, I tagged along with Dorothy Horn to restaurants she was reviewing for her radio show and newspaper column. Our gourmet journey began with Chinese breakfast of fried rice and omelettes at Shirley's. Lunch at Lian's Vietnamese Cafe was foot-long lumpia, wrapped in lettuce leaves, lightly fried and stuffed with pork, bean sprouts, noodles, and topped with sweet plum sauce. For dinner, we relished giant margueritas, ceviche, nachos, and roll-your-own chicken fajitas at Mike's Casa de Fiesta, a Tex-Mex spot on the Tumon strip.

We attended the *creme de la creme* of Sunday brunches at the Pacific Islands Club's Bistro. The Club's beachside grounds, site of the former Continental Travelodge, featured a pool, wedding chapel, and outdoor party pavilion.

The Bistro's maitre d' poured our champagne. Then we helped ourselves to fruit, soup, bread, kelaguen, crab and squid salads, sashimi, sushi, lumpia, beef stroganoff, Spanish fish, roast beef, omelettes, and waffles. When we were sated, the maitre d' gave us each a box of chocolate truffles.

Another day, I had lunch at King's Restaurant and Lounge in Gibson's Shopping Center. I ordered an island favorite—mahi mahi and eggs. The *TV Guam* staff, always dieting, often ate lunch at King's: a plain meat patty with salad, washed down with a vodka and water.

Some of Guam's new restaurants include international favorites, such as Roy's Restaurants at the Hilton Guam Resort & Spa, Hard Rock Café, Outback Steakhouse, Planet Hollywood, Tony Roma's, the Olive Garden, Red Lobster, and Sam Choy's, which offers a taste of Hawaii you can't find anywhere else on Guam.

At the CyberUp Café in Tamuning you can get a sandwich and coffee and sit at one of twenty workstations offering Internet access, color laser printing, scanning, DVD, a digital camera, and electronic games.

There's always a hot time on this hot little island. When the sun goes down, cocktail lounges ease into nighttime entertainment. Guam's nightlife used to run from A to B. Now it runs from triple A to triple Z.

Gone are the days when you could drink, dance, and cavort without mortgaging your house. Thirty years ago, an evening for four at Guam's best restaurants would cost less than $50, including gourmet dinners and drinks. Today, $60 barely covers two sukiyaki dinners, beverages extra, at a Tumon Bay restaurant crowded with busloads of Japanese tourists.

The Duty Free Shoppers complex includes the $32 million SandCastle Entertainment Center, where Las Vegas-style music revue dinners are offered at the 18K gold-plated supper club on Tumon Bay. Prices are so high that as a waitress hands you a check for $85 for each adult, the maitre d' gives you CPR.

This entertainment complex attracts nearly twenty percent of the island's tourists. The area of Tumon where SandCastle sits has flourished and now is perhaps the busiest bit of real estate on Guam. It's a Japanese-style one-stop entertainment building and fits right into the Pleasure Island development.

A Jug of Wine

If the ocean were whiskey, Guam would be floating in seventh heaven. Some say that the tropical sunshine makes people ingest deeply from the booze bag. When the huge orange sun sinks behind purple ocean waves, it's time to kick back with a cold beer or a sip of icy vodka.

Pacific islanders didn't produce or use alcohol until whalers arrived in the mid-1800s. At that time, the American Board of Commissioners for Foreign Missions tried to help islanders resist the whalers' demon rum. Alcohol continues to be a general health and social problem in the islands.

When I lived in Saipan, we used to swim each afternoon after work at Micro Beach. After about an hour in the warm, clear water, someone always quipped, "Let's get out of these wet bathing suits and into some dry martinis."

On Guam, liquor was "so cheap you can't afford not to drink," Trust Territory Counsel, Judge Kinnaire, used to say as he opened a $1.75 bottle of Red Label Scotch. A veteran island-hopper, the judge was a 62-year-old, pipe-smoking bachelor from Chicago. He retired in 1965.

As sales manager for Ambros, Inc., a beverage distributor on

Guam, Judge Kinnaire made Budweiser popular. When he traveled around Micronesia to hear court cases, he toted law books, court records, judicial robes, a cot and bedding, kerosene and stove, cases of food and Budweiser, and bottles of 120-proof vodka.

When the Trukese chief of Lukunor Atoll visited Guam, Kinnaire took him to dinner at the Surf Club. The chief, consuming his second rich dessert, asked the name of the beer Kinnaire distributed. The chief proclaimed that from then on, only Budweiser would be allowed on Lukunor.

Some of the best drinkers on the island hung out in military bars and fraternal clubs. But the Australians outdrank everybody. Employees of the Australian Cable Station lived in spacious houses perched on Guam's western cliffs overlooking the Philippine Sea. The station was a hotbed for booze-ups. Every Boxing Day, the day after Christmas, Tipsy Paddies gathered at the station manager's house to have a drop until the wee hours of the morning.

British tour ships brightened the drinking scene, too. In the days before terrorism, islanders were allowed to visit P&O ships in port. At 11 a.m., little old ladies in tennis shoes gathered in the main lounge to sip sherry, and, during happy hour, Aussies slurped shandys (beer and ginger ale) on deck and watched the sharks race.

Guam's bartenders continually created exotic drinks. For example: Chamorro martinis made with vodka and finadeni—two of these and you'd feel like the captain of the *Titanic*.

Hilton Hotel Manager, Manfred Toennes, invited Press Club members to name the bartender's new drink: a concoction of rum and Galiano served with pineapple in a coconut tumbler. We suggested Hafa Hilton, Dinamita, Marianas Trench, and Galloping Chamorro, but the Surf Cutter won hands down. The contest winner received a bottle of champagne and invited us to dinner in the Hilton's Galleon Grill. U.S. Senators Mike Mansfield and Hugh Scott were sitting at the next table. We media people had no idea the senators were on the island.

With all the cheap booze on this tight little island, it was only natural that liquid reducing diets became popular. Some people thought the fastest way to lose weight was by semi-fasting.

Dorothy Horn once flew to Germany to try a liquid diet, created by nutritionists at the Schroth-Kur Spa in Oberstaufan. The diet reportedly cleansed and rejuvenated the body and prevented obesity, gout, rheumatism, psoriasis, and nettle-rash.

The Spa breakfasts never varied: herb tea, dry toast, muesli, and four glasses of Liebfraumilch. Lunches were vegetable soup and pineapple soaked in gin, sauerkraut and pears soaked in gin, or prune stew made with gin or rum—all washed down with four glasses of wine.

Supper was spare: health bread spread with cream cheese or carrots, chives or chopped cucumber, and Liebfraumilch. After a month of eating liquor-soused fruit and drinking Liebfraumilch, Dorothy lost 30 pounds.

Upon her return, Dorothy invited the *Pacific Daily News* business editor, Dorothy Fritzen; women's editor, Linda Kauss; and myself to sample the diet at her house. We lapped up a lunch of Liebfraumilch, gin-soaked pears and pineapple, and rum-soaked peaches and grapefruit. We drove back to work and, giddily, put out the morning's paper.

Paradise Enow

As the English poet George Gordon Byron said, "Adultery is more common where the climate's sultry."

During my years in Guam, I learned that it wasn't unusual for many Chamorro men, as well as Orientals, to have "a girl on the side."

To Guamanians, who are devout and almost unanimously Catholic, marital relations appear to be broad enough to embrace variety. Sometimes, priests look the other way on such subjects as adultery, incest, and birth control.

I knew many married high government officials, professional

men, neighbors, and co-workers who thought nothing of having affairs. Their wives evidently looked the other way.

When I lived on Saipan, several Guam senators and visiting officials from Washington, D.C., came to the island to cavort with local girls, as well as some female Stateside workers and Peace Corp volunteers.

In my Navy office in Guam, a Chamorro mail clerk and an office secretary, both married, became romantically involved. Everyone knew about it. The secretary had the clerk's baby and passed the child off as her husband's. The couple continued to dally during lunch hours at work.

Whenever I went to the print shop to make headlines for my monthly Navy newsletter, the married Guamanian supervisor chased me around the plant and never ceased asking me for dates. I always refused him, but he never gave up.

Incest, although an outrage against the social system, is often considered to be a private sin. I knew of two cases of incest and abuse on Guam, and I'm sure there were many others.

One Stateside merchant marine officer, who had a Guamanian wife, sired several children by his teenage daughters, whom he would take one at a time on cruises. His wife suffered in silence, too embarrassed to do anything about it and fearing that if she mentioned it, her husband would beat her up.

In another family close to me, the husband and his buddies often came home for lunch and a siesta. The husband/father and his friends, whom the children called "uncles," took naps with the man's teenage daughters. One evening, the youngest girl stuffed her belongings in a paper bag and walked to our house, hoping to stay with my husband and me. Of course, we had to send her home the next morning, but I knew she wanted to get out of that house. Her older sister could hardly wait to go to a mainland college, as far away from her father and uncles as possible.

Micronesians have broad interpretations of sexual relations. The islands' legal code recognizes local customs, and therefore there are almost no trials or cases concerning marital abuse, assault and battery, or sex offenses because relations between the sexes start at an early age in the islands.

In Yap, adolescent girls, regularly violated in Japanese-occupied days, test their ability to bear children before marriage. One Trust Territory teacher on Yap told me one of her students came to her in tears because she couldn't bear children, and her prospects for marriage were almost nil because no man would have her if she couldn't give him heirs.

The birth of children causes no problems in Micronesia because there are plenty of relatives to adopt a child. All children are legitimate, the mother is always known, and there is no disadvantage in being born as the result of a romantic interlude.

Birth certificates issued by Micronesians used to be all but worthless. Even when a woman knew the name of her child's father, which isn't always the case, it made little difference to her what paternal name was on the birth certificate, which is considered just a scrap of paper. Sometimes, Micronesian legal clerks inserted their own names in blank spaces set aside for father on certificates.

A taboo subject on Guam is the sex industry, in which exotic dancers, hookers, and masseurs form the seedy underside of Guam. This is a burgeoning business where strippers make thousands of dollars a week and call girls make that much in one night. It's not just women walking the streets; some are transsexuals, men who think of themselves as women. Some visitors make the trip to Guam with sex as their primary reason for making the trip.

Enforcing Guam's prostitution laws takes a back seat to the fight against drugs and other more serious crimes, while the Department of Public Health strives to regulate the health condition of massage parlors and stem the spread of sexually transmitted diseases, especially HIV and AIDS.

CHAPTER SIX

Up, Up, and Away

This could only happen on Guam: the one millionth Japanese visitor arrived December 7, 1994, fifty-three years to the day after Japan's attack on Pearl Harbor. Island dignitaries rolled out the red carpet to welcome Kazunori Suzuki and his family at the A.B. Won Pat International Airport. I'm sure they were surprised at their bittersweet reception.

Guam's flourishing and sophisticated tourism industry has come a long way since the first European tourist—explorer Ferdinand Magellan—set foot on the island.

In 1935, Pan American initiated regular trans-Pacific airmail service from San Francisco to Manila and back with the China Clipper, a Martin 130. Seaplanes landed at the Sumay base in Apra Harbor. Pan Am constructed a 20-room hotel, the Skyways Inn, at Sumay, to accommodate these early passengers.

When airlines began flying up, up, and away to and from Guam, tourists flocked to the island like seagulls picking at a ship's flotsam. Pan Am, Trans World Airways, Continental Airlines, and Japan Air Lines put Guam on the world map.

Getting to Guam

Decades ago, island-hopping in Micronesia was a thrill a minute. Former wartime airstrips had been turned over to civilian air traffic, and landings were strictly STOL—short takeoff and landing. If the craft wasn't airborne by the time it ran out of runway, medics and ministers had a field day.

Flights between Guam and Saipan were so short that the plane reached maximum altitude above Tinian and Rota, then immediately descended. The stewardesses barely had time to serve beverages.

On those '60s flights, I was usually the only non-nursing or non-pregnant female on board and the only Statesider, to boot. Beside me often sat Chamorro grandmothers wearing Mestizas: a diaphanous blouse atop long, colorful, draped skirts. On those bumpy flights, they ran verbal laps around their rosary beads.

Flying between Micronesian islands was like riding Mexican rural buses. When the plane was full, frequent flyers, wearing nothing but grass around their waists, sat on sacks of onions in the aisle. Tucked under their arms or in burlap bags were crabs, chickens, or turtles. Many passengers, and crew, often flashed red betelnut smiles, thus Continental Air Micronesia's nickname "betelnut airline."

Mainland-bound passengers carried grocery bags filled with hot chili peppers for relatives. Homeward-bound residents toted cardboard boxes filled with San Francisco bread, Vidalia onions, and buckets of quarters from Las Vegas.

In January 1968, Robert F. Six of Continental Airlines founded Air Micronesia, affectionately called Air Mike. After winning a five-year contract to operate in Micronesia, Air Mike began training islanders to be pilots, mechanics, and flight attendants. The company also built hotels in the islands. The first, the Guam Travelodge, opened in June 1970.

Continental/Air Micronesia began flying to Japan in 1976 and adopted a new paint scheme: orange, red, and gold horizontal stripes with a golden tail, thus their slogan was coined: "The Proud Bird with the Golden Tail."

Air Mike pilots were experts at landing on airfields no larger than sea turtles. Laura Atoll is so small that when an Air Mike jet revved up to take off, its backfire blew the island's police shack down and sent the porch of Albater Jamore's bar out to sea.

On one of my numerous trips to and from Honolulu, I was returning to Guam when we landed at Truk during a thunderstorm. The Air Mike pilot set the jet down gently on the rutty, rocky airstrip. After a delay on the ground, we finally took off from the short, rain-slick runway. The Continental Airline official sitting beside me said that was the first time a jet had landed at Truk. He added that some cargo had to be left behind to lighten the load so the jet could get into the air. As I've said before, flying in Micronesia isn't for sissies.

Martin Pray, former Air Mike sales and tourism manager, recalled a time when the airline had trouble keeping DC-6 engines in shape. In fact, they missed the Saipan flight schedule eight times in three weeks.

One flight from Yap to Saipan was delayed, stranding thirteen Japanese tourists who had reservations on the Guam-Tokyo flight. When mechanics got the old engine purring, they flew to Saipan. Meanwhile, ground personnel had picked up the tourists at their hotels and loaded their baggage onto the plane as it touched down on Saipan.

On the way from Saipan to Guam, the hostess asked if there was anything she could do for the passengers. Yes. They wanted to buy liquor at the duty-free shop in the airport terminal. The hostess took their orders, which the co-pilot radioed ahead. When the DC-6 touched down, passengers ran to pay for and pick up their liquor packages while their baggage was checked onto the Tokyo-bound plane—all within ten minutes. In this instance, Air Mike lived up to its motto: we really move our tail for you!

Pray remembered the early days of Air Mike's flights between

Honolulu and Guam when culinary officials didn't think Guam could supply hot food. So they served Corn Flakes for breakfast.

As it turned out, Oriental and Micronesian passengers had never seen dry cereal. They were puzzled when faced with a small box of cereal and a carton of milk. They picked up the cereal in their fingers and munched on it, but asked what the milk was for.

Honolulu officials were finally satisfied that hot meals were available on Guam when Pacific Islands Catering (PIC) opened its doors. PIC served delicious omelettes!

Sometimes pilots in the '70s flew by the soles of their shoes, according to retired Pan Am pilot, Dick Marsh.

Dick, who was also a freelance photographer, remembered one Trust Territory DC-4 flight from Yap to Guam on which many Palauan and Yapese passengers carried baskets of live coconut crabs tied in rubber bands cut from inner tubes. These crabs are so powerful they can open a coconut with their bare pinchers.

When one of the crabs got loose, Matilda, a Trukese stewardess, attacked it with a broom. She missed and it skittered through the open cockpit door. When the pilots saw the crab, they quickly released their safety belts, jumped on their seats, and flew the airplane standing up. The crab disappeared down an access hole to the baggage compartment, and pilots stuffed rags into the hole to keep the crab there.

Pilots radioed ahead to warn baggage handlers to be on the lookout for the crab when they unloaded the plane. For weeks, baggage handlers and mechanics working in the belly of the aircraft lived in fear of being attacked by a mad, starved coconut crab. It was never found.

In another incident, Marsh said bombs bursting in air surprised and frightened PanAm pilots. A TT Grumman SA16 amphibian flying boat, guided by Guam Naval Air Station controllers, was fighting its way through turbulent thunderheads. Giant cumulonimbus clouds were stacked over the mountains and the cliffside runway.

As pilots descended for approach, flares flashed on the thick clouds, "bombs" burst, and "anti-aircraft fire" popped. They thought World War III had started. Not so. Guam was celebrating the Fourth of July with a fireworks display just below the airstrip.

Continental celebrated its 60th anniversary in 1994 by re-enacting its first flight from El Paso, Texas, to Pueblo, Colorado, in a restored DC-3 aircraft. President Six changed the original name of the airline from Varney Speed Lines to Continental after he moved its headquarters, and his wife, Broadway star Ethel Merman, to Denver. He picked the name Continental because the route flew parallel to the Continental Divide.

Continental Micronesia, Inc., which operates 70 percent of all Continental flights out of Hawaii, flies from Honolulu to Guam and Narita, Japan, and island-hops throughout Micronesia. September 2000 marked the final flight of Continental Micronesia's Boeing 727, which was replaced by the Boeing 737-800 series of aircraft.

Guam's tourist industry received a boost with the opening of the Osaka airport in 1994. Continental Micronesia and United Airlines were selected by the U.S. Department of Transportation to provide service from Japan's new airport to Guam and Saipan.

United Airlines also began Osaka-Guam service that connected with Continental Micronesia flights to Bali, Cebu, and Australia.

In 1996, Continental Airlines received the Coast Guard Public Service Commendation for saving lives, reducing suffering, and providing emergency evacuation for burn and diving victims. Air crews have also delivered babies, rescued shipwrecked sailors, and spotted lost and sunken ships.

Chinese Take-Out

Continental Airlines proudly served the United States in April 2001 by flying twenty-four detained air crewmembers from Tainan Island, China, to Guam.

A U.S. reconnaissance aircraft made an emergency landing on Hainan after an in-flight collision with a Chinese fighter jet. The Chinese held the crew for eleven days, then decided to release them as soon as travel arrangements could be made. A U.S. Government-chartered 737-800 Continental plane had been on standby for five days in Guam in preparation for the flight to Hainan.

The following is an excerpt from a personal account written by flight attendant Suzanne Hendricks.

"April 12th was a proud and exciting day for Continental Micronesia.... I had the uncommon good luck, and great honor, of being selected for the crew that escorted them (the VQ-1 crew) on the first leg of their long journey home from Hainan Island, China."

As soon as the Continental crew agreed to take the flight, they had to submit copies of their passports and obtain photographs for visas.

"Bev Haines, Cynthia Iverson, Debby Purcell, Jean Tang, and I were the flight attendants who were proud to represent our Airlines, our island (Guam), and our country.

".... The Repatriation Team consisted of fourteen escorts from the Navy, Marines, and Air Force.... They came aboard with tons of medical, electronic, and personal luggage. The team assembled for Valiant Return came from Whidbey Island in Washington, Japan, Okinawa, and Washington, D.C. It included the commandant and the commanding officer under whom the captured crew served. There were also medical and psychiatric personnel, communications experts, as well as friends who were members of the crew's squadron.

"A commander who taught at the Navy's Survival School briefed us on the care and handling of the men and women we were picking up. These were professional military personnel who had done their job and done it well under extreme circumstances, he explained. They were not to be perceived as patients or invalids. We were told to treat them with the same humor and friendliness that we show all Continental's passengers. But we were also asked to watch for signs of distress or withdrawal.

"Our Boeing 737 aircraft was set up with two fully equipped stretchers and large oxygen tanks that the flight surgeon hoped not to use. Still, he went to great lengths to have them in total readiness: preparing IV bags and other apparatus and equipment, including Continental's on-board defibrillation machine.

"At 2:30 a.m. we lifted off for our five-hour flight to Haikou, Hainan. We served meals to our fourteen passengers upon request throughout the night as they watched movies, stretched out to try to sleep, or worked on papers. The communications men were on the phones or radios constantly. Shortly before arrival, the commandant briefed us about the mission. We did not know if we would be boarded or searched or engaged in conversation. He cautioned his team that no one should allow any of their possessions to be taken, nor was anyone to extend more than the official apology that President Bush had already offered: regret about the death of the pilot and the unauthorized entry into Chinese airspace for the emergency landing."

The aircraft slowed down its airspeed significantly after passing over Hong Kong air traffic control.

"We arrived precisely as planned in the gray, barely breaking dawn at 6 a.m. China time. After landing, we taxied far from the commercial terminal to a huge concrete pad next to buildings in what was possibly a military staging area. We were surrounded by uniforms and vehicles at all times, but never saw a weapon.

"No one boarded our aircraft except a China Air representative who only came just inside the door to give us arrival and departure cards to complete, and collect our passports. No one got off our aircraft except one man at a time. First the pilot to make his walk-around, then one of our mechanics to oversee refueling from two trucks.

"Our ground time was an anxious one and a half hours.... Finally, just as it looked like we were ready to board the VQ-1 crew, an American general came aboard demanding to see the pilot in command. He angrily reported that the whole operation was suddenly in great jeopardy because Continental personnel had erroneously written "Taiwan" on some official documents. Actually they had written Rep. of China, not Peoples Republic of China.... The captain quickly corrected and initialed the papers.

"Then the buses with our passengers arrived. They saluted smartly as they bolted up our stairs and settled quietly in the back of the aircraft. They were all dressed in their flight jump-suits and carried only small items, if anything at all. Although the aircraft was wide open, most of them chose to sit together rather than take separate rows in which to lie down. Even as we took off their mood was somewhat subdued.

"As we broke through the clouds and into the sunlight, leaving China's airspace, I made a casual welcoming over the P.A., telling them how honored we were to be the ones initiating their journey home. I also told them about the airline food they had to look forward to and the fact that our movie would be "Men of Honor," as they were indeed all men and women of honor. The ice was broken as we all cheered for them, and suddenly the aisle was full as they moved around talking for the next couple hours.

"After weaving our way through the crowded aisle numerous times to serve trays of soft drinks and orange juice, we finally initiated the meal service by carrying out trays, two at a time, to see who was hungry. They all were! Although pizza and beer would have probably been more eagerly accepted, we could only offer chicken or ... a boneless trout.

"Slowly they settled in and began to watch the movie as we darkened the aircraft.... Muted conversations continued throughout the flight as medical, officers, and friends began the debriefing process.

"Just prior to arrival in Guam, the Repatriation Team closed the curtains to the forward cabin and transformed themselves into starched, uniformed military officers.... The VQ-1 crew slowly left the plane according to rank, pausing at the top of the stairs for photos. Then they were driven away to ... await a departure time for their next flight that would put them on the ground in Hawaii at a media-friendly time of day.

"When the media finally finished with us, we reboarded to fly our plane twenty miles south to the civilian airport (on Guam). There, the.... jetway was full of balloons and two fire trucks gave us a water cannon salute as we taxied to the terminal. When we reached the terminal our families, friends, and co-workers were all there to welcome us home. We were each given flowers and a Continental Micronesia cooler full of cold Becks beer.

"It was a tremendous honor to participate in this bit of history. A proud day for Continental Airlines and the United States of America," Hendricks concluded.

The crew's arrival at Andersen was tightly controlled. A guard at the gate allowed an organized greeting by the public. Local politicians, businessmen, military officials, and local, national, and international media crews were among those on hand to witness the crew's arrival.

After the plane landed at Andersen Air Force Base on April 12, military officials kept a tight lid on access to the crew, who walked down the steps, saluted, and shook hands with military and Guam government officials.

Governor Gutierrez and Speaker Tony Unpingco welcomed the crew as they stepped off the plane. The governor, who arrived at the air base in a black sport utility vehicle with a yellow ribbon attached to its grille, said, "We are America in Asia, and sometimes people forget that," he said. "I want you to know we are proud Americans here."

As crewmembers left to board the blue Air Force buses, many waved American flags. Some carried Guam Visitors Bureau shopping bags, containing Guam cookies, red Guam shirts, and Guam pins. The crew was driven to military lodging on the air base to shower, shave, and call family and friends. Air Force Captain Michael Escudie said they were served beef tenderloin, mashed potatoes, French bread, and apple pie for their first meal back on American soil.

Later, crewmembers were driven to the airstrip and boarded an Air Force C-17 transport plane, named "The Spirit of Bob Hope," that took them to Hawaii. The plane is based in Charleston, South Carolina.

In an interview, Continental Airline's chief executive, Gordon M. Bethane, said, "We are tremendously proud. It was, of course, the kind of feel-good publicity that companies can only dream of. Guam, the first stop for the returning crew members, is one of four hubs for Continental, which is based in Houston and also works as a military charter."

Over the years, Air Mike's flights have replaced interisland ships as the Micronesians' lifeline. Thousands of tourists arrived by sea during Guam's "glory boat" years, which were a decade behind but just as gala as Honolulu's passenger liner heydays of the '50s and '60s.

The first ship to receive an island welcome to Guam was the guided missile cruiser, USS *Canberra*, arriving on a rainy Sunday afternoon. The sailors were given twelve hours of shore leave, something no major man-of-war crew had received in years. Despite a heavy downpour, the ship was greeted by the Kaululani Dancers, sponsored by the Guam Chamber of Commerce.

Subsequent welcoming festivities were organized by Commercial Port Director, Joe Sarmiento; Guam Visitors Bureau Director, Bert Unpingco; and the late Stanley Rice, Atkins-Kroll shipping agent.

A typical island greeting was extended to Toyo Yusen Line's *Oriental Queen* upon arrival December 6, 1970. The port's transit shed was converted to a terminal where passengers were sheltered from sun and rain. Information, concession, and refreshment booths were set up.

Arriving passengers were entertained by a high school band and local dancers. Members of the Guam Women's Club, clad in long island dresses, gave flower leis and coconut hats to passengers. During the day, an open house and tour of the ship were arranged for Guam residents. At departure, the band played while passengers tossed colorful serpentine streamers from ship to shore.

Port officials agreed that the Navy's ammunition piers should be relocated so a GovGuam-run commercial port could be built on Cabras Island. If Guam couldn't provide a comfortable passenger terminal, tour ships would go elsewhere, they said.

Finally, the new military ammo wharf was completed at Orote Point, and Hotel Wharf was turned over to GovGuam. A passenger terminal was built featuring a gangway entry to ships' upper decks and a viewing area for spectators on the second floor. On the first level were a lounge, dining room, handicraft and gift shop, rest rooms, tour desks, and a covered ramp leading to taxis or tour buses.

During those years, cruise ships made the Pacific circle route, calling at ports in Japan, Australia, Hong Kong, Manila, Taiwan, and Guam. Those ships included the *President Wilson, Himalaya, Sakura Maru, Iberia, Marco Polo, Coral Princess, Cathay, Lurline, Nippon Maru, Fairsky, George Anson*, and *Chitral*, with her 180-member crew outnumbering the 160 paying passengers.

Despite Guam's excellent passenger ship terminal, the Pacific tour ship business tapered off. Most Western Pacific cruise ships ply sea lanes between Australia, Philippines, and Japan, bypassing Guam. However, in 1998 and 1999, Princess Lines and Crystal Cruises began calling at Guam. The *Queen Elizabeth 2* had to stop at Guam in the late 1990s when one of their scheduled ports of call in the South Pacific was canceled.

Tourism

On April 26, 2001, Guam marked the birth of Guam's tourism industry–thirty-four years since May 1, 1967, when 109 Japanese visitors aboard the Pan Am Clipper landed on Guam. Events during May included a "wave" along Marine Drive, the Guam Hotel and Restaurant Association Mini-Fair at Micronesian Mall, a day-long music concert at Ypao Beach Park, and a Second Annual 5K Fun Run/Walk at Ypao Beach Park.

By the late-1960s, the 6,000 visitors to Guam comprised mostly Stateside Americans on their way elsewhere.

There were seventy hotel rooms on the island then, including the first motel, Air-Tel, owned by Mr. and Mrs. Albert Waller. Primitive accommodations were available at Micronesian Inn, located in a Quonset 100 yards off the tarmac at the airport. Most guests were contract workers overnighting en route to Micronesia, and in those days no planes flew after dark.

About that time, the Guam Visitors Bureau and Continental Airlines launched a campaign to make Guam America's Pacific "stopover shopover." North Americans transiting Guam, as well as those landing for a few hours, were entitled to take back to the States an additional $100 in duty-free merchandise.

Posters proclaiming "America's Day Begins in Guam, U.S.A." were distributed to travel agencies, airlines, and steamship offices throughout the world by Rex Wills, executive secretary of the Guam Tourist Commission, and Jose D. Leon Guerrero, director of GovGuam Department of Commerce.

The slogan, borrowed from Wake Island, means that because of Guam's location west of the 180th Meridian, eastbound airline passengers arrive in San Francisco the day before they leave Guam. Guam is on Greenwich Mean Time plus 10 hours: when it's Sunday noon in Guam, it's 6 p.m. Saturday in San Francisco, 4 p.m. Saturday in Honolulu, 11 a.m. Sunday in Tokyo, and 10 a.m. Sunday in Hong Kong. Or, while Californians are celebrating New Year's Eve, Guam's roosters are already crowing about the New Year.

Tourism began in earnest with the Pan Am Clipper touchdown in 1967. These first visitors were young Japanese men who toted tents or sleeping bags and camped on beaches. There were no public restrooms, and on round-the-island tours, Japanese guides told their compatriots, "Cross your regs."

Many older Guamanians did not look kindly on this second wave of Japanese, an invasion of tourists not warriors. Residents remembered when the WWII enemy forced them into slave labor in concentration camps during the occupation, and many people were beaten, tortured, or beheaded. When tour buses jammed roads and parking lots, some islanders wanted to scream, "Tora, tora, tora!"

The Japanese quickly discovered that Guam was a tropical, U.S. outpost with golf, water sports, and duty-free shopping only three hours from Tokyo. Like all of their generation, these tourists vacationed with cameras, golf clubs, scuba gear, and wads of yen.

These snap-happy tourists, too young to remember the war, focused their cameras on the island's lush greenery. They also liked to pose in front of statues, such as the Colonel Sanders at Kentucky Fried Chicken and the revolving figure of Pope John Paul II, nicknamed RotoPope.

In 1965, the Guam Economic Development Authority (GEDA), created by the Eighth Guam Legislature, was the catalyst for a construction boom. Cranes and steel girders formed a new skyline as GEDA offered tax rebates to qualified enterprises, guaranteed hotel loans, and lured outside investors to Guam.

To accommodate increased tourism, the new Guam International Air Terminal was dedicated in March 1966 at the Naval Air Station. Continental Air Micronesia was the main regional carrier.

When I wrote Micronesia's first tourist guide in 1968, there were virtually no visitors and few businessmen traveling to Guam or its neighbor islands.

In 1969, Governor Guerrero formed a tourist commission to attract visitors to Guam. A year later, Governor Camacho restructured the Guam Tourist Commission into the Guam Visitors Bureau (GVB), a quasi-autonomous instrument of government.

Hired to direct the infant GVB was Bert Unpingco, a Guamanian who graduated from the University of Alabama. During Unpingco's ten years' service, the number of tourists and facilities blossomed like tangan-tangan. Unpingco stressed to fellow

Chamorros that they should strive to preserve their culture, traditions, and lifestyle.

When Japan Air Lines initiated flights between Tokyo and Guam on DC-8 jets in 1969, nearly 58,000 Japanese filled the island's 1,000 hotel rooms.

Construction began on the first of Tumon Bay's luxury hotels: the $5 million Guam Hilton with 200 rooms, with J&G enterprises as the driving force. However, the Hilton wasn't completed until 1972.

About that time, businessman Al Ysrael burst into the newsroom of the *Pacific Journal* to ask us to cover the groundbreaking of the island's first tourist hotel. City Editor Carol McMurrough and I laughed him out of the room—Al was noted for his impossible schemes.

As it turned out, construction of Ysrael's building was delayed four years. When completed, it was used for teachers' housing. With the onset of direct Guam-Tokyo flights, Ysrael's partners, the Fujita people, turned the compound into the Fujita Tumon Beach Hotel. It became a popular destination resort. The first luau on Guam was held on the hotel grounds for a group of Japanese single clerical workers, who sat on mats on the beachside lawn at long, low tables. They ate dinner while watching a stage show featuring Tahitian dancers, aka wild waist shows.

New high-rise hotels began popping up along Tumon Bay like glass fishing floats after a storm: Guam Dai-Ichi, Tokyu, Reef, and Okura hotels.

The Tokyu Hotel staged a Chamorro Night. At sundown, a native son, torch in hand, ran across the roof of the hotel, while graceful maidens carried torches to the palm-decorated stage. Tourists lapped up rum drinks in coconut bowls, shrimp kelaguen served in clam shells, and a cultural show accompanied by the music of Frank Cabral and his Ladrones.

Shortly thereafter, the Dai Ichi Hotel invited 180 guests from Japan, including geishas and the granddaughter of the Emperor, for its grand opening.

The opening of the Hilton Hotel took place the same day that President Richard Nixon stopped in Guam on his way to China. The Hilton's logo was a stylized bird once carved on prows of Micronesian *bancas* (canoes).

More than 1,500 residents were invited to the opening of the 18-story, 300-room Reef Hotel. It featured a rooftop cocktail lounge and a wraparound swimming pool with a swim-up bar called the Tuba Korner. The hotel's main dining room, La Sirena, was named for the beautiful legendary Guam maiden who turned into a mermaid.

Not until July 1972 did Admiral G. Steve Morrison, Commander Naval Marianas, grant unrestricted civilian access to the international air terminal at Naval Air Station under a 40-year joint-use agreement with GovGuam.

U.S. Marines never envisioned liberating Guam to make the island safe for a third wave of visitors who stormed the beaches: Japanese honeymooners. For half the price of a Hawaiian trip, honeymooners found sun and sand, an ocean of surfing and fishing, and duty-free shopping on Guam.

These newlyweds sometimes confused hotel personnel, airline clerks, and tour operators. Brides-to-be and grooms-to-be often made separate travel arrangements and obtained passports and visas in their single names. The couple was married before leaving Japan, and when they arrived on Guam, no one was sure they were really husband and wife.

If couples wanted to marry on Guam, they had to wait in long lines at the GovGuam license bureau while locals obtained dog, automobile, and business licenses. When hotel rooms were scarce, honeymooners were often housed two couples to a room.

As the wedding market grew, tour agents arranged packages to include everything from marriage licenses to wedding chapels, receptions, and hotel rooms. Today, all hotel rooms are booked during Japan's honeymoon season each October.

Seoul, Korea, hosted a five-day Weddex 2000 Spring Travel Show featuring Guam as a honeymoon destination.

The Guam Visitors Bureau reports that Guam moved up in rank in the top twenty wedding/honeymoon destinations from eleven to three in 2001. First on the list is Honolulu, followed by Las Vegas, then Guam.

In the early days of tourism, hotels hired local people, but personal service was new to Guamanians. One tourist called room service to get his suit pressed, and the bellhop brought him an iron and an ironing board. At the Cliff Hotel, a guest complained that rain was pouring on him from the window above his bed. A maid moved his bed across the room, out of rain's reach.

For the island's numerous power outages, hotels stock candles and matches for each room. Residents never leave home without flashlights in their purses and cars. When the power goes off, people are asked to park their cars facing stores so business can be conducted as usual. One evening the power went off at the Hilton Hotel and a motorist drove his car, headlights ablaze, straight into the spacious lobby.

Honeymooners aren't affected by power outages. They just go to bed.

In 1979, tourism received a boost when the new International Air Terminal opened. Duty-Free Shoppers was awarded an exclusive concession in the terminal.

Some tourists asked some strange things: When do they turn on the sunset? Where should I stand to get the best view? Who mows the tangan-tangan? Did you find the backpack I lost in Agaña? When does the Marianas Trench open? What time will the whales be swimming by? Where's the W.C.?

Tourist attractions in the '70s were limited. Visitors used to watch B-52s returning in blazing sunsets to Andersen AFB after Pacific bombing raids. Today, tour agencies offer a variety of packages: half-day or all-day tours to jungles, World War II sites, shopping, bar hopping, as well as trolling, parasailing, jet skiing, diving, snorkeling, windsurfing, shooting, golfing, boating, and helicopter rides. There's even a jungle cruise up the Talofofo River.

Guam's latest beachfront high-rise is the 600-room hotel managed by Outrigger Hotels. Outrigger Guam Resort opened in 1998. The company manages a resort at Majuro Atoll in Majuro and a hotel in Koror, Palau. The Outrigger's amenities on Guam include Bon Marche, Louis Vuitton, Dior, Celine, and a Hard Rock Café.

The Guam Marriott Resort, formerly the Pacific Star Hotel, underwent a $13 million renovation in 2000. The Pacific Star Hotel announced an agreement with Marriott International Inc. to manage the 436-room Tumon Bay hotel.

The New Century Hotel Guam, on Ypao Road, opened in February 2000. The $3 million, 48-room hotel took almost three years to build.

In 1980, the Pacific Islands Club bought the former Continental Airlines hotel. Twenty years later, PIC, Guam's largest hotel, was renovated, adding the Royal Tower with an additional 292 rooms. Other PICs are located in Saipan and Phuket, Thailand. The main dining room of the Guam hotel is the Skylight, and other eateries in the hotel are the Rock N Roll café and the Japanese Hanaya and Chinese Toryu restaurants. The hotel has a Mandara spa and a marriage chapel, a 400-seat amphitheater for nightly island shows, boutiques, tour facilities, racquetball court, tennis courts, badminton courts, basketball court, playground, table tennis, billiards, kayaks, beach volleyball, water sports, golf range, two Jacuzzis, swim-through aquarium, a water zoo, and 24-hour movies on command.

The hotel's twentieth anniversary was celebrated by the opening of a new dining room, Le Bistro.

The Japan Travel Bureau, the largest tour wholesaler for Guam, keeps the island's more than 6,000 hotel rooms occupied 89 percent. The peak travel period for most Japanese vacationers is Golden Week, late April to early May. Hotels in Guam are fully booked during this week, thanks to the many inexpensive travel packages to Guam. The top three overseas destinations for Japanese are Europe, South Korea, and the United States mainland. Guam and

Saipan are expected to attract more than one million tourists, according to the Guam Visitors Bureau.

On the downside, the tourist boom has transformed Tamuning and Tumon into an ill-planned, part-American, part-Japanese transcultural clutter. Along Tumon beach and bay, public property has been invaded for private profit with jet-skis, other tourist concessions, and a dinner boat all owned by, catering to and employing mostly non-locals. Dozens of tour companies, car rental agencies, duty-free shops, and branches of Hawaiian stores dot the tourist strip. Vacant lots are filled with Japanese-financed high-rise luxury condos.

Still, tourism is going to be Guam's biggest economic asset in this millennium. Air arrival statistics showed visitor increases from 340,139 in 1983 and in 1996, 1.4 million visitors arrived, 70 percent from Japan. The majority of visitors to Guam are in the 18 to 29 age bracket, followed by 30-39 and 40-49 ages, mostly clerical and sales and students categories traveling for pleasure.

In the year 2000, visitors totaled 326,579 and by March 2001, 356,284 visitors had already arrived on Guam. Most were from Japan, followed by Korea, U. S. mainland, Taiwan, Saipan, Hawaii, Micronesia, Philippines, and Hong Kong.

Officials expect tourist arrivals on Guam to double in the next decade and that hotel occupancy will reach 90 percent. The hotel occupancy tax collected from 1996 to 2001 shows a marked increase: in 1996 $26,205,052; a high in 1997 of $27,778,345; and $20,576,387 in the first six months of 2001.

The goal is to attract two million visitors, according to Gerald S.A. Perez, president of Duty Free Shoppers. This means solving power, water, sewer, and drainage problems in Tumon Bay; landscaping, removing clutter; undergrounding utility services; and opening a police precinct house with visitor-friendly officers in Tumon Bay.

Guam's primary industry in the 21st century will continue to be tourism. The industry will flourish, despite the deadly tragedy that occurred on August 6, 1997. On that rainy morning, Korean

Air Flight 801 crashed and burned on Nimitz Hill, three miles from Guam's International Airport. Most of the 154 passengers aboard the jumbo jet were Korean tourists and honeymooners. Only 28 passengers survived.

Guam has one of the highest standards of living in the Pacific and welcomes tourists from Japan, Taiwan, and South Korea to its clean tropical waters, gorgeous lagoons, waterfalls, and soaring green mountains. But if the island's unique culture and beauty, as well as its sea life, are destroyed, Guam may eventually lose its appeal for tourists.

Heritage tourism is now receiving priority on the island. For instance, local entertainment is presented at the Chamorro Village in Agaña to show tourists what Guam is all about. Cultural home tours, popular with visitors, include traditional Chamorro folkway demonstrations and entertainment.

The Guam Preservation Trust, a nonprofit corporation, was established in 1990 to restore historical properties and support preservation activities. Along with the Trust, the Chamorro Heritage Foundation was created to fulfill the need for arts and humanities programs, such as theater groups, dance schools, and the Guam Symphony Orchestra.

The village of Inarajan has been designated a historical district, and the Trust plans to restore the Inarajan church.

In 1972, the Cruz house in Inarajan became the first to be renovated with federal funds under the Historic Preservation Office. The house, built by Jose Duenas Cruz for his family in 1914, has been a regular feature of the Gef Pa'go Chamorro Cultural Village tour since 1995. The Cruz home features manposteria foundation walls, ifil framing and floors, and walls of horizontal tongue and groove siding.

The Hyatt Regency Hotel on Tumon Bay hired young Phillip Sablan and Neri Blas to give tourists a bit of Chamorro culture. Sablan and his brothers built a hut between the hotel's pools.

Here Sablan and Blas demonstrate how to weave coconut frond hats and flowers. Visitors may also see crabs and fruitbats, take carabao rides, and sample coconut juice.

The Hilton Hotel launched a dinner show in which the Taotao Tano dancers take tourists through Chamorro history in dance and song. Charlie Corn's son, Anthony, public relations manager, says the show is intended to entertain as well as stimulate interest in Chamorro culture.

Recently, the Kiosko at the Plaza de España, an Agaña landmark, was reopened after restoration and repair with Guam Preservation Trust funds. The Kiosko was the site of Sunday Navy Band concerts from 1902 until the beginning of World War II. In a ceremony marking the last public performance by the Guam Navy Band, Lt. Gov. Madeleine Z. Bordallo presented the Ancient Order of the Chamorri to band members. The musicians were transferred to other Navy bands.

Young Guamanians are discovering their cultural roots and making efforts to reclaim land owned for 300 years by foreign forces and the U. S. military.

Many children today speak a Chamorro and English pidgin lingo. GovGuam schools are encouraging a revival of Chamorro language and culture through bilingual programs. The trend to revive the native language resulted in the formation of the Chamorro Language Commission. This commission offers Chamorro language classes to about sixty students a year, runs an all-Chamorro day care center, and translates books into the language.

Guam also has emerged as a regional learning center. Students from Micronesia, the United States, and Asian countries exchange classes with students at the University of Guam. The Micronesian Area Research Center, established at the University in 1967, houses the most complete collection of information about Micronesia.

In 1986, the transformation of TTPI districts, other than the Commonwealth of the Northern Marianas Islands, into the Federated States of Micronesia and the Republics of Marshalls and Palau opened the gates for Micronesian emigration to Guam. Micronesian citizens are treated as U.S. nationals. Since implementation of these compacts of free association, 4,568 Micronesians have migrated to Guam.

Additionally, Koreans, Japanese, Chinese, and a continued legal and illegal inflow of Filipinos, have swelled the non-Chamorro population. These immigrants add heavily to Guam's overloaded educational, health, and criminal justice systems, as well as to housing and utilities.

The federal government in October 2000 delivered a check for $9.58 million to GovGuam to compensate for the social costs of immigrants from the free-associated states in Micronesia. The Commonwealth of the Northern Mariana Islands also received $1 million for this purpose.

As more and more Chamorros migrate to the U.S. mainland, Chamorros will soon be only slightly more numerous than other segments of the population.

Some Guamanians worry that their native culture and language will fade midst U. S. and Asian influences. In 1940, Chamorros constituted 90.5 percent of Guam's permanent population. By 1970, their numbers had been reduced to 72.1 percent. The 1990 census gave a population of 133,152, of which 43 percent were Chamorros, 23 percent Filipino, 14 percent Caucasian, and 15 percent others, 5 percent Micronesians. Guam's 2000 census closed after counting about 45,000 residences; 15,000 more than in 1990.

Shopping

Guam is the place for the "born to shop" crowd. The island's duty-free status means that name-brand merchandise is less expensive than in the country of origin. Each of the resort hotels at Tumon Bay has a lobby arcade, and other specialty shops are within walking distance along Pale San Vitores Road. These stores also carry Micronesian handicrafts, island clothing, and beachwear.

In Agaña and nearby Tamuning, stores sell, at bargain prices, Chinese silk, Austrian crystals, and handmade carpets from India and the Near East. There are also electronic items, sports equipment, CDs, tapes, records, karaoke laser discs, coins, stamps, and shells.

Years ago, Guam had one department store and a few dress shops. The Agaña Shopping Center in Hagåtña banks on the loyalty of long-time local customers. The center and its anchor, Town House Department Store, are owned by Henry Sy and Kenneth T. Jones, Jr. Town House, the only locally owned department store, has built a solid reputation through the years.

Duty Free Shops (DFS) began in 1971 in a hotel lobby on Tumon Bay with 320 employees. Total visits that year were 60,000, all Japanese. Today, DFS serves more than one million visitors and employs 1,500 people. It operates 21 stores in three islands in Micronesia, including 17 hotel shops, airport concessions, and free-standing DFS Galleria flagship stores in Guam and Saipan.

Guam's first large-scale, fully enclosed shopping center, the Micronesian Mall, opened in 1988 between Harmon and Dededo. Recently, Hawaii's top-scale Liberty House opened here. Nearby, Harmon has become a chaotic maze of warehouses, garages, and weekend flea markets.

Kmart's second largest retail store opened in 1994 in a shopping center developed on eleven acres of land on Marine Drive in Upper Tumon. The 24-hour retail store was followed by Price Costco and Walmart.

Ross Dress for Less opened doors at Guam Premium Outlets in October 2000, with 28,000 square feet of retail space. Ross, employing 150 people, has 412 stores throughout the United States and sells clothing, bed and bath accessories, jewelry, and shoes.

Gibson's Town House and Ben Franklin vie for the mid-range

market. Other stores include Crazy Shirts, ABC Discount Stores, and Guam's first factory outlet center.

A unique shopping center is the Chamorro Village, reminiscent of an old Spanish market, centrally located along Agaña Bay. Fresh produce, the catch of the day, local handicrafts, T-shirts, kimonos, and curio shops surround stalls of eateries that serve international dishes. The main hall is used for occasional shows featuring local talent. Chamorro Village was born in the early 1990s to promote Chamorro arts and crafts and to raise the profile of Chamorro culture. Wednesday nights are Chamorro nights.

The Shopping bus and Lam Lam Tours trolleys stop at the Guam Premium Outlets. According to Gerald S. A. Perez, president of DFS Guam and chairman of the Guam Chamber of Commerce, Guam has arrived as a resort destination for shoppers.

Recreation

Many tourists are interested in the World War II sites on Guam. These include the Tank Farm and Sigua Falls, the Last Japanese Command Post, Asan and Agat Invasion Beaches, Mount Alifan Battlefield, Piti Guns, Mount Tenjo, the War in the Pacific, as well as bays, caves, coves, and points that were backgrounds for Japanese and American troop battles.

One of the sights that World War II buffs and dog-lovers should not miss is the War Dog Cemetery and Memorial. The "Devil Dog" cemetery was originally built by the Marines at the war's close in the village of Dededo. Original structures remain there as silent sentinels of the past, but the official War Dog Cemetery was moved to Tiyan.

When the U.S. Marines landed war dogs on Bougainville in the South Pacific in November 1943, it marked the first use of trained military dogs in combat by the United States. Dobermans, the official U. S. Marine Corps War Dogs, served throughout the

Pacific, valiantly leading patrols in the steaming jungles, giving timely warning of the enemy waiting in ambush or hiding in caves, saving untold lives. They guarded exhausted sleeping troops in foxholes by night, preventing infiltration by the foe.

The United Doberman Club dedicated a statue to the courageous Doberman Pinschers that served during the War in the Pacific. The Club-sponsored bronze memorial was created by Susan Bahary and placed at the United States Marine Corps War Dog Cemetery in Guam in June 1994. An inscription reads, "To honor the working dog heritage of the Doberman Pinscher."

The bronze statue, "Always Faithful," is a memorial to the Dobermans who gave their lives on Guam. Some of the war dogs, targets of enemy fire, did not make it home. These dogs made the supreme sacrifice. They lie buried in the War Dog Cemetery in Guam. Their graves are marked with small headstones and a plaque.

The inscription on the memorial commemorating World War II combat dogs says: "Always Faithful, 25 Marine War Dogs gave their lives liberating Guam in 1944. They served as sentries, messengers, scouts. They explored caves, detected mines and booby traps. Semper Fidelis."

In October 2000, a bill was passed by the U.S. Congress and signed by the president requiring military personnel to de-train and put up for adoption military working dogs no longer needed for duty. At this point, the dogs must be adopted by experienced military or ex-military handlers.

Hundreds of *gorufu* fans fly to Guam, Japan's gateway to golf, for weekends on the greens. There are roughly 15 million golfers in Japan, only 1,800 courses, and membership fees in country clubs reach as high as $1 million. Guam offers uncrowded courses, with weekend green fees averaging $115.

The island's first golf course, with 18 holes, was established in 1923 on the Sumay military base. The Guam Golf Club was organized that year.

Another early course, the 185-acre Windward Hills Country Club reported that 25,000 total rounds of golf were played in 1998, and about 12,000 were played during the first half of 1999.

The Country Club of the Pacific, a Japanese-owned course, opened in 1971 on acreage that once housed Duendis, Guam's legendary little people. Its first international tournament attracted sixteen golfers from Japan, Taiwan, and Australia to compete for $100,000 prize money. The golf course is surrounded by villas, a marina, and horseback riding trails. This is supposed to be Guam's healthiest golf course, financially. Sohbu Guam Development Co., which opened this, Guam's second private course, finished paying its construction debt in 1990. Country Club of the Pacific offered annual memberships, which increased to $900 per year in 1993, but in 2000 fell back to the 1988 level of $450 due to competition from other courses.

One golf-condo development built for Japanese tourists rose at Mangilao-Marbo, where half a century earlier Chamorros had huddled in concentration camps under Japanese bayonets. The Mangilao Golf Club is the only course on the island with seaside holes.

LeoPalace Resort hosts tournaments for its members. Some 44,000 total rounds of golf were played here in 1998. The resort offers a Highland Package, comprising a one-night stay at the resort, plus golf rounds and meals. Family members can also use the resort's archery area, rental bikes, swimming pool, and parking facilities.

The Tumon Golf Range opened in May 1999 after a $2 million reconstruction due to damages by Supertyphoon Paka in 1997. The two-tiered facility accommodates 76 players and also includes a putting green and sand trap.

Guam's two biggest tournaments, the annual Charlie Corn and the Marianas Invitational draw big crowds each May. Other weekends are sprinkled with one-day tournaments sponsored by companies, government agencies, schools, and churches.

The number of rounds of golf played on Guam's seven privately owned courses increased in 2000 after three years of decline, peaking in 1996 with 383,000 rounds. That's a lot of golf for a small island: more than one golf course per million people, the standard by which such things are measured. Most of the courses in Guam have been built for tourists, but some say it's a better use of land than growing taro or rice.

Today, Guam has ten golf courses, with another being built in Yona between the cemetery and Jeff's Pirate's Cove. Another three or four courses have been proposed, planned, or otherwise contemplated for the future. When the proposed courses are completed, the number of visiting golfers is expected to balloon from the current 100,000 a year to 800,000.

Recruiting caddies for Guam's new golf courses may be difficult. Golfers might consider using carabaos, as llamas are used for caddies on some Stateside courses.

In 1999 Guam hosted, for the second time, the South Pacific Games (SPG), called the Olympics of amateur sports in Oceania. The SPG were launched in 1963 in Fiji and have been held every three years in New Caledonia, Papua New Guinea, Tahiti, Fiji, and Western Samoa.

The 1999 SPG drew 5,000 athletes from 22 Pacific island nations and territories. Among the competitions were weight lifting, basketball, softball, soccer, golf, triathalons, archery, karate, wrestling, swimming, surfing, yachting, and outrigger canoe racing. Guam International Country Club held the South Pacific Games' golf tournament in 1999.

Also in 1999, Guam hosted the Micronesian Games, aka Coconut Olympics. At the 1994 Micronesian Games, 1,800 athletes from Micronesia, Nauru, and Australia competed in Guam.

The Sydney 2000 Olympic Games was a bittersweet event for Guam. From September 15 to October 1, 10,000 of the world's best athletes from 200 countries competed in 28 sports. There were highs and lows for Guam's athletes, and controversy marred the island's participation. Guam had seven athletes competing in Sydney, but only four completed their competitions.

Guam weightlifter Melissa Fejeran made history when she was among the first group of women to compete in weightlifting, which made its debut at the Olympics. Fejeran placed 15th out of 17 competitors. She carried Guam's flag during the opening ceremony.

Swimmer Daniel O'Keeffe set a new Guam national record in the 100-meter butterfly and finished fourth in his heat.

Sprinter PhilAm Garcia finished 91st out of 95 competitors in the 100-meter dash, but failed to improve his personal best record.

Marathon runner Rhonda Alley placed 44th out of 45 runners in the women's marathon. She carried Guam's flag during the closing ceremony.

Three Guam athletes failed to complete their competitions, including two-time Olympians: cyclist Derek Horton crashed at the start of the men's mountain bike race; cyclist Jazy Garcia did not finish in the men's road race as he was overtaken by the lead pack and he was pulled from the race; laser sailor Brett Chivers and his father and coach, Scott, were pulled from the team and stripped of their accreditation in mid-competition for violating curfew. Controversy surrounded Chivers' removal, as members of the Guam National Olympic committee have yet to accept a Guam Sailing Federation letter apologizing for a member's actions after the Chivers' removal.

Fishing is a lifeblood of Micronesia. Before the coming of Western cultures, the sea's bounty was a key supplement to a diet comprising mainly fruits and vegetables, and, to many today, fish and seafood are still a big part of their meals.

The Chamorros favored hand-thrown *talaya*, crafted by net-making masters, which are still used today. A perfect throw of the net is a vision of artistry and grace that, with luck, adds bounty to the dinner table.

Guam was put on the international fishing map in 1969, when

Gregorio D. Perez caught a world-record Pacific blue marlin off Ritidian Point. This all-tackle record stood until 1983. The fish has been displayed in the lounge at Guam's air terminal ever since.

Guam's tradition of fishing is alive today, but is being threatened. Fishermen can't choose what they catch because too many fish populations have been depleted, partly by harvesting from shore.

Today, Federal and local laws make it illegal to kill, capture, harass, or harm marine mammals. Many pigmy, sperm, pilot, false killer whales, dolphins, and porpoises swimming within a half mile of the coast have been injured by mechanized water craft.

Visiting landlubbers can enjoy underwater sights without getting wet. The SS *Neptune*, an Australian-built semi-submersible vessel, offers trips from Apra Harbor to the Western Shoals. From the boat, viewers explore the world of colorful corals, sea anemones, squid, parrotfish, groupers, mantas, turtles, dolphins, and pilot whales.

Swimmers, snorkelers, divers, boaters, and fishermen are afforded spectacular sights above and below the waterline in Guam, the fishbowl of the Pacific. Hundreds of species of fish, corals, and anemones teem in the waters, as well as conch, cowry, cone, olive, and top shells—if they haven't all been collected by over-zealous shellers.

CHAPTER SEVEN

Celebrity Stopovers

After World War II, GIs called Guam an uninviting place of military exile, where extreme boredom led to rock fever. That image changed rapidly as Guam prospered from 1960 to this century. Distinguished visitors, including presidents, a queen, a senator, a pope, and the first lady, made rewarding visits to the island, and, of course, they made exciting news stories for local media.

Bob Hope

Throughout his career, comedian Bob Hope joked about Guam. On Hope's frequent trips to the Far East to entertain American troops, he often stopped on the island.

At one charity gig at Andersen AFB, Hope quipped, "Guam is a charming, beautiful tropical island. I'll return someday to open a Marriott Hotel."

"Guam's a real historical place," Hope continued. "Did you know that 'Mutiny on the Bounty' didn't really happen on Tahiti, but on Guam? Yeah, Captain Bligh wanted to stay."

He added, "I'm no stranger to the Pacific islands—I've been there and I've got fungus to prove it."

Hope got his come-uppance during a reception following President Richard Nixon's funeral. Robert Underwood, Guam's elected Washington Representative, introduced himself. "Mr. Hope, I just wanted to tell you that I forgive you for all the jokes you've made over the years about Guam."

Hope stared blankly at Underwood. "You're from Guam? I've been there."

Underwood walked away muttering, "I hope I get to Johnny Carson before he gets that old."

On May 29, 2001, Bob Hope celebrated his 98th birthday at his Los Angeles home. His eight-decade career ranged from vaudeville to television, movies, and scores of trips to entertain U.S. troops abroad. He made his last overseas visit to entertain U.S. troops at age 87, stopping in Saudi Arabia in 1990 during Operation Desert Storm.

President Lyndon Johnson

When the White House announced in March 1967 that President Lyndon Johnson intended to hold a conference on the Vietnam situation somewhere in the Western Pacific, the international press corps twitched their collective news noses.

The location was a highly guarded secret, but everyone knew it was going to be America's strategic listening post: Guam. This was to be the first visit of a U.S. President in Guam during its years as a U.S. territory.

Admiral Horace V. Bird, Commander Naval Forces Marianas (COMNAVMAR), coordinated the President's Vietnam conference. Military and local government groups sprang into action to prepare for the event. Streets were cleaned and repaired, official buildings were spruced up, and boonies were cut back. Residents' houses were painted, yards cleaned, and lawns mowed.

On March 20, Air Force One touched down at Naval Air Station and taxied to the airport. Guam's Governor Manuel Guerrero and Admiral Bird welcomed the President and Lady Bird as they stepped out of the plane. On the tarmac, Johnson spoke briefly about the historic occasion. Then he and the First Lady piled into a limousine for the trip to the Navy's COMNAVMAR compound atop Nimitz Hill.

Hundreds of island residents lined Marine Drive to wave at the president. Hilda and Dick Netzley and their two sons bobbed "Welcome to Guam" signs in the air as the cavalcade whizzed through Agaña like a shooting star.

"Johnson certainly couldn't have read our signs," Hilda said later.

The Navy compound was dubbed the "Little White House," surrounded by a coral reef instead of Washington's Beltway, newsmen joked.

The 146 members of the international press corps, including White House correspondents, strained Guam's telephone and wire service systems. While in his hotel room, a *Life* magazine reporter was bitten by a shrew, an incident he cleverly wove into his story.

Some 367 members of the President's staff, advisers, cabinet members, military commanders, and allies immediately began hours of discussion about Vietnam. There were also an untold number of Secret Service men on island with noticeable bulges under their Hawaiian shirts.

After a news briefing the next day, the President was escorted to Andersen AFB, where he decorated airmen and reviewed reasons why America should aid Vietnam, despite anti-war demonstrations at home.

Though on a tight schedule, Johnson attended a fiesta given on the air base. While a U.S. senator, Johnson had garnered a reputation for downing large amounts of Scotch whiskey. At the fiesta, the President didn't disappoint his followers. When he left, Johnson, towering ramrod-straight, was one of the few who didn't stagger. A public affairs officer marveled at the president's capacity for whiskey.

Johnson smiled. "Young man, if you think that was drinking, you should come to a barbecue on our ranch back in Texas."

Johnson and Lady Bird bid farewell to the island, boarded Air Force One and flew away. The 36th U.S. President had been on Guam for 30 hours and 55 minutes.

President Richard Nixon

Richard Milhous Nixon was the only U.S. president to visit Guam three times.

In 1969, Nixon, then vice president, stopped on Guam during a round-the-world trip that included watching the splashdown in the Pacific of Apollo XI, the first moon vehicle.

During his second visit, Nixon gave a news conference at Top of the Mar officers' club on Nimitz Hill. Here he announced his new U.S. foreign policy called the Guam Doctrine, later known as the Nixon Doctrine. This policy stated that no American ground troops would be sent abroad to fight for nations threatened by aggression.

The result of Nixon's policy was that B-52 missions from Andersen AFB, Guam, increased, and tent cities sprang up on the base to accommodate enlisted air crews, while officers filled Tumon Beach hotels.

After Nixon's visit, *Newsweek* magazine described Guam as a coral atoll that was only a fuel stop on the President's round-the-world trip.

Irate, Governor Carlos Camacho shot a letter of rebuttal to *Newsweek*: "Guam is no Pacific atoll. . . . Guam, the home of 100,000 Americans, is of volcanic origin. . . . Furthermore, Guam was no mere fuel stopover on the Presidential trip around the world. To say that is to liken it to a mid-Pacific comfort stop.

"The White House informed us that the President came to Guam deliberately, so that he could be informed of problems of both our island and of the U.S.-administered Trust Territory of the Pacific Islands. The President and Mrs. Nixon spent many of the twenty-one hours on Guam with people from both Guam and the TT. We are proud they visited our island, and you do them an injustice to so casually gloss over the interest and attention they evinced in this developing American community.

"The President's stop on Guam won the island international renown because the new U.S. policy on military assistance to Asian nations which Nixon enunciated at his Agaña news conference has been labeled by the press as the Guam Doctrine," Camacho wrote.

Guam was one of the few communities in the United States to loyally support the Vietnam War. Governor Camacho flew to Vietnam in 1969 for a five-day visit at Christmas. Camacho carried gifts for Guamanian servicemen. He was accompanied by Johnny G. Sablan, a popular Chamorro singer. Guamanian troops, the governor, and his entourage sang Chamorro songs at a mini-fiesta of rice, roast pork, kelaguen, and finadene.

The week before Nixon's third visit to Guam, in 1972, the island was secured by FBI, Secret Service men, and a Chief Petty Officer assigned to the White House. They chased civilians off Nimitz Hill and checked everything from accommodations to watermelons. They even made ice cubes from bottled, not tap, water. Nixon's luggage was enough to make a carabao stagger. He brought his own makeup man, a special bed, and shower head—everything except a toilet, said a Navy aide.

Most of the president's advance party, along with Henry Kissinger and newsmen Walter Cronkite and David Brinkley, stayed at the Cliff Hotel. The group brought its own phone switchboard to the Guam "White House."

On February 20, Air Force One touched down at Guam International Airport within five minutes of the ribbon-cutting ceremony at the Guam Hilton Hotel's grand opening. Nixon made a brief address from the tarmac. According to some reports, he commented, "Ladies and Gentlemen: Don't tell me that the Hilton isn't open yet?"

Then he and Mrs. Nixon, clad in her famed "Republican cloth coat," shook hands with some of the crowd gathered to welcome the couple. Nixon picked up a few babies, one of whom piddled on him.

The public lined Marine Drive to wave at Nixon and Pat, who were whisked in a black limousine to Nimitz Hill for an overnight stay in the Admiral's guest house.

The next morning, I was assigned to take pictures of the President's departure. My press pass allowed me to get in front of the public barricade and jostle into position in a pack of reporters and photographers, but still I had to use a telephoto lens.

As the first couple waved "Hafa Adai" from the steps of the aircraft, I snapped pictures as fast as the Minolta's shutter would open and close, hoping for one picture that would make the front page of the newspaper. Suddenly, I heard "click, click." My camera ran out of film just as Nixon had assumed his traditional pose: upstretched arms flashing the V-for-victory sign (his coat puckering behind his neck because he forgot to unbutton it), a frown of concern on his brow, shifty eyeballs, coupled with waggling jowls.

Luckily, UPI stringer Dick Williams gave me a few of his shots to go with my story. Nixon went on to China, where he sipped ceremonial wine with Communist leader, Chou En Lai.

Nixon was interested in the Trust Territory of the Pacific Islands. During his administration, he transferred the responsibility for Micronesia from the Department of Interior to his personal representative, Franklin Haydn Williams.

Lee Marvin

In October 1967, Academy Award winning actor Lee Marvin brought his yacht to Micronesia to search for a movie location. He and his producers decided that Palau would be the perfect spot to film "Hell in the Pacific." During filming, it was reported that war nearly broke out again as the American, English, and Japanese film crews and actors relived old battles.

On screen, Marvin was the quintessential badass. It was all acting. Though he was no stranger to foul language, looked menacing even when overjoyed, and drank a lot, in reality, he was kind, intelligent, well-read, an art enthusiast, a deep-sea fisherman, and a gourmet. His interests varied from studying the inner working of industrial machinery to making tortoise-shell jewelry.

He was perfect for Palau. Of all the cast, Palauans liked Marvin best. He didn't take himself too seriously and was fond of closing the bars each night—a trait Palauans admired. Marvin invited Palauans to play poker on his yacht, then delighted in winning Palauans' hard-earned government salaries. While playing cards, they savored lobster tails and taro chips and downed beers.

Most of the movie was filmed on a narrow, white-sand strip under a jungle-covered, coral-limestone cliff. The beach became known as Lee Marvin Beach, and, today, is the locals' favorite spot to snooze, picnic, guzzle beers, and munch on lobsters roasted over driftwood fires. (For more about Palau, see Chapter Nine.)

In 1970, Marvin's yacht was brought to Guam on an LCU. Tied up at Dillingham's pier in the Commercial Port, the sleek yacht underwent minor electrical and bilge pump repairs. Later, the boat was available for charter.

Born in 1924 in New York City, Marvin dropped out of high school to join the Marine Corps. His unit was sent to Saipan, which was occupied by 30,000 Japanese soldiers. One of the deadliest battles of the Pacific War took place on the island. In 1944, Marvin was wounded just below the spine and his sciatic nerve was nearly severed. One of six survivors from his unit, Marvin was hospitalized for 13 months before being discharged.

In 1951 Marvin appeared in the Broadway production of "Billy Budd," then made screen appearances the next year. Tall and rugged, Marvin usually played the brutal heavy. He won an Academy Award for best actor in his dual role in "Cat Ballou" (1963), and starred with Clint Eastwood in "Paint Your Wagon," filmed partly near Black Hawk, Colorado. Marvin died in 1987.

Cameron Mitchell

One day Wilfred Hagen, Continental Travelodge manager, called me to say that Cameron Mitchell was on island. The actor had just finished filming a segment of the TV series, "The American Sportsman," on Truk.

I met six-foot-tall Mitchell and his wife, Maggi, on the terrace of the Continental Hotel, where they were resting after a grueling week in Truk. Over mai-tais, Mitchell said that he dove with Paul Tzimoulis, publisher of *Skin Diver* magazine. While in Truk, Mitchell also did promotional films for Continental Airlines and Hotels.

"Before I made this episode of 'American Sportsman,' I had never scuba-dived. A day after a crash course in Los Angeles, I dove 100 feet into the Truk Lagoon. They thought I was too old to do it. It was a challenge to me," said the 55-year-old actor.

"I was flirting with death. Each morning when I kissed Maggi goodbye before diving, I thought, I'll never see her again," he said.

Maggi, his wife of nine months, frowned. "He's either the world's bravest man or the biggest idiot."

Mitchell said he could handle the diving but the sharks frightened him. He felt exalted, yet dwarfed, by sharks and giant seafans, he said. At the bottom of the 40-mile-diameter Truk Lagoon, he explored a few of the almost undamaged sunken Japanese warships, destroyers, and cargo ships.

"After eleven dives, I was glad to take off my wet suit without a drop of blood on it," Cameron said. He gave away $500 worth of scuba equipment when he left.

Mitchell was born November 4, 1918, in Dallastown, Pennsylvania. The son of a minister, he decided on acting as a career, to the dismay of his family. "All the men in our family as far back as I can remember were ministers," he said.

After a World War II stint as bombardier, Mitchell moved to Los Angeles and signed with MGM. He made his film debut in 1945 and appeared in more than 90 films. In New York, he worked as a Radio City page before landing a stage job in the 1939 production of "The Taming of the Shrew," starring Alfred Lunt and Lynn Fontaine. Mitchell gained stature after his portrayal of Happy in stage and screen versions of "Death of a Salesman." He starred in the TV series "High Chaparral" and appeared in an episode of "Murder She Wrote" with Angela Lansbury. His films included "They Were Expendable" (1945), "Les Miserables" (1952), "The Klansmen" (1974), "How to Marry a Millionaire," and "Carousel." He appeared overseas as Julius Caesar and other historical figures in foreign-language films. His last movie was the 1986 "Band of the Hand."

Sportsman Mitchell won several golf tournaments and caught huge marlins off the coast of Bermuda. When his wife, who inherited stock in the Southern 500 stock car race in Darlington, South Carolina, introduced him to stock car racing, he was hooked.

Mitchell spoke proudly about his poem entitled, "Born of a Simple Woman," the story of the birth of Jesus and Mitchell's deep faith in humanity. He wrote the poem on a plane en route to a muscular dystrophy benefit in Nashville and cut a recording of it.

In July 1994, at age 75, Mitchell died of lung cancer at his home in Pacific Palisades, California.

Hollywood Pacific

Guam's assets are perfect for television shows and motion pictures: brilliant sunshine, predictable temperatures, dramatic skies, spectacular landscapes and seascapes, and plenty of talented Chamorros.

In the '70s, Japan's Tokyo Chuo Eiga Company shot scenes for the movie, "Kagero," on Guam. This was a tragic love story set on Saipan and Guam, portraying the effects of the atomic bomb on two generations of Japanese. Jimmy Dee of the Guam Visitors Bureau, Pauline Rosenzweig of the Hilton Hotel, and several policemen were among the extras.

The Guam Tokyu Hotel was the setting for a TV motion picture, "The Play Girl," which was aired January 4, 1971. The crew of the Toei Movie Picture Company and actors Ryoichi Tamagawa, Makoto Satoh, Yoko Nogiwa, and Tamaki Sawa sailed to and from Guam aboard the *Oriental Queen*, a passenger ship of the Toyo Yusen Lines.

When I worked for Navy Public Works Center, I gave permission for a Japanese TV crew to film a commercial in front of headquarters. Brilliant red hibiscus bushes in front of the whitewashed metal building caught the cameramen's eyes. When I left for lunch, I noticed that the female model was wearing a fur coat.

After lunch, I found a message tacked on my office door ordering me to report to the captain. Evidently, Navy civilian and military personnel driving during their lunch hour on Marine Drive nearly ran off the road as they gawked at the nude model, her fur coat draped over one shoulder. They reported the sight to the admiral, who called my boss. Thereafter, PWC was off-limits to visiting camera crews.

Although films made on Guam weren't prime-time successes, a central casting file of local people was established by Gem Productions, headed by Gordon Mailloux, jeweler, jade collector, former Guam senator, and election commissioner.

Gem Productions made several films on Guam, one of which was the action picture, "Noon Sunday." Directed by Australian Terry Bourke, with art director Barry Adler, the movie featured a cast from 13 countries and 300 local people. One ad went out for an extra: a woman with a head as bald as a cue ball.

"Noon Sunday" action began with a treacherous mission to liquidate a guerilla general on the grassy slopes near Agat, with

WW II machine gun nests in the background. Episodes were grisly: guerilla troops trapped two villagers and a priest above a Harmon Field quarry; badly wounded mercenaries, Darmody and Cootes, rested on coral rocks at low tide on Tarague Beach to await rescue by helicopter; and the Umatac Church of San Dionisio was "burned" to the ground in the dramatic conclusion.

The world premiere of "Noon Sunday" was held on Guam in January 1971. Top-billing stars were John Russell, Mark Lenard, Keye Luke, Danny Pacic, Linda Avery, and local actor Cynthia Kop.

Russell, a tall, handsome man who often played second lead and smooth heavies in Hollywood, portrayed the mercenary Darmody. He had been on the screen since the late 1930s, with time out as a Marine. He was most famous in the "Lawman." In "Cannon for Cordoba," he portrayed General Pershing. His last movie was "Honky Tonk Man" (1982).

Lenard played Jason Cootes in "Noon Sunday." In one scene, boonie dogs chased him into a creek near Inarajan—they probably just wanted to get into the act. Lenard is best known for his memorable portrayal of Sarek, Spock's father in the "Star Trek" episode "Journey to Babel," the animated "Trek" adventure "Yesteryear," several "Trek" films and two "Next Generation" episodes. Lenard also narrated several "Trek" audionovels. He died in November 1996 at age 68.

Keye Luke

When I learned that Keye Luke was playing guerilla leader Colonel Oong in "Noon Sunday," I arranged an interview.

I had met Luke when I was fourteen years old. My mother and I were breakfasting in a Miami coffee shop when I spotted Luke. I went to his table to tell him how much I had enjoyed his performance the previous evening in the film, "Dr. Gillespie," and, afterwards, on stage at the Olympic Theater. He invited me to sit down.

That interview was one of my first articles published in the *Washington Sunday Star*. I received a dollar for the piece, which appeared in January 1946.

Luke, whose parents emigrated to the United States from Canton, China, grew up in Seattle, Washington. He planned to become an architect but worked as a commercial artist designing layouts for movie theaters. This led to a job doing artwork for Graumann's Chinese Theater in Los Angeles. Later, he became a staff artist with Fox and RKO. He served as technical advisor on Hollywood films with Chinese themes.

In 1934 Luke debuted as an actor in "The Painted Veil" and appeared in supporting roles in "The Good Earth" and "Across the Pacific." His 150 films included "Dragon Seed" (1944), "Love Is a Many Splendored Thing" (1955), "Gremlins," "Around the World in 80 Days," and "The Painted Veil" with Greta Garbo.

Luke starred in the TV series "Hawaii Five-O," but is perhaps best remembered for his role as Charlie Chan's "number one son" in 13 episodes of that detective series. He also played Master Po in "Kung Fu." He appeared in "Dr. Kildare," "The Green Hornet" and was a regular on ABC's daytime serial, "General Hospital."

Making his stage debut in 1958 in Broadway's "The Flower Drum Song," Luke remained with the company in New York for two years and in the national company for another year.

My second interview with Luke took place in August 1970 in his room at Earl's Huts in Tamuning, headquarters of the cast and crew of "Noon Sunday." The settings of our two interviews were similar: sand and palms under tropical sun and sky, but oceans and 25 years apart.

While Luke read my 1946 article, I glanced around the room. On the dresser sat two pipes, a bottle of brandy, and a foot-high pile of books. He said he reread novels and listened to classical music in his leisure hours between scenes. Heavy rain had delayed shooting, so he had time on his hands.

The thunderous electrical storms that hovered over the island were "frightening," Luke said. One night during the storm he awoke to see a pool of rainwater, driven by the wind beneath the door of his motel room.

Although he liked warm weather, he wasn't used to Guam's high humidity. He suffered most when he wore the colonel's heavy uniform.

I thought he hadn't changed much since we first met in Miami.

"The years have been good to me," he said. He added that he often had to be made up with wrinkles and grey hair to appear older.

Luke, who had just completed work in "The Chairman" with Gregory Peck and "The Hawaiians" with Charlton Heston, said Guam's locations were "wonderful . . . hard work, but well worth everything."

"It's so far!" Luke said when he was asked to come to Guam to play the colonel. When he arrived at the Guam airport, the Customs official called him Senator, the role he played in "Hawaii Five-O."

Luke was surprised at the number of cars. "Marine Drive looks like a freeway." En route to locations at Merizo, Umatac, and Chalan Pago, artist Luke enjoyed the colorful scenery and seascapes.

"When Lenard and Russell arrived on Guam two weeks ago, most of my major scenes had been done during a full week of shooting. Although I led the soldiers in pursuit of the two stars, I don't appear in any scenes with them," said Luke.

He had been waiting for weeks to "die" from a mercenary's grenade in front of the Umatac Church. The rain had held up the assassination scene, which involved synchronized special effects and action sequences.

Luke praised Director Terry Bourke and the cast and crew of the movie. He said the crew comprised a mini-United Nations, with people from Australia, Canada, Holland, Hong Kong, Philippines, Japan, Guam, and the U.S. Each person was an expert in his field.

Luke was a complete artist: singer, painter, actor, at home on stage, motion pictures, and TV. He enjoyed doing classical Chinese painting and calligraphy, and had just completed a tempera mural in a decorative lineal style for his son's house. He practiced singing to keep his speaking voice in shape, because he never knew when he'd be called to play a singing role again. He enjoyed musical drama because it combined acting and singing.

During his early Hollywood years, Luke married a French-Irish girl. They had two sons, four grandchildren, and two great grandchildren.

One of the founders of Screen Artists Guild, Luke toured with Bob Hope while entertaining American troops with the U.S.O. In 1986 Luke was honored with the first Lifetime Achievement Award bestowed by the Association of Asian/Pacific Artists.

On January 12, 1991, while playing Dr. Yang in Woody Allen's film, "Alice," 86-year-old Luke died of a stroke.

Tiny Tim

One afternoon in October 1972, the Guam Press Club interviewed Tiny Tim. He had come to Guam after a gig at the Holiday Inn in Torrance, California. He was starring in an act billed as "The New Tiny Tim" for a Guam Women's Club charity event held at the Cliff Hotel.

We reporters had just settled onto chairs placed in a semicircle in a conference room when Tiny Tim and his wife, Miss Vicki, entered.

Tiny Tim plopped onto a seat facing us. This last remaining flower child blew kisses at us and set his trademark shopping bag on the floor. He had long, frizzy reddish-brown hair, his nose protruded under wayward eyebrows, and his belly bulged slightly over his belt. He wore his traffic-stopper outfit: a vest with a ukelele embroidered on it, a ruffled shirt, and a bow tie under a rumpled business suit.

Tiny Tim soon had us laughing at his humorous, yet sincere responses to our questions. When he talked of astronomy or baseball, his encyclopedic knowledge awed us. This gentle soul believed, or so he told us, that "Hollywood is Shangrila—fairyland of the imagination."

He once sent a videotape from his home in Des Moines, Iowa, to Paramount Pictures to audition for the role of an old woman in "The Naked Gun III: The Final Insult." He was rejected. "I just kept on going," he said.

In 1959, under the name "Larry Love, the Singing Canary," Tiny Tim played Hubert's Museum and Live Flea Circus of New York. The singer left Hubert's when he was asked to sing in a lower register.

In 1968 and '69, Tiny Tim was a frequent guest on "The Tonight Show Starring Johnny Carson." On December 17, 1969, 63-year-old Tiny Tim and Miss Vicki were married on Carson's show. Carson was the reason Tiny Tim played his "banjolele" rather than the electric ukelele he had long favored. "I did send Mr. Carson my ukelele, the electric one. I didn't want any publicity, and I didn't send it to him because I wanted him to call me on his last show. Two or three days before, I sent it express mail. Apparently he does have it. It was just a matter of appreciation to thank him for being on his show in 1968 and plugging my first album," he said.

At the end of the interview, Tiny Tim grabbed his uke and sang his fluttering falsetto rendition of "Tip-Toe Through the Tulips With Me," the 1968 song that made him famous. As he left, he said, "Thank you and God bless you all." He smiled, blew kisses and rolled his eyes heavenward.

During the interview, Miss Vicki had been leaning against a wall in the back of the room. She didn't answer questions. Five years later, she and Tiny Tim were divorced. Tiny Tim died at age 64 in December 1996.

Queen Elizabeth

When Ricardo J. Bordallo was elected governor in 1975, First Lady Madeleine set about renovating Government House. Redecorating was completed just in time for the May 3 visit of Queen Elizabeth II, the Duke of Edinburgh, and British government officials.

The Bordallos moved back to their Yoña home so the dignitaries could stay at Government House. At the last minute, however, the fall of Vietnam and the ensuing chaos changed the Queen's plans.

When the Queen and her entourage arrived on a British Airways 707 at Guam's airport on May 3, they were whisked to guest quarters at Andersen AFB for an overnight stay instead of Government House.

Tere Rios Versace covered the Queen's arrival for *TV Guam* magazine. Despite barriers between the Queen and the press, Tere took several pictures, but missed the best shot of all. As the Queen walked down the line of people waving British flags, a child whispered something in her ear that broke the Queen up with laughter. The Queen's laugh suddenly changed her appearance from a stuffy *grande dame* into a warm, responsive person, Tere recalled.

The next morning, the royal couple attended church services at the Air Force base chapel and strolled along Tarague Beach. Madeleine and Ricky Bordallo, who had moved back into Government House, gave a reception for the Queen and her party before their afternoon departure.

Bicentennial Warner

Guam pulled out all the stops for America's 200th birthday. Senator John Warner, executive director of the American Revolution

Bicentennial Administration (ARBA), Washington, D.C., came to Guam March 22 and 23, 1976, to kick off celebrations. He was accompanied by Kent Williams, San Francisco regional director of ARBA.

Before Warner's party arrived, Governor Ricky Bordallo organized "happy labor" to spruce up the island. New state and territorial flags and flagpoles were raised on Flag Day, June 14, in Skinner Plaza. At Anderson AFB, airmen had painted bicentennial murals on the outside walls of barracks and other buildings.

The local ARBA committee staged sports events, a Yankee Doodle rock concert, arts and craft displays, taotaomona horseshoe contest, executive slow-pitch softball tournament, youth fishing derby, and an essay-speech contest for school children. Bicentennial events culminated on July Fourth in a ceremony at the Statue of Liberty.

Upon arrival, Warner and Williams met with local officials and attended—what else?—a fiesta staged by the 19th Guam Legislature. Speaker Joseph Ada opened the ceremony and introduced Warner, who unveiled a mural on the front of the Legislature building. Painted by University of Guam students, the mural depicted Guam's history from pre-civilization to present.

During his visit, Warner stayed at the Nimitz Hill guest house and renewed his long-time acquaintance with RADM Kent Carroll, COMNAVMAR. Warner also found a few hours to scuba dive, one of his favorite pastimes.

The next morning in front of Government House, Warner and Williams boarded the Navy's Bicentennial bus, "Spirit of '76," a school bus repainted red, white, and blue. Also on the tour were local ARBA officials, Madeleine Bordallo, military officers, and myself.

The trip began at Two Lovers' Point, Guam's tallest sea cliff. As the bus rattled along the narrow road, I was reminded that the director of Guam's NASA station told Press Club members that the road to the point was comparable to the surface of the moon. Constantly in need of grading and resurfacing, the rough road caused car tires to blow out and vehicles to get mired in the mudholes.

The visiting bicentennial group walked around the point, where during Spanish rule, a fair Chamorro maiden was ordered by her father to marry a Spanish army captain. She refused, having fallen in love with a handsome Chamorro warrior. After the two tried to escape, they were chased by the Spanish army to the edge of the cliff. Rather than surrender, the legend goes that the lovers tied their long black braids together and plunged together 334 feet to their death in the dark water below.

This point was to be the site of the proposed Bicentennial Latte Stone Memorial, one of Governor Bordallo's dreams: a 200-foot-tall tower in the shape of a latte stone, topped with a civic auditorium, with an estimated cost of $20 to 25 million.

Warner suggested that 200 steps should be placed inside the giant latte stone to commemorate America's 200th birthday. He said the latte stone represents early Chamorro culture and should be a quiet place to reflect on the beauty of the surroundings.

When Bordallo left office in 1978, more than half a million dollars had been raised by private fund drives for the memorial trust fund. By 1993, there was a balance of $1,737,389 in the not-for-profit Latte of Freedom organization. The giant latte was never built and still remains Ricky's vision.

Today, two bronze figures, fifty feet tall, embrace at Two Lovers' Point. The statues honor the legend of the Two Lovers, a key part of the Chamorro culture. The legend is described in four languages, and the view is fantastic.

Instead of the spirits of the two lovers frolicking in the ocean below, visitors see ice-cream cups littering the ground. An admission fee is charged at the overlook, flanked by a Häagen-Dazs stand and postcard booth. The statue was blown down in a banana typhoon recently, but was reinstalled and guyed in place.

While Two Lover's Point is billed as a sacred Chamorro site, few Chamorros ever visit. The only visitors these days are the occasional Japanese couple who get married there.

Next, the bicentennial group stopped at the replica of the Statue of Liberty at Paseo de Susana, strode through the Farmer's Market, and examined a 50-foot-long flying proa being carved from four breadfruit trees.

The bus sped past Piti, Polaris Point, the U.S. Naval Station, and Agat. It paused near the Old Spanish Bridge. A local official told the visitors that in the 1700s travelers rowed canoes from Agaña to Piti, then jiggled in bullcarts along an old trail, and crossed the Taleyfac River on this double-arched stone bridge.

At the Cetti Bay overlook, the group admired the view of Cocos Island, located on Guam's only barrier reef, and Cetti Bay's pristine coastline, later to be designated as the Territorial Seashore Park.

Passing Magellan's monument in Umatac, the bus circled the parking lot at Fort Nuestra Señora De La Soledad, a well-preserved Spanish fort built in the early 1800s to spy on English pirates entering Umatac Bay. Atop this scenic point, Guamanian boys charged tourists to pose for snapshots on carabaos in front of a stone sentry box. They also sold feathery tangan-tangan leis.

When Williams asked what tangan-tangan was, a Navy officer explained that the island's vegetation had been destroyed during World War II. After the war, to prevent erosion, Americans reforested the land with a Latin American tree: *Leucaena glauca*, called tangan-tangan. The plant is used for firewood, food for cattle, and poles for hut and fence supports. It grows profusely, covering everything in its path.

As the bus drove by Merizo Pier Park, we saw Japanese tourists piling into glass-bottom boats for the mile-and-a-half trip across the bay to Cocos Island. There they would picnic, swim, and snorkel midst colorful corals and sea creatures in the crystal clear lagoon.

Farther along the shoreline, we stopped at Delfina Aguigui's house, where lunch was waiting for us. Kindergarten children sang and presented handmade tangan-tangan and shell leis to the guests. A table was laden with woven coconut baskets filled with fruit and betel nuts, and dishes of fish, kelaguen, and Chamorro red rice. Tuba was served in coconut cups.

Back on the bus, the visitors learned that Merizo, or Malesso in Chamorro, means full of leso, or the tiny fish called manahac. Similar to California's grunions, the fish spawn on shore in May and June in Agaña, Agat, and Umatac Bays. The delicacies are barbecued over beach fires or pickled in salt and lemon.

After lunch, we traveled through Inarajan, where brightly colored, tin-roofed houses, shaded by palms, cycads, and banana trees, lined the narrow streets. Outside the village, we passed Inarajan's salt water pool, formed by continuous wave action on the reef. The community had added an overlook, walkways, and picnic grounds around the diving pool.

We didn't have time to stop at the black sands of Talofofo Bay Beach Park, where surfers rode waves formed where the Talofofo river, Guam's longest river, empties into the bay.

We stopped at the Mangilao Youth Center, where Warner had been invited to share cake and punch with the youngsters, proud of their new center.

Near the end of the trip, I asked Warner about Guam's tourism industry.

"I'm not too optimistic about luring American tourists to Guam, since Americans can find similar scenery in Hawaii or other islands closer to U.S. shores," he answered.

On legalized gambling, he said, "I don't think Guam casinos would attract international gamblers, who frequent Las Vegas or Monte Carlo."

Warner had been responsible for allowing Guam Power Authority to extend service to new hotels on Tumon Bay. He said that military spending would continue to be a major part of Guam's financial base. The Guamanians he met were warm, friendly people who seemed happy with their unique culture and environment, he added.

ARBA executives said goodbye at Government House and continued by plane to the Far East. Several months later, Warner became Elizabeth Taylor's seventh husband.

His Holiness

His Holiness Pope John Paul II visited Guam in 1981 and celebrated an open-air mass before thousands of people at the Plaza de España. He unveiled a sign to change the street in front of the Dulce Nombre de Maria cathedral from Saylor Street to Chalan Santo Papa Juan Pablo Dos.

Later, a monument was erected to John Paul II. This life-sized bronze statue, designed to rotate 360 degrees, was placed in a traffic island in the middle of the street in front of the cathedral.

The statue stopped turning years ago. In 1998, the Guam Shipyard rebuilt the statue's electric motor, checked its gears, and had it working again. Four months after the repair, it broke down. It is still motionless in 2001.

There is no religious significance to the direction the Pope's statue faces, but when the statue is rotating, residents tell time by it, depending on the direction the statue faces.

In 1984, Pope John Paul II elevated the Diocese of Agaña to an archdiocese as part of a worldwide church reorganization. The Vatican named Guam's Bishop Felixberto Flores as the first metropolitan Archbishop of Agaña, and designated Agaña's cathedral as a basilica.

The Pope also announced in 1984 the beatification of Sanvitores, the Jesuit martyr. A mass was held in celebration at the Sanvitores memorial on Tumon Beach, where he had been killed by Chamorros. Today the shrine is rarely visited because it is overshadowed by the high-rise Reef Hotel and blocked from Tumon Beach by restaurants and tourist concessions.

The Former First Lady

In September 1995, Hillary Rodham Clinton, now a U. S. Senator from New York, stopped in Guam en route to the United Nations Fourth World Conference on Women in Beijing. During her three-hour visit, Mrs. Clinton was welcomed at a fund-raiser held at the Hyatt Regency Guam Hotel.

At the reception, Mrs. Clinton compared the War of 1912's burn marks, evident on the White House in Washington, D.C., to the prominent signs of World War II occupation that are still evident on Guam.

"Your sacrifices were instrumental in ridding the world of tyranny and establishing the peace we have all enjoyed during the past 50 years. . . . America thanks you," she said.

CHAPTER EIGHT

Hams and Gams

The Guam Press Association was organized in 1966 by GDN Editor Joe Murphy and a handful of media types during a game of Yahtze. Patterned after the National Press Club of Washington, D.C., the association held weekly luncheons, highlighted by guest speakers, and staged annual no-holds-barred Gridiron Shows.

In the shows, jungle journalists roasted Guam's teachers, the bishop, utility managers, pothole politicians, and mother nature. We told stories by singing, dancing, and cavorting about news that, for some reason or another, had fallen between the cracks on the newsroom floor.

During intermissions, we presented Golden Coconut Awards to the Best Newsmakers and Top Newsmaker of the Year. Proceeds went toward journalism scholarships at the University of Guam.

As a charter press association member, I sang and danced in gridiron shows. For one gridiron program, I wrote an introduction entitled, "What is a Gridiron Show? Or, What's a nice girl like me doing in a show like this?"

"I had the dubious honor of hoofing it and singing in all but one Guam Press Association Gridiron Show," I wrote. "No, a gridiron show has nothing to do with football, unless you consider that roasting is similar to kicking newsmakers the way a pigskin gets kicked around the field during a game. It's the highlight of the year for members of the Fourth Estate who have spent their working days and nights trying to make sense out of the news from Government House, the Legislature, the tourist business, show business, and monkey business."

Reporters had fun writing, singing, and dancing in the annual hams-and-gams shows. Most of us cast members, chained to typewriters, were unfamiliar with front-center stage, pretty flat in the music department, low in acting talent, didn't read too well (what do you expect of proofreaders?), and couldn't memorize lines.

Chorus girls, using the term loosely, opened and closed each show and most acts. We wore costumes from gunny sacks and shortie muumuus to tutus. We weren't the Rockettes—we seldom hit the beat or clapped and kicked at the same time—but we loved to ham it up.

We encouraged drinking before, during, between, and after acts, so restaurants or hotels could make a profit while we trashed their stages. Through an alcoholic haze, the audiences roared, shrieked, jeered and cheered. The public was having as much fun watching the show as we had putting it on, and few could watch us without laughing so hard they wet their pants.

In early 1967 after two weeks of loose rehearsals, the Guam Press Association staged its first Gridiron Show at the Surf Club in Asan. Cast members read from dog-eared scripts, missed a few cues, and lost one entire skit. One hundred people in the club giggled and sucked 'em up for hours.

I almost missed the second gridiron show held in February 1968 at Hong Kong Garden's Panciteria. Two hours before the performance, Carol McMurrough phoned and told me to get my tail down to the Legislature. During an hour-long special session, senators passed a casino gambling bill. I sped to the *Pacific Journal* office, where Editor Garrison was holding up the front page for the story. I told him I had to get to the Panciteria for the opening number of the chorus line, but he turned a deaf ear.

When I finished writing the story, I raced to the Panciteria, climbed into my gunny sack, tossed a plastic lei around my neck, and jumped into the chorus line just as the curtain was going up.

My gambling story made the front page of the morning edition, but the governor vetoed the bill.

That Gridiron Show's theme was "O.O.G. (Only on Guam)." President of the Press Association, Carol McMurrough, introduced the show: "Every booboo up for fixit . . . No use heading for the exit! So . . . Relax, and suck 'em up!"

We played to 500 persons, lampooning every island official—military and civilian. We took digs at power and telephone problems, the paucity of hotels, beauty contests, and government junkets. In one skit, the "governor" presented "President Johnson" with a key to the Legislature's men's room.

From the 1968 Gridiron Show, "O.O.G.—Only on Guam."

(Tune: "King of the Road")

Quonsets we've got for rent
Shacks to let, patched up tent.
No roof, no floor, no can
You've gotta take it as it am.
Ah, but ten years' government lease,
Means we can do what we please.
It's your house of dreams, by no means
Only on Guam.

Peeling paint, leaking rain
Broken window, clogged up drain
Worn out, twisted, rusted, bent
For this we pay 200 rent.
What a sweet deal we have found,
And we've only broken ground.
There'll be more schemes, by all means,
Only on Guam.

Hong Kong Garden's Panciteria in Tamuning was perfect for gridiron shows. It was then the only nightspot that had a large stage with dressing rooms in back, tables and chairs for 500 people, and could dish up delicious Chinese-American dinners. The beach setting was air-conditioned by muggy, sometimes putrid, breezes wafting off the Philippine Sea. Beneath each table a mosquito coil was lit to zap mosquitoes, but sometimes hot coils singed hems of long dresses and bell-bottomed trousers.

In one of her columns, Glenda Moore suggested that the Panciteria could stand a coat of paint and new carpeting to bring it up to par with newer nightclubs. A few days later, the club manager announced that the Garden had been painted, carpets had been ordered, and an acoustic ceiling had been affixed. The new ceiling was covered with cardboard egg cartons, which did help lessen the din of raucous laughter from the stage as well as the audience. Never underestimate the power of the press!

The third show, "Expose '68" was staged also at Hong Kong Gardens, January 25, 1969, and directed by David Brinkley (not *that* David Brinkley). The show attacked the Guam Power Authority for its great blackout, held a raucous wake for the deceased *Pacific Journal*, and wondered why the Federal comptroller was coming.

From "Exposé '68."

(Tune: "Sweet Betsy from Pike")

Oh, have you heard tell of Joe Murphy of Guam,
He came to the island no one knows where from,
He crossed the broad ocean, decided to stay
He edits the paper you read every day.
Singing toorali, toorali, toorali-a.

Now everyone knows he's a writer of sorts
And no one will question he's king of good sports.
His motto is "Write it as long as it's news."
Why search for the truth if it wears out your shoes?
Singing toorali, toorali, toorali-a.

The stories get jumbled, they're lost or they're late,
Mis-spelling, mis-printing, why blame it on fate.
We shouldn't complain if our Joe's not so hot
Let's face it, folks, he's all that we've got!
Singing toorali, toorali, toorali-a.

The fourth show—and probably our most lewd and popular—was called "'69, The Impossible Scene." It was directed by Allen Carroway and MC'ed by Bill Gibson. We poked fun at President Nixon, shipping problems, lack of rest rooms for round-the-island tour groups, radar patrol cops (we hit a real cop on the head), Air Micronesia, corruption in GovGuam, acquisition of the GDN by Chinn Ho (played by Press Club President Phil Behr), a committee for decency protesting blue movies at the Johnston Theater, and The Gold Room scandal skit in which Lillian Sekt, Mae McCarter, and Montie Protasio, clad in skimpy gold lamé dresses, strutted their stuff.

From the 1969 Gridiron Show, "Impossible Dream '69"

(Tune: "Those Were the Days")

Once there was a pretty little island
Where they raised a coconut or two.
A ship or two came in 'bout every season,
But if they missed, the islanders made do.

Now they're building hotels down at Ipao
For Japanese on trips and honeymoons.
You can't see the ocean anymore now,
But cash registers are playing pretty tunes.

Those were the days, my friends,
But now they're at an end.
They import everything but mountain dew.
If you're not broke, you're bent
From paying bills and rent.
You gotta pay. Oh yes, you gotta pay.

The Gridiron Show's last performance at the Panciteria was in 1970. That year, chorus girl Karmee Dolley toted a gallon of screwdrivers backstage. We slopped up the screwdrivers before and during the show. I was so tipsy doing my softshoe tap number, I almost tumbled off the stage. By the time the show was over, our Guam Hymnals (songbooks) were drippingly orange. After that, the law was laid down: no drinking for the cast until the show was over!

We didn't have a Gridiron Show in 1971 because the number of working press could be counted on one hand. The club was reorganized and its name was changed from Guam Press Association to Guam Press Club. Besides active press workers, membership was opened to those engaged in public affairs, promotion, and advertising. Thirsty souls who flocked to Fourth Estate watering holes joined. They included priests, nuns, military public affairs officers, hotel public relations people, and government employees.

In 1973, we paid a professional actor to direct the Fifth Gridiron Show, entitled, "Come On In! This is the Second Year of the Erection." The director's expertise didn't make an iota of difference in our feast of ham and corn.

Since we'd had a year to catch up on the island's never-ending problems, the show featured old skits that still applied: telephone tribulations (ting-a-ling, you call us, we can't call you), government spending (junkets make GovGuam go round), gambling (but Bishop baby, will blackjack ever replace bingo?), and snakes in the boonies (where have all the birdies gone?).

One skit became the joke of the decade. In it, the First Lady went to a mainland finishing school to help her be the best governor's wife she could be. Back in Guam, a reporter asked what she had learned. She answered, "I learned to say 'fantastic,' instead of 'bullshit'!"

The Sixth Gridiron Show, "We're a Grand Ole Press," was held October 26, 1975, at the Grand Restaurant in the Zee Complex. Cocktails, a teriyaki steak dinner buffet, and show for $10 a person—a bargain at twice the price!

One of the most hilarious dance numbers of all times was the "Breadfruit Ball," a spoof of Governor Bordallo's inauguration ball. Male hoofers tucked away their manhoods into veggie and fruit-of-the-loom costumes that looked like the world's largest condoms.

The 1976 Gridiron Show, "One BLEW Over the Cuckoo's Nest, or Washington's Pet Rock," celebrated Supertyphoon Pamela. One song, "A Million-Dollar Latte with a Giant Concrete Floor," was about the ground breaking ceremony for the million-dollar phallus. Planned as a tribute to Chamorros' heritage, the giant latte hasn't yet seen an erection.

From the 1976 Gridiron Show, "One BLEW Over the Cuckoo's Nest"

(Tune: "She Was Comin' Round the Mountain")

She was comin' toward the island when she came,
She packed winds of a hundred ninety when she came,
She left terrible destruction,
Tore down half of Guam's construction,
She was comin' toward the island–then she came.

She wrecked all the phones and power when she came,
And who should fix them up became a game.
When the Navy said, "Our men will,"
Ricky said, "We should, and then bill
Admiral Carroll, there'll be millions we can claim."

She brought FDAA and food stamps when she came,
She brought cash and Red Cross vouchers when she came.
Stores got rich–Town House, Ben Franklin,
Guam's a mess, but Ricky's thankin'
God that this time typhoon Pamela's to blame.

Also from the 1976 Gridiron Show
(Tune: "Million Dollar Baby at the Five and Ten Cent Store")

We witnessed at our Bicentennial,
Ground-breaking ceremonies for:
To build a million dollar latte
With a giant concrete floor.

To pay a tribute to Chamorros,
The strength and sustenance they store,
Will stand a million dollar latte
With a giant concrete floor.

Why build another youth club
Or buy supplies for schools?
Can't use funds for something useful
Like sidewalks or swimming pools.

We'll have a million dollar palace,
A monument you can't ignore,
Erect a million dollar phallus
With a giant concrete floor.

The 1977 show, "The Merry Old Land of OOG, or The Wizard of OOG," was held at the Hilton Hotel. OOG (Only On Guam) songs lampooned the millionth honeymoon couple, the ding-dong phones, and "Sing a Song of Corruption" (a pocketful of dough, one and twenty senators, lined up in a row).

From the 1977 Gridiron Show, "The Merry Old Land of OOG"

(Tune: "Ding Dong, the Wicked Witch is Dead")

Ding dong, my phone is dead
I tried to call
I went instead
Ding dong, my ding dong phone is dead.

I tried hard to place a call
Couldn't call no place at all
Ding dong, my ding dong phone is dead.

I always receive my bill . . . they know just where I am
When I need some service, they don't give a damn.
So hi ho, the merry O..Guam is weird and nuts I go
But we all know that GTA is dead.

Ding dong, the power is dead
No more lights . . . no more brights
Ding dong the GPA is dead
Hi Ho, the merry O . . . sing it high . . . sing it low.
Ding dong, the GPA is dead.

After I left Guam, I received two Gridiron Show programs in which the songs and skits were so familiar they could have been taken from our old shows.

For instance, the 1985 Gridiron Show held at the Pescador Nightclub in Tamuning, was called "Jeopardy Island 1999." Based on the TV game show, "actors" portrayed famous broadcast celebrities who tried to raise $6 jillion to pay for Ricky Bordallo's sticky fingers and to pay off GovGuam's deficit.

The 1986 Gridiron Show, "Paradise on Parade," was held at Fernando's on Camp Watkins Road, Tamuning. Skits poked fun at Star Wars, RotoPope (cannot spin, this my friends is a cardinal sin), and Ricky Bordallo's embezzlement. The show featured marching units from the GovGuam judiciary, Department of Labor, and Guam Federation of Teachers.

If the Guam Press Club still exists, here are some skit ideas for the year 2001 Gridiron Show:

—Marine Drive construction nears completion

—Guam Power Authority needs generators to end power rationing

—Tourists hold noses while sewage spills along Tumon Beach

—Public Utility Agency of Guam experts identify areas with low water pressure and contamination

—Department of Education defends low test scores and studies feasibility of air-conditioning schools

—Battle over ex-Naval Air Station land goes to Supreme Court

—Smelled any mustard gas lately?

—Stepped on any live bombs?

—Is the hospital still open?

—The Guam Commonwealth Act causes riots in U.S. Congressional hearings

—You take Agaña and I'll take Hagåtña!

CHAPTER NINE

Sailing Through Micronesia

My first trip through eastern Micronesia was thirty-four years ago, but little has changed except for the construction of new airports and renaming places. That first trip and my return island-hopper visit in 1990 are chronicled in this chapter.

My husband, our three-year-old Silky Terrier, Chichi, and I boarded the Motorvessel (MV) *Gunners Knot* the evening of February 25, 1967.

Our departure was like a scene from the movie, "The African Queen." We were delayed several hours while a Humphrey Bogart lookalike fiddled with the engines. Three hours after we boarded, he declared the ship seaworthy. The ship shuddered as the anchor was sucked, clanking, into her bowels. We steamed out of Apra Harbor under a full moon.

The *Gunners Knot* carried 30 cabin passengers and about 100 people on deck. The ship was so overloaded she had only two inches of freeboard.

The ship carried tons of copra, aka Micronesian gold, from the islands to Japan, where it was processed into oil, margarine, soap, and glycerine. During World War II, the Japanese made fuel and ammunition from copra. A ton of copra equals the meat of 4,500 coconuts, exudes a sour, musty odor and is paradise for millions of tiny bugs that invade every cranny of the ship.

On the second afternoon at sea, the *Gunners Knot* waited outside Truk's reef for high tide, as the thundering surf curled over the coral reef heads. My nostrils flinched at the first whiff of *Eau de Truk*, a melange of copra, exposed coral, and pools of stagnant water filled with dead fish, fractured clams, wounded lobsters, and rotting seaweed.

The 30-mile-wide Truk Lagoon, the world's largest lagoon, is Micronesia's geographical center. The Japanese called this lagoon a natural aircraft carrier.

Comprising 100 islands, of which 40 are inhabited, Truk was discovered in 1565 by Spanish explorer De Arellano. Spain ruled Truk until the 1890s, and then Germany took over until 1914, when Japan annexed Micronesia and established military administrative headquarters there.

Early on February 17, 1944, U.S. forces attacked Japan's Truk base in Operation Hailstone. While Nipponese pilots were sipping saki across the lagoon on Weno Island, American forces disabled dozens of enemy planes and sunk freighters.

At the end of the war, the scrap-hungry Japanese initiated salvage of these sunken vessels, which had been constructed in part from scrap purchased in the United States. This was a full cycle of international trade: America's sale to Japan of steel scrap, fabricated into instruments of war, destroyed in turn by the U. S., subsequently reduced once more into scrap, and ultimately winding up yet again in Japanese mills.

Today, this lagoon, an underwater graveyard of dozens of Japanese warships, destroyers, and cargo vessels, is one of the finest sport diving spots in the world.

Villages dot the water's edge of the seven square miles of Moen Island. The lowlands along the water rise to a plateau and culminate in two tall peaks from 1,200 to 1,500 feet high. The highest, Mount Tonochon, looks like a top hat. Truk's port is on Moen, which means man in Trukese.

The administrative center comprises a hotel, hospital, bank, post office, cafes, and houses. In a metal warehouse, the Truk Trading Company sells clothing, food, notions, appliances, spears, books, handicraft, beer, liquor, and wine.

Many drunks roam around Moen, as well as many other islands in Micronesia. These people who used to drink the native tuba now guzzle ice cold beer. Visitors, especially Americans, are advised not to be out alone at night.

Our voyage in 1967 coincided with the visit of the Seventh United Nations Inspection Team, who had already inspected Saipan, Yap, and Palau before embarking on the eastern leg of their trip.

The day after the *Gunners Knot* arrived at Truk, TT's DC-4 arrived with the U.N. mission team. Delegates were Dr. Angie Brooks of Liberia, chairman; Pierre Jules Basdevant, France; Richard Neil Posnett, United Kingdom; N. Rifai, Syria; R. Wathen, U.S.; Henry Astwood, U.S.; Norma Chai, Trinidad; B. R. Devarajan, Ceylon; and Australian Kenneth Henry Rogers, who hobbled around on crutches after an accidental fall during the inspection trip.

One hundred smiling Trukese, music, and sunshine greeted the U.N. team on the small airfield, bordered by ocean on three sides and a mountain on the other. Welcoming ceremonies were staged from a truck decorated with flowers and palm fronds. Members of the Trukese-American Women's Association, wearing blue dresses and marmars (headbands), presented flower leis to the visitors.

From the tarmac, Dr. Brooks addressed the crowd. "We're here to listen to your problems and report the progress of the TT government to the U.N. Trusteeship Council, especially with respect to recommendations made by our 1964 visiting commission."

For the next several days, the delegates met with magistrates, members of the Congress of Micronesia and Truk Legislature, and Peace Corps volunteers, and then they toured schools and public facilities.

Missionaries and Peace Corps members drifted to Micronesia like birds of passage. They developed fierce urges to protect islanders from denture commercials and golden arches, especially after visiting torch-lit villages where men carved canoes from breadfruit trees and children swam naked in lagoons. The slogan of the Peace Corps' advertising campaign was, "The toughest job you'll ever love."

When Peace Corps officials, with their bureaucracy, silliness, and patronizing attitudes, came out from Washington on inspection tours, they ingratiated themselves to these young, idealistic people by telling them, "You're doing fantastic work here. Aren't these wonderful islands?" For most of those visitors, it was merely a free trip to the Pacific. They hadn't the slightest idea of what the starry-eyed youngsters were doing, and when they left, they were still unaware.

A 20-minute motorboat ride from Moen lies Udot Island, where an on-the-spot training center was set up for Peace Corps volunteers. At the camp, groups of young men and women, clad in T-shirts, shorts, and zoris, sat cross-legged in circles below clusters of palm trees. These recent college graduates had come to teach the natives, who had been farming and fishing for thousands of years, how to farm and fish, not to mention play softball, yodel, and guzzle whiskey.

The young people lapped up the primitive life: no haircuts, no make-up, no ties, no stockings, and no jewelry, with one exception. Almost every man and woman wore a large tortoise shell and cowry necklace made by native women in precious spare moments after birthing babies, tilling taro fields, and fishing in the lagoon.

Peace Corps members were advised not to be too visible, too friendly, or too involved with the natives. One girl, stationed in Yap, didn't believe in keeping a low profile. She decided to go native–discarding her bras and shirts. After a while she acquired a deep tan, and didn't stand out too much in a crowd of bare-breasted Yapese women, who customarily wore only grass skirts. She was the topic of conversation (not always favorable) in the Peace Corps community as well as everywhere else in the islands.

In the early '70s, Continental-Air Micronesia invited press

members to check out the company's new hotel on Truk. We arrived at the Truk Continental Travelodge to find victims of Typhoon Amy staying there. The typhoon had swept through the islands the previous month, destroying homes and damaging the hotel's roof.

The next stop on our freighter trip was Ponape and, again, the *Gunners Knot* waited outside the reef.

Ponape, the second largest island in Micronesia, is one of the rainiest spots on earth. Some 200 inches a year of rain fall along the coast and 400 inches in the jungles, thus the name Garden Island. Clouds usually obscured Sokehs Rock and the interior volcanic peaks that snare rain, producing waterfalls and lush vegetation.

One of the shortest place names in the world is U, a municipality of Ponape, sometimes spelled "Uh."

One of Micronesia's beachcombers, James F. O'Connell, dubbed the Tattooed Irishman, arrived in Ponape in 1826 as a castaway from an American whale ship. He married one of the chief's daughters and served his father-in-law as interpreter and trader for seven years before returning to the United States. O'Connell published a book about his experiences and became a professional entertainer known as "The Celebrated Tattooed Man—A Sailor of the South Seas."

(Many newscasters, writers, and officials, all of whom should know better, refer to Micronesia, erroneously, as the "South Seas.")

An hour later, the clouds lifted, revealing channel markers in the narrow coral reef passage and Sokehs Rock, a 2,000-foot basalt landmark, called Micronesia's Diamond Head. The ship entered the lagoon and tied up to the dock on Langar Island. Cargo and passengers were loaded into LCUs and speedboats for the mile-long trip across the water to the district center of Kolonia.

After dinner on the ship, the captain and I took a boat to shore and got drenched in a heavy downpour. Island boats don't have canopies or tarps to keep the rain off passengers, who squat under black umbrellas.

A ship's agent drove us to Kolonia to pay a courtesy call on Ponape's District Administrator (Distad), Robert Halvorsen. At the Distad's home, Poneapean Assistant Distad Leo Falcam and his Hawaiian wife, Iris, were sipping cocktails beside a Japanese garden and fish pond, which the Distad had built in his living room.

A bachelor from Chicago, Halvorsen lived with assorted terriers, monkeys, parakeets, and Ponapeans. He served in the Navy in the Pacific during World War II. He took a Navy course on Micronesian affairs at Stanford University in 1946 and immersed himself in Micronesia ever since. He performed many marriages, including one at the ruins of Nan Madol, and couples have named children after him.

Reputed to be TT's best host, he was authorized to spend $450 to entertain the U.N. delegation that week. He knew he'd have to add his own money, recalling that he once spent $800 to treat an earlier U.N. team.

The next morning, we took a dinghy to shore and borrowed a friend's car. Kolonia's roads were the worst in TT, so rocky we couldn't possibly drive as fast as the 15-mph speed limit.

Kolonia is the major town on Ponape, situated on the north coast next to the wide harbor. There were no traffic lights or names on the rutty roads, more frequented by dogs than cars. We walked up the steps of the old walled Spanish city, then strolled along Kolonia's main street, bordered by the Distad's office, hospital, Kaselehia (aloha) Inn, Mayor Martin's bar/bowling alley, and Sepio Bermanis' wholesale store.

Driving beyond town, we tunneled between a row of stately royal palms to TT's agriculture station, directed by Hawaiian Kazu Matsumuro.

The station's Japanese-built administration building was surrounded by lush acres of guava, star apples, breadfruit, cherries, mangosteens, chestnuts, bananas, coffee, and coconuts.

Islanders use coconut palms for shade, food, drink, and building material. Palm leaves are woven into fans, baskets, hats, skirts, and roofs. Coconut husk fiber is turned into ropes and fishing nets, and polished and carved coconut shells become cups and utensils.

Micronesians reused the shards of civilization for years before recycling became cool. The remains of World War II fighters were converted to dog and chicken shelters. Halved plastic fishing floats made chicken and pig food dishes. Washed-up bottles stored rainwater or decorated family graves. Plywood and metal sheets formed walls of thatched-roof huts.

In the early 1960s, cultivation of black pepper (*Piper migrum*) was introduced in Ponape. The pepper vine is grown around a wooded trellis or posts of fern log and mangrove. When the pepper is ripe, it is picked and sorted. Dried peppercorns are packed in plastic bags and decorative bottles for sale in Kwajalein and Micronesia, and some is also shipped to U.S. mainland and world markets.

On Friday, March 3, the captain and I couldn't get a hot lunch at the Kaselehlia Inn because cooks were preparing food for the U.N. delegates. We and six Peace Corps volunteers settled for glasses of iced tea and canned tuna sandwiches.

From the breezy dining room on the hill, we watched TT's SA-16 land in the lagoon and taxi up the seaplane ramp on Langar Island. U.N. delegates climbed into speedboats for the half-hour ride to Kolonia. Accompanying the team was Robert Wenkam, a Honolulu photographer.

Children sang as the motorboat approached the dock, where residents and a police honor guard greeted the visitors. Girls Scouts, whose uniforms were merely green headbands, gave each visitor a flower lei. After lunch, the U.N. team toured schools and government facilities.

That evening in the Ponape Community Club, the delegates were welcomed at a reception attended by Ponapeans, TT employees, Page Communications personnel, Peace Corps volunteers and, a new arrival, Bob Krauss, columnist for the *Honolulu Advertiser*.

The club was decorated with palm fronds, red ginger, hibiscus, and fruit. The buffet table was laden with salads, fish, pork, rice, taro, breadfruit, sushi, and Distad Halvorsen's intoxicating vodka and fruit punch.

After dinner, Dr. Brooks, wearing a long, two-piece dress of Liberian design, spoke briefly. "We are impressed by your new schools, medical clinics, and economic development since our 1964 visit."

On Saturday, delegates met with twenty business leaders. Without an interpreter, local leaders wouldn't discuss economic, business, and agricultural problems because they thought their English wasn't good enough to get their ideas across.

One member of the U.N. team asked Carlos Etscheit, a Belgian planter, about business conditions. Etscheit, a long-time resident, said Ponape was producing the best copra, cacao, and pepper in the world. All the cacao was sold to Ghirandello's in San Francisco, he added.

Among TT's problems was the sad state of equipment, often abandoned in disrepair because of lack of money, spare parts, or mechanical knowhow. For instance, engines had been ruined by filling with salt water instead of fresh water. M-boats and LCUs used for cargo operations sat idle because no one could repair them.

A Ponapean summed up Micronesians' concerns in an article in the *Senyavin Times*, published by a Peace Corps volunteer in Kolonia: "I would like to understand more about the equipments that are here, such as the bulldozer, the cars and trucks, ditch digger, and the LCU, etc. . . . I think the High Commissioner sent these equipment for us to pray to and worship because these equipments are sitting idle. . . . I am surprised that the U.S. government has been administering these islands for more than 22 years, however, the improvements they have made up to date hardly surpassed half of what the Japanese Administration accomplished. . . ."

Saturday evening, the captain and I accompanied the U.N. team to the village of Kapingamarangi, where Polynesians live in thatch huts without electricity. Polynesians also live on the islands of Nukuoro and Kapingamarangi.

The village chief, clad in a lava-lava, invited us to help ourselves to the food spread out on a table lit by kerosene lanterns. We put fish, clams, taro, and breadfruit in baskets of woven coconut leaves and ate with our fingers. A hot coconut drink was served in half-coconut shells with woven coconut leaf saucers.

When we left, we were given a choice of gifts: woven mats, handbags, shell leis, and carved wooden canoes handcrafted by the Kapingamarangis.

Back in Kolonia around midnight, the captain and I went to the Community Club for a nightcap. Four members of the U.N. team walked in and ordered two hamburgers each. The British delegate said he enjoyed the food at Kapingamarangi, but it wasn't what he was accustomed to. Dr. Brooks ordered a hamburger sent to her hotel room.

The club's kitchen was out of hamburger buns and a waitress was sent to get some from a grocery store. The captain and I munched on boiled crab, fried breadfruit, and banana chips, while the delegates played ping pong. An hour later, the waitress returned with several loaves of bread. She delivered a hamburger to Dr. Brooks.

The next evening, the Distad hosted a farewell dinner for the delegates. Among the 50 attendees were Bob Krauss and Kolonia Mayor and Mrs. Martin. Halvorsen served green salad, fried chicken, shish kebob, onion bread, and ice cream topped with creme de menthe. The U.N. team said his dinner was by far the best of their trip.

In the morning, delegates motored by boat to Metalanim, location of the Farm Institute and Ponape Agriculture and Trade School. The next day, the UN mission flew to the Marshall Islands.

Since cargo operations weren't finished, the captain and I hitched a boat ride to Metalanim. En route we stopped at Nan Madol, a deserted, mysterious Pacific Venice like nowhere else on earth. Nan Madol is one of the remnants of megalithic cultures that dot Micronesia: basalt ruins in Kosrae, taga stones in Tinian, terraces in Palau, stones with Easter Island-like faces in Palau, and huge stone money of Yap.

Nan Madol comprises about 100 mangrove islands connected by canals. These walls of huge hexagonal columns of interlocking black basalt have survived storms and high seas for centuries. At high tide we motored up Nan Madol's narrow canals to the mangrove islets where crabs skittered.

On shore, we explored the multi-angular, 15-foot-high basalt blocks, which were sacred temples, ceremonial halls, royal houses, and burial vaults built at the behest of the 13th-century Saudeleurs' dynasty. Tons of prismatic blocks were quarried and brought from Sokehs on the other side of Ponape, the only place on the island where columnar basalt is extruded.

The Saudeleurs conquered Ponape and reigned in Nan Madol for centuries. These ruins, surveyed by German archaeologists at the beginning of the 20th century, have been radiocarbon dated, tracing human habitation to 200 B.C.

On Metalanim we toured the trade school with Father Hugh Costigan, a Catholic priest who had been a member of a New York bricklayers' and plumbers' union since high school. On Ponape, he organized the Metalanim Housing Cooperative, whose members built a dock, warehouse, and concrete block houses.

Father Costigan presided over the mission in the village of Tamori, Ponape, several hours by outboard motorboat from Kolonia. He was a Sunday-school teacher in a Protestant church, a skilled construction man, and the parent by adoption of a Ponapean boy. He taught Sunday school at the atoll of Pingelap. Born in 1914 and raised in the Bronx, Costigan entered the priesthood. In 1965 he opened the Ponape Agriculture Trade School.

When we arrived back on the ship at Ponape, a speedboat driver was waiting to take us to shore. Sepio Bermanis had invited us to join him at Mendiola's Restaurant for a feast of roast suckling pig, sashimi, rice, two vegetable dishes, and a full bar.

After dinner, the captain and I went to a Kolonia bar for a nightcap. In one corner of the room, local men and women were drinking sakau, once a drink of Micronesian nobility.

A slightly narcotic beverage the color of dirty dishwater or motor oil, sakau is brewed from the mashed roots of the pepper shrub. It smells like licorice or anise. The pepper roots are chopped into little pieces, then pounded on metates, adding water to make a pulpy mass. Then the pulp is placed on hibiscus bark and twisted to form a long tight roll. The liquid is collected in coconut shells and served in cups.

Sakau gives users a kick, like a narcotic Sneaky Pete. It's so powerful it's been used for a dental anesthetic. Sakau can make a person numb so that he or she can't stand up, and they sink to the floor or onto a chair. There are scores of sakau bars in town and thatched, open-air bars around the islands.

At sunrise, Monday, March 6, the *Gunners Knot* left Ponape. On board were the TT cooperatives officer, four Peace Corps volunteers, and a dozen deck passengers.

Our next stop was tiny Kusaie, Ponape's sister island. Kusaie is a beautiful high volcanic island, with endemic ferns, mosses, and palms. We waited outside Lelu Harbor for high tide, then entered the narrow channel in the reef. The lagoon, surrounded by mountains, is as idyllic as a Swiss lake.

Anchoring in the center of the tiny harbor, the crew tied the ship to coconut trees on each side. M-boats, speedboats, and outrigger canoes carried passengers, magazines, beer, cigarettes, and generators between ship and shore.

Bully Hayes, a modern buccaneer, lost his vessel on Kusaie's reefs. He frightened the peaceful Kusaians by landing a number of fierce and warlike Ocean and Gilbert Islanders, who brewed coconut-toddies and staged carousals and orgies. Hayes' legend had him burying $250,000 on Kusaie, his favorite haunt. The Boston missionaries on Kusaie were convinced that Hayes was a devout Congregationalist. But another tale had him so irritated by the intrusion of the *Morning Star* mission ship at Pingelap in the

Marshalls, that he forced the mission party to dance themselves to exhaustion to the music of his accordion.

What became of him isn't certain, but he was thought to have been imprisoned in Manila for helping convicts escape from Guam. Hayes' conversion to Catholicism moved the Bishop of Manila to intercede for his release. He returned to the States as a destitute seaman, at public expense.

After the copra was loaded, the *Gunners Knot* left on the midnight tide. Meanwhile, the U.N. mission had already arrived in Kwajalein (aka Kwaj) in the Marshalls Islands.

The coconut wireless announced that Dr. Brooks had pulled a quickie. Instead of resting when they arrived, Dr. Brooks and French delegate Basdevant convinced the Marshall Islands Distad, Dwight Heine, to take them to Ebeye.

Travel writer David Stanley called Ebeye the "armpit of the Pacific," one of the twelve worst places in the world.

Ebeye was an overcrowded ghetto occupied by thousands of Marshallese, who were displaced from their home atolls which had been contaminated by nuclear debris. These people lived in squalor only three miles from Kwaj's country-club atmosphere enjoyed by American missilemen and their families.

From 1946 to 1958, the U.S. conducted nuclear tests in the living laboratories of Eniwetok and Bikini atolls. The largest American above-ground nuclear explosion was Bravo Shot, March 1, 1954. The 15-megaton bomb was 1,000 times stronger than that dropped on Hiroshima. Hours before the test, winds changed and the fallout contaminated 13 islands populated by 239 people. Tragically, thousands of islanders and a few American soldiers were unwitting guinea pigs. On Rongelap Atoll, 100 miles away, 200 residents died.

Bravo and 65 other nuclear tests in the Marshalls exposed islanders to high levels of radiation that caused cancer, leukemia, miscarriages, and other health problems. The U.S. government paid the Marshallese $183.7 million for their suffering, but nothing compensated for their exposure to lingering radiation, resulting in the highest rate of thyroid tumors in the world.

Today, Bikini's islands and the ocean bottom, once deadly with radioactive poisons, have been pronounced safe for visitors. Islanders are developing a resort, which they hope will rival recreational diving sites of the Truk and Palau lagoons.

On the day of their scheduled visit, the U.N. team toured the atoll with Dr. William Vitarelli, TT's Ebeye Representative. Delegates were concerned about Ebeye's crowded conditions, as well as poor water and sanitary facilities that caused frequent epidemics. The U.S. Army was completing Phase 1 of the Ebeye Rehabilitation project, which included building 300 apartments, and installing fresh and salt water systems and a power plant, and dredging the lagoon to make more land for residents.

March 11 at sunset, the *Gunners Knot* steamed slowly past 20 low islands and through the channel in the reef that encircles Majuro's lagoon.

The Marshalls, 2,300 miles southwest of Hawaii, comprise 29 atolls in two coral reef chains called Ratak (sunrise) and Ralik (sunset). From the air, atolls look like Key Lime pies: sand crusts, limeade lagoon fillings, and meringues of white-capped waves crashing on reefs.

The Pearl Harbor attack in 1941, launched from the Marshalls, was almost immediately followed by a push from the Carolines to the west, the south, the east, and even the north. Within a month, Guam, Wake, the Gilberts, and Philippines were in Japanese hands.

The rare tourists who find their way to the Marshalls discover plentiful fish, lobsters, crabs, bananas and coconuts, as well as ideal swimming and snorkeling beaches.

When the ship's gangway was secured at Uliga dock, stevedore gangs were waiting to start discharging cargo by floodlight. At most ports in TT, stevedores usually had to be rounded up from homes or bars.

Our ship carried passengers, watermelons, air compressors, engines, beer, cigarettes, sodas, rice, and air mail to Majuro, the Marshalls' district center.

The M/V *Mieco Queen*, a small ship owned and operated by

Micronesian Islands Import-Export Company (MIECO), was docked beside us. Its skipper, Captain Oscar De Brum, came aboard to invite us to a dinner party at MIECO headquarters to welcome the U.N. team.

Captain De Brum was a descendent of a Marshallese seafaring clan, but he learned modern navigation from the U.S. Navy. When I asked him whether he ever used bamboo stick charts to navigate, a tradition with Marshallese sailors, he said no but his ancestors had used them.

Bamboo strips on the charts represent wind and sea currents, and shells mark locations of stars and atolls. Generally, the straight horizontal and vertical sticks of the navigation charts are intended as supports for the map, though they may represent the direction of swells. The diagonal and curved sticks represent the swells produced by the prevailing winds which travel in a direction at right angles to each stick on the concave side. The shells tied to the sticks represent the position, remarkably accurate, of most of the islands in the group. To this day, some fishermen use these charts, but most charts are sold to tourists for wall decorations.

On Majuro atoll, only a few hundred yards separate the lagoon from the ocean on the other side. The island center was typical: scattered tin-roofed cafes, stores, churches, bungalows, and the Coconut Rendevous Club, a watering hole where Micronesians imbibe and play shuffleboard.

Within a whisper of the surf were four L-shaped houses built by TT public works for the Distad and his assistant. Nearby, Peace Corp volunteers had erected their own A-frame houses, complete with kitchens, bathrooms, and walls decorated and insulated with burlap copra sacks.

Located on the waterfront, MIECO'S three-story building housed offices, stores, legislature meeting hall, and an air-conditioned hotel, bar, and restaurant.

During the welcome party held in the second-floor restaurant, Distad Dwight Heine and Dr. Brooks greeted guests, who included Assistant Distad and Mrs. Dan Akimoto, Dr. and Mrs. Lanwi, Judge and Mrs. Goss, and MIECO employees.

After dinner, U.N. delegates admitted this was the first time they had slept in windowless hotel rooms. At least the rooms were air-conditioned, they said. Due to the water shortage, toilets were flushed by pouring buckets of water into the bowls. One delegate suggested that MIECO devise a salt-water system so guests could "flush with success."

At a public meeting in the Uliga Church, the U.N. team discussed problems of island-wide electricity, water rationing, improvement of roads, discontinuance of U.S. Department of Agriculture food for schools, the problems of Eniwetok residents, who were relocated on Ujelang when their island was taken for atomic testing, and the political future of the territory.

On Monday, March 13, the U.N. mission was given a farewell dinner at Uliga Park, in front of the pier. A brass band of young boys, directed by Catholic Father Hacker, played lusty marches, while students performed native dances and women placed baskets of food on the picnic tables.

Years ago, there had been a struggle in Majuro for musical superiority between a Protestant children's choir and a Catholic boys' band. The Catholic band was formed by Father L. G. Hacker, a Jesuit from Buffalo, New York. He had been in the Pacific for 25 years and at Majuro since 1952. This dynamic man built a school and, although he wasn't a musician, taught Marshallese adults and children to play trumpets and trombones.

It was unthinkable to hold any celebration at Majuro without the brassy participation of Father Hacker's band, which consisted of trombones, trumpets, French horns, tubas, snare drums, bass drums, cymbals, and castanets, all procured from Navy and Army surplus.

On a wet Tuesday morning, March 14, TT's DC-4 arrived to fly the delegates to Saipan. Again, Father Hacker's brass band bid *Yokwe Yok* (aloha) to the gift-laden visitors. No one noticed the downpour, badly needed to replenish Majuro's dwindling water supply.

The *Gunners Knot* sailed from Majuro to the world's largest atoll, Kwajalein, a 176-mile strand of coral reef enclosing a 1,100-square-mile lagoon. Kwajalein is a dog-legged, 80-mile-long lagoon. Japan's Imperial Navy battle fleet sailed out of this lagoon on their mission to strike Pearl Harbor.

From the water, Kwaj looked like a mass of futuristic white domes and odd-shaped buildings with towers rising among the palms. Nike missiles from Kwaj intercepted Strategic Defense Initiative (star wars) ICBMs fired into the Pacific from Hawaii and Vandenberg AFB, California.

During World War II, the U.S. Marines landed on Kwaj, Japanese headquarters for the Marshalls. The Marines found maps and intelligence indicating that the coral atoll of Eniwetok was weakly defended. On February 19, 1944, U.S. forces sailed into Eniwetok's lagoon, bombed the enemy installations, and secured the northern part of the atoll. At the same time, battleship and cruiser guns pounded nearby Engebi.

After the war, Engebi became the site of U.S. H-bomb tests. The atoll was wired with every atomic device available. Someone pushed a button and blew it sky high. Some say the island doesn't exist now; others say it exists but only rats live there.

Kwaj was, and still is, off-limits to everyone except Department of Defense personnel working at the test site and employees of Global Associates, contractors for the Army. Even Micronesians are prohibited entry without special permits, except people commuting to Ebeye.

A press card opens many doors, but not Kwaj's. Honolulu newspaper columnist Bob Krauss was put under house arrest when he arrived. Officials kept Krauss in his room until his plane left for Honolulu.

An employee of Global Associates drove the captain and I around the unclassified parts of Kwaj. Being a reporter, I was not allowed to wander around the base unescorted.

The veil of secrecy surrounding the atoll hid the fact that thousands of Americans were living luxuriously with all the amenities of civilization in air-conditioned houses and shopping in air-conditioned stores in a community of manicured lawns and stately palms.

The next day, we sailed from Kwaj, passing many small islands, including Ebeye. Through binoculars we saw shacks, palm trees, rain catchment towers, and dredges on the atoll.

Arno Atoll in the Marshalls was once a strict Protestant outpost. No liquor was permitted, residents sang hymns, and church bells pealed at 5:30 each morning. When the University of the Arts of Love was supposedly founded on Arno, anthropologists flocked there like parrot fish at spawning time. The university was a finishing school in which older Marshallese women taught young girls how to make men happy. The faculty taught students, who averaged fourteen years old, libidinous dances, patterned on movements of waves and winds. Some say it wasn't a school, but a brothel for Japanese colonists, or it was totally invented by transient anthropologists to titillate the U.S. Navy. The school's graduates were coveted as wives.

The ship's engines chugged laboriously and hull timbers creaked as we sailed, crablike, west to Ponape and Truk.

At Truk, we loaded on deck a giant turtle bound for a private zoo on Guam. Every few hours, sailors hosed the turtle down to keep it from dehydrating. However, either Trukese sailors or deck passengers slashed the turtle's eyes out with knives. Tragically, the sea giant died before we arrived in Guam.

When we anchored in Apra Harbor, Guam's quarantine officer wouldn't let Chichi go ashore. While we had been away, a number of pets had contracted rabies, probably spread by shrews. The Navy had issued an embargo on importing dogs and cats, requiring animals entering Guam to be quarantined for 120 days unless they came from rabies-free areas.

I showed the inspector Chichi's up-to-date rabies shot record, but only my fast talking convinced him to let me take her home. That was the end of Chichi's sailing days.

Returning to the Scene

In July 1990, twelve years after I moved from Guam to the U.S. mainland, I returned for a visit. To get the most bang for my $900 round-trip airfare, I chose Air Mike's island-hopper from Honolulu to Guam. The trip takes ten hours and a day.

In my absence, new airfields and terminals had been built, place names had been changed, and island-nations had been formed. I wanted to see the changes for myself before I began writing the first edition of this book.

At Honolulu International Airport, I waited with three dozen Micronesians. These frequent fliers, wearing T-shirts and rubber zoris, carried cardboard boxes tied with string, aka Portuguese suitcases. Air Mike announced that our flight was delayed and gave us coupons to get breakfast in the cafeteria. Five hours later, we boarded the Boeing 727, as the airport chaplain sprinkled us with holy water.

Every seat on the plane was occupied by Micronesian college students, government officials, businessmen, and families. The only Statesiders were myself and my seatmates: a contract engineer and his bride bound for Kwajalein.

The jet soared above the Pacific Ocean to 38,000 feet, where cumulus clouds streamed under the fuselage like yogurt. I dozed off after attendants from Saipan, Koror, and Guam served breakfast, the second for us early airport arrivals.

Two hours later angelic voices, high and clear as a waterfall, woke me. Bronze-skinned coeds, returning from mainland colleges, were singing hymns in the lilting language of Kosrae (the name was changed from Kusaie in 1986).

The aircraft bounced down roughly on Johnston Atoll: 60 acres of palms, ironwood trees, three runways, a few houses, bunkers, gooney birds, and a U.S. Army atomic weapons test and disposal site. For 20 minutes, military police, armored vehicles, and guard dogs aimed their rifles, canons, and teeth at us.

Johnston Island, once the home of migratory birds and valuable for rich deposits of guano, was claimed by the U.S. and the Kingdom of Hawaii in 1856. After the Second World War, the Air Force converted this idyllic atoll into one of the most toxic places in the Pacific. Used in 1950s and '60s for nuclear testing, one end of the atoll remains radioactive. Since 1971, thousands of tons of mustard gas and nerve gas, which are periodically incinerated, releasing dioxin and furan into air, have been deposited on Johnston.

We weren't allowed to deplane, but I didn't take it personally. In 1985, William F. Buckley, Jr., was forbidden to set foot on the atoll when he and his yacht crew anchored offshore. After buying fuel and ice, Buckley was ordered to cast off.

During the two-hour hop to Majuro in the Marshalls, we ate breakfast number three and crossed the International Dateline. Monday became Tuesday.

Four years earlier, the Republic of the Marshall Islands, along with the Federated States of Micronesia, were molded into independent island-nations in free association with the U.S.

From above, Majuro's airfield looked like a postage stamp. I recalled Art Buchwald's play, "Sheep on the Runway," which could have been set on Majuro. Before landing, pilots used to buzz the short coral and sand runways two or three times to chase off wild pigs. The pigs fled to the boonies when the runway was topped with concrete. Airfields were lit by automobile headlights for rare night operations.

Nowadays, these paved and lighted airstrips range from 4,700 to 7,000 feet. Our pilot brought the plane straight down for a smooth landing on the reef runway, about 13 miles from the district center of Majuro.

Outside, a rainbow arced over the welcoming sign, "Yokwe Yok." Lizards and land crabs skittered on the seawall and waves washed onto the runway.

The terminal gift shop was crammed with Marshallese handicraft: shell leis; woven bags, hats and mats; feather and tortoise shell fans and purses; carved wooden bowls, masks, and figures; and navigational stick charts.

Amata Kabua, who was descended from a family of chiefs near Bikini, was president of the Marshalls until his death at age 68 in December 1996. Speaking before 15 South Pacific nations in Brisbane, Australia, Kabua offered a tiny contaminated island to be sacrificed for a disposal site for nuclear waste and warheads from Japan, South Korea, and Taiwan. Kabua said that revenue received from leasing one island for a dump would pay for rehabilitation of other radioactive islands, which could be resettled by their cancer-riddled owners.

Kabua reportedly also bid on a multimillion-dollar plan to import nontoxic waste from the U.S. West Coast to the Marshalls to use for landfill. Islanders were to receive millions of dollars in exchange for adding inches to their atolls and becoming the world's largest trash dump.

The Republic of the Marshall Islands has come a long way. Visitors can go scuba diving and sports fishing, visit World War II historical sites, or take a scenic drive to peaceful Laura Beach.

The Alele Museum, in downtown Majuro, showcases traditional and colonial history of the Marshalls, such as authentic tools and artifacts, canoe displays, and photos from the German, Japanese, and U. S. colonial eras. There's also an elaborate shell collection from Mili Atoll.

Peace Park Memorial, just past the airport, pays homage to all soldiers who fought and died in the Pacific during World War II. The memorial, constructed by the Japanese government, features an upright granite stone and a picnic area.

There's also a 1918 Typhoon Monument located on the lagoon side of Laura Beach, a great picnic spot. The sandstone monument commemorates the Japanese Emperor's donation of imperial private funds toward the rebuilding of Majuro atoll after the devastation by the 1918 typhoon, which caused 200 casualties and destruction of churches, homes, and businesses in Majuro.

A unique activity for visitors is touring the RRE Clam Farm, a giant clam holding and raising facility featuring state-of-the-art aquaculture technology.

There are first-class hotels and motels in the Marshalls these days. Majuro's largest is the Outrigger Hotel and Resort, with 150 rooms. Accommodations are also available at the Hotel Robert Reimers, Majuro Royal Garden Hotel, and other small hotels.

What a surprise to learn there are hotel rooms today on nearby Ebeye at the Anrohasa, Midtown, and DSC hotels. Nearby Jaluit offers the MEC Hotel, with 2 rooms and 6 bed spaces, and the Wau Cottages in Mili, with 7 rooms and 21 bed spaces.

Visitors from around the world are attracted to the Marshalls' pristine coral reefs teeming with marine life. Yet the country faces formidable challenges, such as environmental degradation, rapid population growth, accelerated sea-level rise, and the legacy of nuclear testing.

The U.S. nuclear testing program conducted in the Marshall Islands will not go away–with good reason.

Recently, major discrepancies were discovered pertaining to radiation dose estimates previously cited regarding population groups exposed to Bravo Shot on March 1, 1954. S. Cohen & Associates, Inc., under contract to the Public Advocate of the Nuclear Claims Tribunal, has identified errors in dose estimates published by Brookhaven National Laboratories regarding external whole-body exposures and thyroid doses.

Preliminary data suggest that whole-body doses associated with Bravo were a factor of two higher, and thyroid doses may be up to 10-to 20-fold higher than previous estimates. A full disclosure of these findings is being prepared.

The Marshalls Islands lies in open ocean, vulnerable to waves and storm surges. Although the islands have by no means been free from weather extremes, they are frequently referred to in folklore as "jolet jen Anij," or gifts from God. The relative safety that the islands have historically enjoyed is now in jeopardy.

For many years, the Marshalls' government has been concerned with global climate change. The 1,225 islets, scattered over three-fourths of a million square miles, have an average height above sea level of two meters. The highest land area is Likiep Atoll, where the elevation reaches an altitude of six meters.

The Marshallese would become environmental refugees, if evacuation is necessary before the islands are completely inundated. The Marshall Islands are referred to as a "front line state" with regard to the climate change issue. The potentially catastrophic effects are beginning to appear, and it may be too late to prevent further warming that will threaten all of the world's coastal regions.

On my 1990 trip, an hour after leaving Majuro, the aircraft floated like a feather down to Kwajalein. A sign on the gate boasted: "U.S. Army, Kwajalein Atoll, USCINCPAC Representative, Republic of Marshall Islands. The Army's Community of Excellence in the Pacific."

My seatmates were the only passengers who disembarked. On the tarmac, a Collie sniffed off-loaded boxes, and a guard made sure no one else deplaned.

In nearby Bikini Atoll, surveys have declared that it is habitable, so long as residents don't eat too many coconuts. Early in 1997, four elderly women, who were evacuated from Bikini more than fifty years ago, returned to begin the ceremonial process of cleaning up their radioactive island where twenty-three nuclear explosions had been conducted in the 1940s and '50s.

Bikini residents are inviting tourists to their white sand beaches, fringed with swaying coconut palms, with fish and sea turtles swimming within a coral reef in a turquoise lagoon. Divers can explore wrecks of nineteen ships, including an aircraft carrier, sunk during U.S. atomic testing. The Bikini Dive Resort has with 7 rooms and 14 bed spaces.

From Kwaj, our plane barely reached cruising altitude when it descended over Kosrae (formerly Kusaie), where the singing angels gathered their belongings and deplaned in a drizzle.

The people of the Federal States of Micronesia are culturally and linguistically Micronesian, with a small number of Polynesians living on Nukuoro and Kapingamarangi atolls in Pohnpei. The four states are separated by large expanses of water. Prior to Western contact, this isolation led to the development of unique traditions, customs, and language, but the influence of European and Japanese contacts can be seen. English is the official language, and there are eight major indigenous languages: Yapese, Ulithian, Woleaian, Chuukese, Pohnpeian, Kosraean, Nukuoro, and Kapingamarangi.

Each of the four states has its own culture, folklore, and tradition, but common cultural and economic bonds are centuries old. Cultural similarities are evidenced by the importance of the traditional extended family and clan systems found on each island.

The islands have a rich oral history, with traditional music carried down from generation to generation. Local radio stations broadcast Micronesian pop music, influenced by traditional tunes, American country and western, reggae, and modern Europop.

The basic economy of the islands is based on cultivation of breadfruit, banana, coconut, citrus trees, and root crops, such as taro and yam. Fishing supplements the islanders' diet and economy.

The religion is predominantly Roman Catholic and Protestant, with other faiths also represented. The population in 1994 by ethnic group totaled 105,506 people, of which the largest is Chuukese, followed by Pohnpeian, Kosraean, Yapese, and others.

In September 1991, the United Nations General Assembly admitted the Federated States of Micronesia (FSM) and the Republic of the Marshall Islands to full membership, thus endorsing the decolonization of the Trust Territory of the Pacific Islands.

The Foreign Investment Act of 1997 barred foreigners from investing in business activities in the FSM, such as manufacturing, minting of coins or printing currency, nuclear power or radioactivity-related businesses. Foreign investment is restricted in fishing, banking, telecommunications, air transport, and shipping.

Today, the FSM economy stands at a crossroads as it continues to negotiate for continued U.S. funding that is key to its economy. For two decades, the U.S. government has provided $1.08 billion in funding to the FSM under the compact, but the FSM government doesn't have much to show in terms of developing its private-sector economy despite this funding. An existing financial aid agreement under the compact ends this year. The FSM will have a chance to state its case during the third round of compact talks, scheduled to take place in mid-2001 in Honolulu.

Kosrae's misty volcanic peaks tower 2,600 feet above rainforests, waterfalls, tropical fruit gardens, mangrove swamps, and isolated beaches. The island's mysterious Lelu Ruins are similar to but not as extensive as Nan Madol on Pohnpei (formerly Ponape). Both sites contain basalt houses and temples built by 13th-Century rulers.

Before the airstrip was built in 1986, Kosraens were isolated from the outside world except for the arrival of occasional copra ships and seaplanes. Today, scuba divers explore coral shelves and shipwrecks in Lelu Harbor, including pirate "Bully" Hayes' ship sunk in Utwe harbor in 1874.

Now, visitors can enjoy the Kosrae Nautilus Resort, with a private beach, swimming pool, and restaurant; the Pacific Treelodge, with rooms nestled in tree tops near the ocean; and the Kosrae Village Resort, offering scuba diving trips; and two smaller hotels.

As lei-bedecked Kosraen passengers boarded Air Mike's 727, a Stateside boy, who had boarded in Majuro, said, "Mom, everybody's gift-wrapped."

The sun set during the hour's flight to Pohnpei. At 7 p.m., the pilot announced our descent to the 6,000-foot coral runway built in 1970. Pohnpei was doing what it does best—rain. We waited, silently, descending through baroque clouds enveloping hilltops.

Suddenly the plane banked, soared, circled, and tried to land again and again in the rainy abyss. Finally, the pilot said he was running low on fuel and was heading for Chuuk (formerly Truk).

Pohnpei these days has tourist-class hotels that offer degrees of comfort and amenities, ranging from fan-cooled thatched cottages to hotel rooms with air-conditioning, cable TV, mini-bars, and restaurants. The hotels include the Ocean View Plaza, Village Hotel, C-Star Apartelle, and Snow Land Hotel (what snow?).

An hour later, Chuuk's airstrip, lit like a pinball machine, welcomed us. As passengers disembarked, Air Mike agents gave Pohnpei-bound passengers coupons for hotel rooms and tickets for flights from Chuuk to Pohnpei the next day.

Recently, the FSM public auditor reported that $1.5 million was spent in Chuuk on cars and boats that were simply given away to individuals for their personal use. The U.S. Embassy in the FSM described such spending as "cars and boats for votes." A written response from the FSM government response says that spending wasn't a misuse of compact funds because the boats are transportation needed for the livelihood of islanders.

These days, Chuuk has accommodations at the Truk Stop Hotel with oceanfront rooms, restaurant and diving activities; Blue Lagoon Resort, Chuuk Pacific Resort, Chuuk Star Hotel, Pacific Garden/Falos Beach Resort, and the live-in ship, *Truk Odyssen*.

We soared away from Chuuk into a sky ablaze with stars and constellations so bright I could almost reach out and touch them.

After an hour and 25 minutes (and six hours late), we skimmed over the villages of Umatac and Merizo as we descended to Guam's Won Pat International Airport.

On the ground, the heat and humidity hit me like a 4x6 board. It was one of those dog-under-the-house evenings when the temperature hovered in the mid-90s and the humidity was equivalent to pea soup. But the sweet scents of plumeria and hibiscus mingling with salty breezes embraced me.

The new terminal was air-conditioned. The departure lounge had plenty of seats, double the number of immigration booths, an observation lounge to view arriving and departing passengers, a Duty Free shop, cafeteria, portable bar service, and a renovated Blue Marlin lounge.

My visit coincided, accidentally, with the 14th anniversary of Typhoon Pamela.

Phyllis Rice had invited me to stay with her in Santa Rita, two blocks from where the captain and I had lived. Two days later, in keeping with Pamela's anniversary, the power and water went out in Santa Rita and southern villages. Without air-conditioning and electricity, Phyllis' house was dark and hot, and I couldn't see the myriads of geckos crawling in and out of my shoes and suitcase.

I moved to the Tamuning Plaza Hotel on Marine Drive, between Agaña and Tumon. For $50 a night I had a spacious, air-conditioned room with a kitchenette. Built for Japanese businessmen, instructions to operate appliances were in Japanese. One sign translated as, "Danger—do not swim across the reef. It is razor sharp and there are sharks that will eat you. Besides, it is dangerous."

The next morning I awoke to Guam's natural alarm clock: the fanfaronade of barking dogs and crowing roosters. When I first moved to Tamuning, I complained about the cocks crowing at sunrise. My neighbor shrugged, "This is Guam. Cocks must crow."

Tamuning was a maze of duty-free shops, shopping malls, a hospital, and residences.

Tumon has become Japan's tropical mecca. San Vitores Road, once a narrow lane skirting Ypao Beach, is a four-lane thoroughfare with traffic lights and turning lanes. It's walled with high-rise tourist hotels, mostly owned and managed by Japanese. Every square foot of land is crammed with plush resorts, restaurants, nightclubs, gun clubs, karaoke clubs, pachinko palaces, and fast-food chains serving hamburgers and milkshakes to hundreds of thousands of Japanese vacationers yearning for a taste of the U.S. wild west.

I drove to Ypao Beach to check out the handicraft and agricultural fair taking place. People crowded around the many vendors' booths at the beach park. Some people, to get out of the hot sun, gathered in pavilions and sat on concrete benches, which had been donated by senators, whose names were etched on them.

In the public rest rooms, I saw Guamanian women washing clothes, as well as splashing water on themselves to cool off on that warm day. I strolled farther up the beach, and saw World War II concrete bunkers decaying in caves behind the Pacific Star Hotel and Pacific Islands Club.

In 2001, Governor Carl T.C. Gutierrez announced that GovGuam plans to renovate Ypao Beach Park to the estimated tune of $10 million. Improvements will include a botanical garden, cultural center, concession building, a three-story parking garage, and a site for the interment of ancestral remains returned to Guam the previous year.

The park belongs to GovGuam and will continue to be run by the Department of Parks and Recreation. The contribution by the private sector is to clean, maintain, and provide security for the park.

On another morning I drove to Agaña, which is still a sprawling, disordered capital with a small-town flavor. I went to the *Pacific Daily News* building for old time's sake.

PDN's editorial offices are very modern, compared to my days on the newspaper. Today there is air-conditioning. Carpeting on the floors and halfway up the walls and partitions separating sections deaden the editorial noise. Still, when the power goes out, the floor is dark. Candles light the way to and inside the windowless bathrooms.

After a brief talk with Publisher Lee Webber, Joe Murphy invited me for coffee at Take Five cafe, a hangout for local businessmen.

Joe and I talked about how Guam has changed since we both arrived thirty years ago and since my absence in 1978. The island has progressed from a strictly military island to a civilian island, run by island people. The transition was caused almost entirely by tourism, which provides a base for the civilian economy. Tourism has certainly built up from the days when the first visitors had to sleep in tents in Tamuning, we agreed.

Another day, I parked at the Paseo de Susana, a spit jutting west from Agaña near the mouth of the Agaña River.

In Paseo Park, created with massive amounts of rubble from the buildings of Agaña destroyed during World War II, vandals had knocked the head off the Statue of Liberty, erected by Guam's Boy Scouts. Nearby stood a memorial to four Marines awarded Congressional Medals of Honor while liberating Guam.

I gazed for the first time at the larger-than-life bronze statue of Chief Quipuha, which dominates the center of the traffic circle at Marine Drive and the Paseo. Quipuha was an ancient Chamorro warrior chief who welcomed the first Jesuit missionaries to the Mariana Islands.

Only seven months earlier, in January 1990, 62-year-old Ricky Bordallo had ended his life at the Chief's feet.

Ricky had been found guilty of forcing an engineer to lie to federal officials about a $60,000 contribution from a group of Japanese businessmen. During his trial, Bordallo said the money was a campaign contribution. He was convicted on ten counts of exchanging political favors for payoffs and sentenced to nine years in prison. A Federal appeals court reversed eight of those counts and set aside the sentence.

Bordallo's situation worsened when he blurted out at a University of Guam lecture, and again at a Chamber of Commerce luncheon, that he had received a $10,000 gift from businessman Ken Jones. Later Jones pleaded *nolo contendere* to a misdemeanor for exceeding campaign donation limits and paid a $20,000 fine.

In November 1989, Bordallo's troubles escalated when a federal grand jury handed down a superceding indictment against him on 17 counts. New charges stemmed from Jones' gift and for bribes relating to a $300 million municipal bond project, as well as a new extortion charge that involved government contracts.

The next month, Bordallo was fined $10,000 for witness tampering and conspiracy to obstruct justice. He was sentenced to four years in federal prison. Bordallo appealed, awaited the appellate court's decision, and began writing his memoirs.

The Ninth U.S. Circuit Court of Appeals reversed four of Bordallo's bribery-related convictions and four extortion-related convictions, but upheld the convictions of witness tampering and conspiracy to obstruct justice. Bordallo was sentenced to a four-year term in the federal correctional facility at Boron, California.

On the day Bordallo was to fly to Boron, he drove his jeep to the Paseo Loop. Dressed in a T-shirt, faded blue jeans and jacket, and a wide-brimmed straw hat, he parked near Chief Quipuha's statue.

Bordallo sat down with his back to the rear of the statue, placed a Guam flag around his shoulders, and set handwritten placards around him: "I regret I only have one life to give for my island" and "I choose death before dishonor." Other signs called for justice and a halt to the deculturation of the Chamorro people.

Ricky held the barrel of a .38-caliber pistol against his right temple and squeezed the trigger. He was still breathing when police responded to a call from workers filling potholes on Marine Drive. The former governor died at the U.S. Naval Hospital.

During my drive around the southern loop of Guam, I saw one of Ricky's follies: at the north end of Umatac, a turreted, cantilevered bridge spans a gulch on the main road. This gaudy structure seemed more appropriate to the transplanted London Bridge in Havasu, Arizona, than to sleepy Umatac.

On the way back to Tamuning, I stopped for a delicious Guamanian plate lunch at Jeff's Pirate's Cove, a long-time favorite spot for residents and tourists alike. This Talofofo landmark opened a mini-museum in December 2000, featuring historical photographs, artifacts of the area, and memorabilia of the capture of Sgt. Shoichi Yokoi. Jeff's also displays a laminated serious of photos of the collapse of the Royal Palm Resort when it was destroyed after the 1993 earthquake.

After Ricky Bordallo's death, his wife, Madeleine, and Carl T. C. Gutierrez ran for governor and lieutenant governor in the November 1994 election. They won, and Madeleine became the first woman elected to that position on Guam.

Madeleine, who graduated with a voice major from St.

Katherine's College, Minnesota, had been active in the Guam Women's Club, Guam Theatre Guild, Guam Symphony Society, and the Women's Democratic Party of Guam. She was president of Beauty World (Guam) Ltd., the local sponsor for the Miss World Beauty Pageant, the oldest international beauty contest held annually in London. Daughter Deborah won the Miss Guam World title and was crowned Miss Universe in 1971.

On January 1, 1995, Archbishop Anthony S. Apuron offered an inaugural Mass at 4 p.m. in Dulce Nombre de Maria Basilica. Prayers were offered in 17 languages commonly heard in Guam, and a merienda was held behind the Cathedral.

The next day, the inaugural ceremony began at 4 p.m with despedida speeches given by outgoing Governor Joseph F. Ada and Lieutenant Governor Frank F. Blas. This new event was created to smooth the transition from one administration to next.

Madeleine took the oath of office on a Bible used by her late husband, Ricky, when he was sworn in as governor. "I stand here for all the women of Guam," Madeleine said. "How fortunate I am to live among people who consider women their equals. My greatest sadness is that the one individual who, more than anyone else, made this possible, can't be here. Ricky, this one's because of you and for you," she said.

After Gutierrez took his oath of office, the fiesta warmed up. Some 10,000 citizens enjoyed the inaugural fiesta in Skinner Plaza.

Gutierrez and Bordallo claimed their inauguration ceremonies didn't cost taxpayers a cent. Volunteers from Talofofo and Inarajan built 24 hexagonal huts for food, drink, and ceremonial cakes in Skinner Plaza in Agaña. There were 19 cakes, one for each village. The archway at Plaza de España was afire with blood-red ginger and white orchids, interspersed with birds of paradise and white and red carnations. A stage in the Plaza de España was erected and painted white to match tables and benches scattered around the Plaza. More than 5,000 people were invited to the events, including local and foreign dignitaries. About 100 godchildren of Carl and Madeleine were there, along with their relatives.

Eight pigs were prepared and each family brought a casserole, salad, or bread for the event. Although the food and entertainment were free, citizens were advised to bring cash to purchase gift baskets of locally made products and commemorative medallions. Pictorial souvenir programs sold for $5 each, and ads in the publication helped defray expenses of the gubernatorial campaign.

Governor Gutierrez's wife, Geri, quickly set about renovating Government House, which hadn't been remodeled since Madeleine Bordallo had done it 13 years earlier. The house had sustained considerable damage during recent typhoons and the 8.1-magnitude earthquake in 1993. The 42-year-old First Lady helped cook for dozens of workers and volunteers during the renovation project. Guam Department of Public Works did most of the construction work, with help from 15 prisoners from the Department of Corrections.

Renovation of the building's interior and exterior and grounds cost GovGuam $1 million and taxpayers $1.2 million. Since the opening ceremony, January 16, 1996, it has been called *Guma' I Taotao Guam*, or House of the People of Guam.

The evening before I was to return to Honolulu and the mainland, I drove to the Hilton Hotel for happy hour to watch the sun set over the Philippine Sea.

As I walked from the hotel's parking lot to the lobby, I heard a familiar voice. "Hafa adai, Janet."

I turned to see Bert Unpingco, former head of the Guam Visitors Bureau, coming toward me. He hugged me.

"Bert. What a surprise!"

"Let's have a drink," Bert said.

"That's exactly what I was going to do."

We sat at a beachside table on the terrace, but the waiter asked us to move to a back corner table. He explained that a busload of Japanese tourists were coming for happy hour.

"It's all your fault, Bert." I smiled at him. "If it hadn't been for your decade of dynamic leadership at the GVB, most of these tourists wouldn't be here today."

Bert grinned.

We talked about how life was treating us and what each of us was doing these days. When Bert left to attend a business dinner in the Hilton's dining room, I sat for a while to enjoy the beach and sea view at sunset. Then, I returned to my hotel to pack.

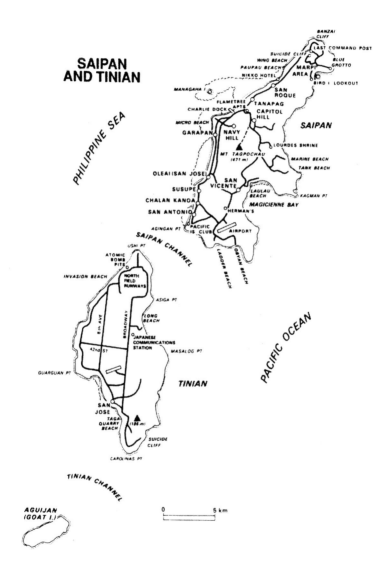

CHAPTER TEN

Island Hopping

Guam is the ideal base for island-hopping. While living there, I traveled around the Micronesian islands several times by air and sea. This chapter describes Saipan, where I lived two years while working for the Trust Territory government, and profiles other islands which are not described in detail in other chapters. As mentioned earlier, Micronesia, once known as the United Nations Trust Territory of the Pacific, has emerged in the past few decades as the Republic of Palau, the Federated States of Micronesia, and the Commonwealth of the Northern Mariana Islands.

Yap

I first visited Yap in 1965 while on a freighter trip from Saipan to Palau and Japan, and I returned on a later trip arranged for the media by Air Micronesia.

Yap is the most traditional corner of Micronesia. The 10,000 inhabitants, who are mostly Roman Catholic, are determined to protect their traditions, to ensure that the state doesn't become another Guam or Saipan. Yap is now a part of the Federated States of Micronesia.

Yap comprises 118 square kilometers, including the large adjoining islands of Yap, Gagil-Tomil, Maap, and Rumung, plus fifteen outer atolls, in the Western Caroline Islands. The main islands are linked by bridges, but Rumung is accessible only by boat. A coral reef surrounds the cluster. Yap, alone among the other large islands of the Carolines, is of sedimentary origin, not volcanic.

In 1525 Portuguese navigators in search of the Spice Islands of Indonesia came upon Yap and Ulithi. Later, Spanish expeditions made the first European contact with the islands. Spain established a colonial government on Yap and claimed the Carolines until 1899.

In the early 1900s, Yap fell under the administration of Germany, which tried to establish sovereignty over the islands.

The Yapese were, and the outer islanders still are, great voyagers of the Pacific, sailing incredible distances in outrigger canoes, with only the stars and waves to guide them. The word Yap means paddle in the Yapese language.

Yap is well known for grass skirts, thus (loincloths), stone money, and handicraft.

For centuries, Yapese women have worn only grass skirts. Missionaries tried to force women to wear colorful muumuus, but the women saved those gowns for special occasions. When a container of T-shirts arrived, the almsgivers hoped Yapese women would wear them. The women wore the shirts, but they cut holes in the front to bare their breasts. Today, few women on Yap Island proper wear grass skirts.

Young boys and some adult men still wear the native thu.

The big circular stone money of Yap resembles a flat gristmill with a hole in the middle, so two men can carry it on a pole. The largest piece, on Rumung, is four meters across and takes a dozen men to move it. Although important, size is not the only factor in determining the value of a coin; a smaller piece may be worth more due to its age and history. Stones are seldom moved since who owns each piece is common knowledge. Sitting or standing on stone money is forbidden.

Yapese craft items include lava lava, woven from hibiscus and banana fibers; grass skirts; woven baskets to carry betel nuts; men's combs with long bamboo teeth; mother-of-pearl shells tied with woven coconut fiber; carved wooden spoons; shell belts and necklaces; model canoes; and woodcarvings.

Yapese, who like to dance on special occasions, can dance from any position—marching, sitting, standing. They often use bamboo sticks for rhythm.

Visitors can be quite comfortable, if not luxurious, in Yap's main town of Colonia. Accommodations include the Rai View Hotel, located on a hill overlooking Colonia Bay, with ten air-conditioned rooms with color TV and a restaurant; the ESA Bay View Hotel, on the south side of the lagoon, with sixteen air-conditioned rooms and private baths, TV, and refrigerators; the Manta Ray Bay Hotel; Ocean View Hotel; the Pathways Hotel, an eco-resort that overlooks the lagoon and has an open-air restaurant; and Traders' Ridge Resort, with a full-service diving operation.

Belau (formerly Palau)

Southwest of Yap lies the archipelago of Belau, consisting of six island groups and twenty islets, totaling 200 islands in the Western Carolines chain. The terrain varies from the mountainous main island of Babeldaob to low, coral islands fringed by large barrier reefs. Natural resources include forests, marine products, gold, and deep-sea minerals.

A unique feature of the Belau archipelago is the hundreds of Rock Islands. These are large or small, uninhabited, turtle-shaped humps of limestone, covered with pandanus and palms. The islands are the pitted remains of coral reefs thrust out of the sea long ago by the forces of undersea volcanoes.

Carbon-dating of artifacts found in the oldest known village sites on the Rock Islands and on the terraces of Babeldaob place civilization in Belau as early as 1,000 B.C.

The most noteworthy first foreign contact took place in 1783 when the vessel *Antelope*, under the command of English Captain Henry Wilson, was shipwrecked on a reef near Ulong, a Rock Island. Koror's High Chief Ibedul helped Wilson and his men rebuild their ship. From that time on, many explorers called at Palau.

Pope Leo XIII asserted Spain's rights over the Caroline Islands in1885. Churches were established by two Capuchin priests and two brothers, resulting in the introduction of the Roman alphabet and elimination of intervillage wars.

In 1899, Spain sold the Carolines to Germany, which established an organized program to exploit the islands' natural resources. Germans transformed Jaluit Atoll into a commercial capital and set up a trading shop in Palau. On Babelthuap, children used to sing "Die Lorelei" and "Stille Nacht," inherited from the former German overlords.

After Germany's defeat in World War I, the islands were passed to the Japanese under the 1919 Treaty of Versailles. Japan's influence on the Palauan culture was immense, as it shifted the economy from a subsistence to a market economy and property ownership from the clan to individuals.

Palauans are Micronesia with Malayan and Melanesian admixtures. English and Palauan officials languages, but also Sonsoral, Tobi, and Angaur are spoken.

For the most part, Palauans strongly identify with their traditional culture. Several of the traditional ceremonies, such as the omersurch birth ceremony, ocheraol first-house ceremony, and kemeldiil funeral services, are widely practiced today, and the beliefs adopted by Palauan forefathers are still revered.

The most noticeable aspect of Palauan culture is the close connection with the sea, the main source of their livelihood. The people are knowledgeable about the currents and phases of the moon and the behavior of fish.

Traditionally, it was the men's duty to go to sea to harvest fish and battle against enemy villages. Women generally stayed on land or along shallow reefs and spent days tending to their homes, family, and taro fields.

In 1922, Koror, today's capital, became the administrative center for all Japanese possessions in the Pacific. The town was then a stylish metropolis with factories, shops, public baths, restaurants, and pharmacies.

During the Second World War, U.S. Marines fought many bloody battles and defeated the stubborn enemy, who were entrenched on Palau's limestone knobs. One of the most atrocious fights took place on Bloody Nose Ridge.

Following Japan's defeat in WWII, the Carolines, Marianas, and Marshall Islands became the United Nations Trust Territories of the Pacific Islands, under U.S. administration.

After three decades as part of the Trust Territory, some 18,766 Palauans chose independent status in 1978 rather than join the Federated States of Micronesia. Palau's national holiday is Constitution Day, July 9, 1979. A Compact of Free Association with the U.S. was approved, not without controversy, in 1986 and ratified in 1993. The United States provides for Belau's defense, and, in turn, nuclear-powered vessels are allowed to dock in the island's ports.

At the invitation of Continental-Air Micronesia in the 1970s, I accompanied a group of press members to sample the company's new hotel, the Palau Travelodge. The hotel perched on a cliff overlooking the mushroom-shaped Rock Islands, not far from ruins of stone images and monoliths hidden in the jungles. These five-ton blocks of basalt once supported immense bais, or meeting houses.

While there, we attended the Palau Fair, featuring colorful island songs and dances and handicraft, such as carved wooden storyboards, woven goods, and batiks.

Palauans were learning to make batik from artist Harry Conley, a retiree who somehow wound up in Micronesia. He was a middle-aged Gauguin, sporting a paint-spattered shirt with the tail hanging over faded shorts and zoris on his feet. While he taught painting to students, pretty Palauan girls vied to satisfy his every need.

To accommodate the 1988 Micronesian Olympic Games, Palau built a swimming pool, volleyball court, basketball stadium, a running track, baseball field, and a gym for weightlifters.

Recently, a golf course proposed for Aimeliik, ran into opposition from the Palau Conservation Society, which went on record to request that the Environmental Quality Protection board deny the permit. The Society said Palau's infrastructure was inadequate to accommodate the 198-acre development, and the erosion caused by construction of the golf course would damage the mangrove swamps.

Although Palau's Foreign Investment Board has issued seven licenses for golf courses, only two, including Palau Golf, appear to be moving forward. The other is planned for Airai State.

Micronesia Investment and Development Corp. contends that a golf course in Palau will bring more visitors to the islands and create jobs for locals. Palau Golf Inc. says the $25 million, 18-hole course in Aimeliik is scheduled to open in 2002. The clubhouse will overlook Koror, Belau's capital.

A new attraction for visitors opened in 2001: the Palau International Coral Reef Center, featuring outdoor display pools and exhibit areas, indoor aquariums, and a gift shop. Additionally, there are research laboratories, an education laboratory for students, a multi-purpose conference/lecture room, scientific research library, and apartments for researchers.

Belau's economy is primarily subsistence agriculture and fishing. The government is the major employer of the work force, relying heavily on financial assistance from the U.S.

Famous for its quarter-ton giant clams, there are 400 varieties of hard corals and 200 species of soft corals in Belau's waters. The sea also has its hazards: sea snakes, stinging jellyfish, venomous cone shells, poisonous lionfish, crown-of-thorns starfish, stonefish, fire coral, crocodiles, sea urchins, and sharks.

Long-run prospects for the tourist sector are optimistic, as Belau is one of the divers' paradises in the world. In October 2000, 44,233 tourists visited Belau. The Bank of Hawaii released in February

2000 its Republic of Palau Economic Report, predicting that Palau's gross national product will jump from 9 to 27 percent annually between the years 2000 and 2004.

Still, all is not rosy in Palau. There are problems with inadequate facilities for solid waste disposal; and threats to the marine ecosystem from sand and coral dredging, illegal fishing practices, and overfishing.

Accommodations include resorts, hotels, motels, and home-visits. Koror has two major department and grocery stores, banks, gifts shops and hotels. Today, a new capital is being built about 20 kilometers northeast of Koror.

The Café@Palau, in downtown Koror across from the post office, has five computers providing Internet access and two computers for general computing use and games.

The Northern Marianas Islands

The Commonwealth of the Northern Marianas (CNMI) hosts a harmonious and eclectic mix of Western and Asian residents. Indigenous Chamorros and Carolinians share the islands with people of the Philippines, Korea, Thailand, China, Japan, Micronesia, India, and the United States.

This self-governing commonwealth is composed of 22 islands and islets in the Mariana Islands, a chain of volcanic mountain peaks and uplifted coral reefs. The Northern Marianas have a land area of 184 square miles. The principal islands are Saipan, 47 square miles; Tinian 39 square miles; and Rota, 33 square miles. These islands, together with Alamagan and Agrihan, are inhabited.

Rota, the southernmost island, consists of a volcanic base capped with coral limestone, giving it a terraced appearance. Four southern islands, Farallon de Medinilla, Saipan, Tinian, and Aguijan, are composed of limestone and have gently rolling elevations and few mountains.

The islands farther north are volcanic peaks. Mount Pagan erupted in 1922 and again in 1981, 1983, and 1988; Farallon de Pajaros, also called Urucas, the northernmost of the Marianas, and Asuncion are active volcanoes. Agrihan volcano, the highest of the Northern Mariana group, rises to 3,165 feet.

The Northern Marianas enjoy a tropical marine climate with abundant year-round sunshine and refreshingly clean air and water. The average year-round temperature of 84 degrees Fahrenheit, an average humidity of 79 percent, gentle northeast trade winds, and occasional rain showers create a nearly perfect climate.

The islands have more than forty indigenous and introduced bird species, rare deer, monitor lizards, and fruit bats. Despite the islands' proximity to Guam, the Brown Tree snakes do not plague the Northern Marianas, although a few snakes have arrived in Saipan on airplanes and ships.

The surrounding coral reefs abound with tropical fish, marine turtles, and manta rays. The oceans are home to marlin, mahi-mahi, tuna, barracuda, Ulua, and bottom fish. The islands are afire with colorful hibiscus, orchids, ironwood, banyan, tulip, papaya, banana, plumeria, and flame trees.

Saipan

From the air, Saipan, the capital of CNMI, sprawls like a friendly dog snoozing in the sun, legs stretching eastward. Flaming trees line pine-fringed beaches that taper into limeade lagoons, where azure waves crash over coral reefs.

For nearly fifteen years, the Chamorros of the Northern Marianas fell under the administration of Germany, which also acquired the Marshall Islands and the Caroline Islands. Germany encouraged establishment of Catholic and Protestant missions. One way or another, Germany by 1900 was mistress of a miniature Pacific empire, except American-owned Guam.

Germany tried to make the islands profitable, concentrating on the production of copra and tinkered with cotton-planting. Unlike the Spaniards, the Germans did not bring a garrison force. The German governor on Saipan tackled problems of public works, health, safety, and education. He established an agricultural experiment station and imported two foresters and seeds from Berlin. He dredged Tanapag Harbor so trading ships could call at Saipan. The First World War ended German administration in the Northern Marianas.

Saipan was the scene of blood-drenched WWII battles in the American campaign to retake this Pacific stronghold from Japanese hands. At Invasion Beach, a humble helmet atop a cross marks the spot where the Second and Fourth Marine Divisions charged ashore on June 15, 1944. While liberating Saipan, 14,224 U.S. soldiers, sailors, and marines were killed or wounded.

The interior jungles harbor World War II armaments, aircraft, and graveyards of thousands of American and Japanese troops. Hulks of sunken ships lie offshore.

From 1949 to 1962 in Saipan, the Central Intelligence Agency (CIA) operated a top-secret enclave, under cover of the Naval Technical Training Unit (NTTU). The CIA-backed NTTU trained Nationalist Chinese guerillas there, and supported China's preparations to invade mainland China from Taiwan. NTTU built a $20-million base in the central mountains of the island. The project was so secret that official visitors were flown from Guam to Tinian and taken by M-boat to Saipan. Washington closed NTTU in 1962.

When the Interior Department resumed jurisdiction over the Northern Marianas from the Navy in the early 1960s, the Trust Territory of the Pacific (TTPI) headquarters was moved from Guam into the CIA's former concrete offices and residences on Saipan.

Americans in Micronesia, even if forewarned, could not have any idea of what they were getting into when they cast their lot with a handful of American executives, office workers, teachers, doctors, and construction engineers on the islands.

I was among those early American civil servants contracted to work for TTPI in Saipan. I was housed in the single employees' Donnihill Apartments, the former CIA's barracks, high up on Capitol Hill. The road to Capitol Hill climbs from sea level up around steep hairpin curves and past a quarry of coral rock used to build roads. During tropical rains, the coral aggregate is slippery, and maneuvering the curves is hair-raising.

A short hike beyond Donnihill is 1,554-foot Mount Tagpachau, Saipan's highest point. During World War II, Chamorros hid religious icons in hillside caves there.

Only days before I arrived in Saipan, a typhoon swept across the island, stripping leaves from bushes and trees. Olive Horne, a teacher from Philadelphia and my upstairs neighbor, hid in a kitchen cabinet during the Christmas storm.

When I moved into the unair-conditioned singles' quarters, I was told that Americans must hire maids to clean their apartments and take care of their laundry because the tropical heat was debilitating to Statesiders. I had never had a maid in my life, but I figured, when in Rome. . . .

One day, Maria, a middle-aged Saipanese woman, knocked on my door and offered her one-day-a-week services for $1.50. I accepted. She washed my clothes, ironed, changed bed linens, and mopped the tile floors in the kitchen, livingroom, bedroom, and bath. Sometimes I'd notice items disappearing, such as a bottle of my favorite Hawaiian perfume. I'm sure Maria or her teenage daughter, who used to help her, "borrowed" it. Micronesians, as well as Polynesians, don't concern themselves with personal possessions; they believe in community property. If I left any food in the refrigerator that I planned to eat for lunch or dinner, it was gone by the time I came home from work.

We American employees on Saipan learned to disregard the nasty shrews crawling through the unscreened wooden louvers placed close to the floor and ceiling of the apartments so the cool night air could circulate.

In my day, roads on the 47-square-mile island were sparsely

traveled by surplus jeeps, derelict junkers, free-ranging cows, and carabao carts. There were no traffic lights. The custom was to smile and raise two fingers from the steering wheel to greet passing drivers.

There was one store, Joe Ten's, owned by Jose Tenorio. There we could buy food, beverages, hardware, cars, fishing licenses, and rural mailboxes, even though we had to pick up our mail at the post office.

In the '60s, we were lucky to buy Spam® and Australian corned beef, cabbage, and potatoes, and we groaned over tough beef imported from Japan. We bought fresh bread at the bakery and eggs from a poultry farm on Beach Road. On Fridays, we'd dicker on the docks for shrimp, lobster, and tuna caught by fishermen. There was a plethora of Chivas Regal and Seagrams at $1.75 a bottle.

On the interisland road, the benighted ghosts of Amelia Earhart and Fred Noonan haunt the old Japanese prison hidden in the boonies. Nearby is a village where Carolinians, relocated after a tidal wave devastated their atoll, live in shacks and wear traditional grass skirts and thus.

North in the Marpi area, Navy Explosive Ordnance Demolition (EOD) teams, in the '60s, attempted to get rid of unexploded ammunition by blowing up a dump. As a result, live ammunition spewed in every direction without being detonated. Many areas were declared off-limits, but we employees tiptoed guilelessly through fields of live 60-mm mortar shells to explore Marpi's beaches.

Micronesians used to fish with explosives and frequently had their fingers blown off. While searching for shiny playthings, boys removed brass burling bands from live shells and often lost their hands or arms.

Demolition teams have cleared Marpi, making it so safe that honeymooners and executives wearing silly hats and shorts hit golf balls across former shrapnel fields.

Young Japanese now snap pictures at Peace Memorial Park. Bursting with the joy of life, these tourists are too young to know that their ancestors had forced Saipanese to work in sugar cane fields, producing ammo and fuel for Japanese military forces. They clap and bow before shrines honoring their ancestral war dead. They learn history from maps at the Last Command Post, where in 1944 Hirohito's commanders made a final stand before committing harikari.

Shell-scarred Banzai Cliff stands as a reminder of the bloody campaign when U.S. forces attacked Imperial troops in June 1944. From 50,000 to 74,000 Japanese soldiers and civilians opted for suicide by leaping from the craggy rock cliffs 800 feet below into the sea.

Saipan's east coast is dotted with tranquil coves and pink coral beaches. At the Blue Grotto, expert divers climb 100 feet down a steep rope stairway over a limestone scarp. Below, they swim amid starfish and damselfish and blue and lace corals in an inky pool connected to the ocean by two passageways. Cowries, spider conchs, and driftwood wash onto the warm sands of secluded Profile, Tank, Wing, and Marine Beaches.

On the southeast tip of the island, history buffs bushwhack through tangan-tangan to explore a Japanese pillbox and ancient latte stones near Obyan Beach.

During my 1990 visit to Guam, Dorothy Horn and I flew to Saipan, where she rented a car so we could tour the island. It was my first trip back to Saipan in twelve years.

Gone were the friendly gestures drivers used to make to other drivers they passed on the road. Nowadays, motorists careened in and out of traffic behind windshields tinted like gangsters' sunglasses. The six-mile-long Beach Road, once alive with carabao carts and rusty old American cars, was now jammed bumper-to-bumper with yellow school buses, 4-by-4s, and Toyota sedans.

Modern mini-malls and hotels of the honky-tonk '50s Waikiki variety bordered both sides of the two-lane Beach Road. Behind rows of motels, hotels, and restaurants, basked the main village of Chalan Kanoa, a dusty collection of houses, banks, offices, and general stores, built with concrete walls and corrugated tin roofs.

At Duty Free Shoppers, Ltd., Japanese tourists snatched up designer shirts, perfume, watches, and Scotch—possessions as out of reach for them at home as membership in a mega-priced Tokyo golf club.

Most tourists stay in Garapan, which claims to have the world's most equable temperatures: from 67 to 88 degrees Fahrenheit.

Garapan has changed from its pre-war role as a military port, where restaurants, geisha houses, a hospital, jail, and railroad terminal catered to 29,000 Japanese expatriates. During one of my moves in Guam, a box disappeared that contained a photo album given to me by Saipanese friends. In the album were historical, irreplaceable photographs of people, activities, and installations of Japanese-occupied Garapan. Though movers denied they had lost the box, I've often wondered whether it had been stolen so I couldn't duplicate or publish the pictures.

In the shadow of new beachfront hotels lies The War In The Pacific Park, where graceful palms and poincianas shade rusty tanks and guns collected from battlefields around the island.

Now, seaside lots sell for as much as Malibu ocean frontage. This Nipponized resort offers air-conditioned rooms, color TVs, swimming pools, tennis courts, golf courses, duty-free shops, shooting galleries, and karaoke clubs.

Farther north, feathery ironwood trees framed Mañagaha Island, a two-mile boat ride across the limeade lagoon. Here, islanders and visitors picnic, explore sunken war relics, and share a kaleidoscopic seascape with stonefish, puffers, octopus, shrimp, eels, manta rays, and sea turtles.

In 1990 when Dorothy drove past a factory building, she told me that hundreds of Asians had been brought to Saipan, as well as to Yap, to work in textile and clothing plants. The blouses and other goods made are sold in the States and labeled "Made in USA—Saipan, Mariana Islands" and "Inspected by Soo Lin."

Some 40,000 foreign contract workers, mostly from China, Bangladesh, and the Philippines, were imported to Saipan to work in the garment industry that exploits Saipan's exemption from a number of American labor and immigration controls. This allows the garment factories, mostly run by Chinese or South Korean firms, to pay foreign laborers substantially less than the minimum wage, but still export nearly $1 billion worth of clothes annually to American markets, free of duties and quotas that usually apply to products made in China and Korea.

In 1998 the factories in Saipan were criticized for being sweat shops, using slave labor. These workers are like indentured labor, and the Northern Marianas administration is being pressured to clean up the sweatshop practices or face a federal takeover of immigration and labor controls. Some workers paid a $2,800 recruitment fee in China. One Bangladesh woman paid a $6,000 recruitment fee.

Abuses of contract workers are widespread. Asian women, lured to the islands to work as maids or in the factories and farms, are physically and sexually abused. Some women are forced to work as prostitutes in Saipan. One 14-year-old Filipina, who came to Mariana Islands in 1995 to be a dancer, was forced to dance nude.

The Northern Marianas garment workers' law suit against major national retailers was settled in March 2000. The companies were to pay about $5.7 million to workers and set up a monitoring system.

Three Saipan nightclubs–Club Happiness, Maytenth Club, and Club Micronesia–were ordered to pay their employees $2.75 million for time the club's waitresses were restricted during nonworking hours spent in confinement in their barracks in 1990 and 1991.

Today, Saipan's thirty-five hotels are located all over the island, from the capital of Chalan Kanoa to outlying villages. Accommodations include the Aqua Resort Club Saipan, Chalan Kanoa Beach Club, Dai-Ichi Hotel Saipan Beach, Hafadai Beach Hotel, Holiday Inn Saipan Resort Club, Hotel Nikko Saipan, Pacific Gardenia Hotel, and Pacific Islands Club. The Hyatt Hotel opened in late 1997, as well as the $80 million, 460-room Le Meridien Saipan Resort and Spa.

The Aquarius Beach Tower, an all-suite hotel, opened in Chalan Kanoa on the ocean front and beach protected by coral reefs. The Tower is located fifteen minutes from the dock where visitors board the Tinian Express for a quick trip to the Dynasty Casino.

Golf enthusiasts flock to the Coral Ocean Point Resort Club, Kingfisher Golf Links, LaoLao Bay Golf Resort, Mariana Country Club, and Saipan Country Club. Increased hotel occupancy in early 2001 means increased golf activity, much to the glee of resort managers.

The Pacific Mall was built on Navy Hill, once the site of an abandoned lighthouse, Navy housing, and the Saipan Hotel. The mall includes a Liberty House store, Foot Locker, Radio Shack, Sharper Image, Blockbuster Video, Baskin Robbins, Kentucky Fried Chicken, plus five movie screens.

JoeTen Department Store and Supermarket in Chalan Kanoa have been going strong since World War II. These retail stores are run by Jose Tenorio, head of a large Saipanese family.

There are so many restaurants on Saipan these days that the Marianas Visitors Authority lists them by ethnic specialties: Chamorro, American, Japanese, Chinese, Korean, Filipino, Thai, Italian, Mexican, Mongolian, Spanish, and French. Fare ranges from American hamburgers and fried chicken to Spanish rice and tortillas, from Chamorro coconut crab and fruit bar or octopus, to Japanese sushi and tempura.

Dorothy and I ate delicious shrimp and vegetable sukiyaki and shared a piece of Kahlua and pecan pie for lunch at the Pacific Gardenia Hotel, on the beach in Saipan.

While on island, we learned that businessmen Henry M. Sablan and Ben M. Sablan had opened a $2 million cultural center in Chalan Kanoa in August 1989. This facility included a cockfighting area and a small zoo.

Water sports are, of course, dominant in the islands: jet skiing; charter boats; sea walks under water; glass bottom boats; parasailing; wind surfing/Hobie Cats; snorkeling; diving; fishing; trolling for marlin, mahi-mahi, barracuda, jack, and tuna; submarine cruises; and sunset dinner cruises.

Saipan's first tourists were Japanese who collected bones of their ancestors killed in battle. Some 654,000 Japanese visited Saipan in 1995. The visitors bureau expected a million visitors in the year 2000, and by October, the Marianas Visitors Authority reported that 439,792 visitors had arrived so far that year.

The tropical sun, sand, and sea, as well as the lack of a visa requirement, bring tourists to the Northern Marianas, often from some unexpected locales as Vladivostok, Russia.

The U.S. Postal Service held a ribbon-cutting and dedication ceremony in January 2000 for its new 13,564-square-foot post office in Chalan Kanoa. It houses 5,500 postal boxes. And the same month, the Saipan Chamber of Commerce celebrated its 40 years of existence.

Annual events on Saipan include the Garapan Street Market, swim meets, windsurfing, runs, boxing, the Annual Flame Tree Arts Festival, Taste of the Marianas, volleyball, walks, Liberation Day Festival, and the unusual Annual Snow Festival, during which snow is flown in from Japan.

Saipan is served by Asiana Airlines, Continental Micronesia, Japan Airlines, Northwest Airlines, and inter-island service by Freedom Air and Pacific Island Aviation.

Tinian

Only six miles southwest of Saipan, Tinian consists of a series of layered limestone plateaus covered by tangan-tangan. Tinian was once the world's greatest producer of cane sugar, but only scattered wild clumps of it grow today.

U.S. and Asian fishing boats use Tinian's spacious harbor to transfer tuna caught in the waters to refrigerated freighters bound for U.S. canneries. This presence, together with explosive-laden vessels of the U.S. Military Sealift Command stationed here, explains the number of bars with Filipina hostesses in San Jose, the main city.

Before World War II, Tinian had a population of 15,000 Japanese and Korean civilians. All were repatriated. In 1948 the inhabitants of the present capital of San Jose were resettled there from Yap. The island's current population is about 2,631.

Tinian was also the site of a Tinian School for displaced Japanese and Korean children in the Mariana Islands. In 1941, the U.S. Navy officials found that only twelve officers in the entire service were fluent in Japanese. The Navy trained Americans in Japanese, producing a cadre of 1,100 men and women who served as interpreters, translators, and code breakers. These veterans shared a common starting point: the University of Colorado (C.U.) at Boulder, which became the site for the U.S. Navy Japanese Language School from 1942 to 1944. Until 1940, the school had been located in Tokyo. In 1941, the program was transferred to Berkeley, but the internment of Japanese ancestry people on the west coast of the U.S. following the Pearl Harbor attack deprived the Berkeley program of most of its teachers, forcing Naval officials to search for an alternative site. One of the students of the C.U. language program ran the Tinian School.

In 1944, American Seabees began rebuilding a captured Japanese airstrip at the north end of Tinian. Less than one year later, North Field was the largest airfield in the world, with four vast 2,600-meter runways, where a total of 19,000 combat missions launched against Japan. Two divided highways were built across Tinian to carry bombs from the port to the airport. As the island is shaped something like Manhattan, GIs named the roads Broadway, 8th Avenue, and 42nd Street.

A marker beside one of the runways indicates the pit where the world's first atomic bomb was loaded into an American B-29, the Enola Gay, to be dropped on Hiroshima on August 6, 1945. Some large concrete Japanese buildings and bunkers are hidden in the brush nearby. To the west is Invasion Beach, where 15,000 U.S. soldiers landed on July 24, 1944.

The U.S. military pulled out of Tinian after the war, but today is making a comeback. In 1983, everything north of the present airport was leased for the next fifty years. The island is already being used for amphibious exercises by Okinawa-based Marines.

Japanese visitors, the mainstay of the tourist business, visit the historical House of Taga and Taga Beach, as well as WWII sites and memorials, such as the Atomic Bomb Pit, the Shinto Shrine-American Memorial, a SeaBee Monument, and the former Japanese communications station. This latter structure is now the slaughterhouse of the Bar K ranch, built by Guam's businessman, Ken Jones, on leased land. Jones used to run 4,500 beef cattle across a third of the island.

At Suicide Cliff on the southeast side of Tinian, die-hard Japanese troops held out for three months after the rest of Tinian had fallen. There is a Japanese peace memorial here now.

Gambling was legalized in 1990 in Tinian. Residents want to develop a mini-Las Vegas to bolster the island's economy. The first casino opened in 1995, but closed a few months later.

Tinian's Gaming Commission issued licenses in 1997 to the Hong Kong Entertainment (Overseas) Investments Ltd. and CNMI Touring and Entertainment Inc, owned by a Philippine national and a Hong Kong importer-exporter. Both groups planned to open $100 million, 5-star, hotel-casinos.

Today, the Tinian Dynasty Hotel and Casino welcomes gamblers to its opulent structure. Past the marble foyer are the Jackpot Lounge, nonstop games of baccarat and roulette, a recreation center, gym, and tennis courts. Hotel guests enjoy ocean views from their suites, serviced by a multilingual staff from twenty-two nations.

Other accommodations on Tinian are the Fleming Hotel and two smaller hotels. Restaurants offer American, Japanese, Chinese, and Korean food at the casino. Activities include triathalons, fishing, bike racing, Thai boxing, and fiestas.

Rota

Rota, southwest of Tinian, is smaller than Guam, but similar in geology, flora, and fauna. Rota's years of isolation have preserved the most authentic Chamorro culture and traditions in the Marianas. Residents feel that the economic goals of tourism must tie in with preservation of their culture and environment.

Rota is the last Chamorro community which continues to wave and smile to friends and strangers as they pass one another by car or on foot on the road. Rota's main city is Songsong, and the island's population is 3,500.

Rota's Mayor Benjamin Manglona, former lieutenant government of the CNMI, has had village streets paved, built a hospital, and beautified the island with parks, monuments, and statuettes.

For years, residents made a good living by selling freshly grown fruit and vegetables to Air Mike passengers who stopped there briefly on flights between Saipan and Guam. A ground-breaking ceremony was held in October 2000 for the $3.3 million Rota runway Rehabilitation Project. Construction was expected to be completed in July 2001.

Recently, Rota's forests have been cleared to make way for three golf courses owned by Japanese companies. A Japanese marketing company in 2000 visited the Rota Resort and Country Club to look at the possibility of converting 15 or 20 units to time sharing to accommodate Japanese golfers. Located on the coast with magnificent views, the resort is called Micronesia's best kept secret. It nestles on a green hillside with panoramic views of the ocean and more than 560 acres of coconut trees, flowers, and birds. It features American, Chamorro, Japanese, and Filipino restaurants; a luxury pool with swim-up bar; and poolside massages. The country club has an 18-hole golf course, as well as ocean views and lush jungle backdrop.

Rota Resort has maintained the highest per-night rate for its hotel units in the Mariana Islands at $185, and has seen the number of golf rounds for the local market, mainly Guam, grow by 14 percent in 2001. Overnight golf packages are available to Rota with Freedom Air and Pacific Island Airways.

The island has a small airport, 100 hotel rooms, a golf course, and good beaches for swimming and diving.

Historical and cultural sites of Rota include the shipwreck of the *Santa Margarita;* Taga Stone Quarry; Mt. Tapingot, called Wedding Cake Mountain; a Japanese World War II locomotive and cannons; sugar factory ruins; the zoo; and the Peace Memorial Park.

Pinatang Park features a natural salt water swimming pool with bridges, water slides, picnic tables, and a giant salt water aquarium. There is a wildlife conservation area that preserves coconut crabs, fruit bars, and deer. A bird sanctuary protects hundreds of marine birds.

Annual events include bike races, volleyball, swimming, fishing, marathons, and fiestas.

Farallon de Medinilla

This Northern Mariana island, home to twelve species of migratory birds, is concerned about naval bombing exercises. Bombing began quietly in 1976 on the uninhabited 200-acre island.

The northern end of the island, about fifty acres, is designated a non-impact zone, which means the Navy cannot bomb that area. Much of the island's bird population lives in this zone. The birds are continuing to breed, but they're taking a beating.

In 1996, the U.S. Fish and Wildlife Service refused to issue the Navy a permit to continue to bomb the island, but the Navy claimed the migratory bird act didn't apply to federal agencies. In 2000 a lawsuit was filed in Washington, D.C., by the Earthjustice

AFTERWORD

Guam certainly has changed in the last century. Outrigger canoes and carabao carts have been replaced by motor boats and Toyotas. Many old Chamorro words, as well as their calendar, in which two months were named for fishing seasons, have disappeared. Traditional customs, such as *manngingi*, kissing the hand of elders to show respect and humility, have practically been forgotten.

When I first arrived in Guam in 1965, there were no buildings higher than two stories, no elevators, a handful of civilian restaurants, a dozen military clubs, no tourists to speak of, and one traffic light.

In the past two decades, new traffic lights and high-rise buildings have been erected helter-skelter, and rents and property taxes have skyrocketed, raising Guam's cost of living above Hawaii's.

Today, Guam's blue skies, sunshine, warm ocean water, clean beaches, history, culture, golf, water sports, duty-free shopping, excellent food, friendly people, and first-class hotels draw more than one million tourists, mostly Japanese, each year.

But the more things change, the more they stay the same. Since the Second World War, Guam has progressed economically from a third-world to a first-world territory, despite Government of Guam's manifold inadequacies: budget woes, power outages, mercurial telephone system, gridlocked roads, and inadequate health-care.

These problems haven't changed much in the new millennium. They've just "become more sophisticated," according to *Pacific Daily News* Publisher Lee Webber.

GovGuam spends 80 to 85 percent of its budget on salaries,

leaving almost nothing left for roads, schools, water systems, parks, and recreation areas.

Yet, compared with other United States' territories, Guam looks good. The June 1992 Interior Department report on the State of the Islands concluded, "The Government of Guam is perhaps the best administered of the U.S. insular governments."

The Department of Public Works hasn't solved the problem of the enormous growth of vehicles. Tens of thousands of Japanese-made trucks and cars were imported in the '80s. By 1990, 100,796 vehicles were registered to a population of 133,152. These days, the number of cars on Guam equals the population figures.

The island's main road is outdated, but it is difficult to cut into a mountainside or expand a highway into the ocean. Marine Drive's six traffic lights from Agaña to Tamuning don't do much to ease the non-stop, snail-like traffic at peak hours. The island-wide speed limit is 35 miles per hour, unless otherwise posted, but drivers rarely reach that speed in this congested area.

One local politician said Guam's highways have become war zones. Chamorros seem to have lost respect for one another on highways, he said, and their social code of behavior and respect seem to have eroded dramatically.

Unfortunately, violent crime has reared its ugly head on Guam. When I lived there, two of my news beats as a reporter were the police station and federal and local courts.

The police blotter was always filled with arrests for driving under the influence of alcohol, possession of drugs, prostitution, robberies, and bar brawls. Many of the court cases concerned disputes over land ownership or zoning rights. Once I covered a sensational case in which a local businessman was acquitted of murdering his girlfriend by beating her head against a fan's metal blades.

As tourism increased, muggings of visitors became more frequent along the hotel strip in Tumon Bay. During my 1990 visit, I was surprised when friends warned not to drive to Cabras Island alone, day or night, because it wasn't safe. One of my regular beats used to be Cabras Island, where activities at the USO, the Seaman's Club, and maritime news were fodder for my weekly columns. The area has become a hangout for gangs and thugs.

In March 2001, a violent shooting took place at the Seventh-Day Adventist Clinic. A former employee killed a nurse and his wife, from whom he was separated, before he was fatally wounded by police. Four other victims recovered from gunshot wounds.

When the dockets of Guam's criminal courts became more and more jammed up, the need for additional detention facilities was apparent. In late 2000, two new facilities were opened, one in Hagåtña and the other in Mangilao.

The Air Force Base, Navy base, and nine other Defense Department facilities cover one-third of Guam. Military personnel and dependents account for one-fifth of the population, and federal and territorial administrations employ half the civilian work force.

During the buildup for the Vietnam War, Guam had dozens of B-52s at Andersen Air Force Base. There were bomb trucks roaring down Marine Drive from Naval Station north to Andersen. Guam had a submarine base, a viable Naval Air Station, busy Navy Communications Station, a Naval Magazine, Naval Hospital, public works, and ship repair facility.

Since 1994, the military presence on Guam has been downsized. Part of Guam's denuded military force was created by an agreement, signed by the United States and Japan, that allows U.S. troops, planes, and ships to be stationed in Japan and Okinawa. Under this relationship, the U.S. helps provide for the defense of Japan. In return, the Japanese government pays billions of dollars to maintain this defense posture.

There are signs that the U.S. military now recognizes the importance of Guam in the Western Pacific, and it's not about to leave the island.

The Nimitz Hill headquarters of Commander Naval Forces

Marianas, Fleet Weather Central, and Naval Air Station are gone. The Naval Air Station was closed and Brewer Field was transferred to civilian control.

Agaña is almost a ghost town since GovGuam offices moved to Tiyan, the former Naval Air Station. GovGuam offices at Tiyan include the Chamorro Land Trust and Language Commissions; Commerce, Agriculture, Education, Labor, Police, Energy, Fire, Power, Parks and Recreation Departments; Public Health and Social Services; Environmental Protection Agency; Veteran's Affairs; and the museum and public library.

The former Naval Station and Naval Magazine were consolidated to form Naval Activities Guam. Raytheon Technical Services Guam, with more than 1,000 employees, officially took over many naval base operations in April 2000. The Navy is seriously thinking of spending $45 million to dredge Apra Harbor.

When the Navy's Ship Repair Facility (SRF) closed, the plants were converted for industrial use. In July 1999, a 21,975-ton floating dry dock, AFDB-8, arrived in Apra Harbor. The dry dock, one of the largest in the United States, was given to GovGuam by the U.S. General Services Agency. GovGuam subleased the dock to the former SRF, which has increased its employees to complete a contract, won in January 2001, to repair the USN *San Jose*.

In mid-August 2001, three Navy ships, with crews totaling 4,500, arrived for a ten-day port visit to Guam for rest and relaxation (R&R) as well as to refuel and restock supplies. The USS *Boxer*, USS *Cleveland*, and USS *Harper's Ferry*, amphibious ships from San Diego, were docked at Apra Harbor, wrapping up a six-month tour of the Western Pacific. While on shore liberty, the crew members were expected to spend $200 a day at restaurants, hotels, and shops. The Guam Chamber of Commerce estimated that the port visit would inject at least $3.5 million into the island's economy.

Another large military port visit was in April 2001 when the USS *Kitty Hawk*, with a crew of 5,000, arrived in Guam to conduct flight training exercises and to give the crew R&R.

At Andersen AFB in late 1988, SAC's 43 Strategic Wing traded its nuclear deterrent role for a conventional mission. In 1990, the Wing's last 14 B-52Gs were phased out, but the Helicopter Combat Support Squadron Five and headquarters staff of the 13th Air Force, which directs air operations throughout the Pacific and Indian Oceans, remain. The 613 Contingency Response Squadron, activated as part of the 13th Air Force, provides the Pacific Command with a mobile, self-sustaining, rapid-response unit which can deploy within 24 hours.

It's apparent that the Air Force is not going to abandon its Andersen Base any time soon. In August 2001, two schools were opened on base for military dependents. The schools, located on ten acres of land, were constructed with $40 million from the federal fiscal 2000 budget. Accommodating more than 1,000 students, the elementary school has 50 classrooms and 35 specialty rooms, and the middle school has 20 core rooms. The campuses will share a cafeteria and multipurpose gymnasium. A full-sized soccer field was built, too.

Through the postwar years, the military's benevolent activities on Guam, such as air and sea search and rescue, weather reporting, and the Naval Hospital, have created jobs and have been priceless assets to the people of Guam.

In 1994, former Governor Joseph A. Ada lobbied in Washington, D.C., for 3,200 acres of Navy base land to be returned to the Guamanians. "I am the governor of a non-self-governing people. I am a member of an ethnic group, a Chamoru, that has been denied the right of self-determination by the colonial powers that have administered us, Spanish and American," Ada said.

Recently, the Committee for Traditional Land, *Komitea Para Tiyuan*, has requested that the U.S. Government return 27,000 acres of prime land that was grabbed by the Japanese after the invasion, then put behind U.S. military fences after the Second World War.

Guamanians began debating their political status back when leaders of the First Guam Congress spoke about the island's right to determine its political destiny. In 1984, the 18th Guam Legislature established the bipartisan Commission on Self-Determination to determine political status. The commission, chaired by Governor Bordallo, called for Guam to remain under U.S. sovereignty, but to allow citizens control of their own government under their own constitution.

In a 1986 plebiscite, Guam residents voted for commonwealth status. The people seek a broad commonwealth arrangement with the U.S. that includes measures of autonomy, such as determining its immigration policies and labor laws and setting minimum wages.

Guamanians hope that the U.S. Congress will approve the Commonwealth Act of Guam, H.R. 1056, introduced by Washington delegate Robert Underwood in the 104th Congress. The Act appears to be dead in the water for now. Even if this Act is passed, Guam would still not become a member of the U.S. Electoral College and citizens could not vote in presidential elections.

According to the coconut grapevine, Underwood is thinking about running run for Governor of Guam at the next election. If he wins, he could be instrumental, with all his Washington connections, in getting the Commonwealth Act passed by Congress.

Underwood, in a recent address at the University of Guam looked toward the future: "The challenge for us in the next millennium is to apply our own genius.... We will launch new initiatives... which will eliminate the last vestiges of our colonial status.... And we will launch these initiatives while being mindful of the proud traditions and culture of our 4,000-year-old launchpad."

Although Guam is tied to the U.S. political structure, it depends on Asia's economy. The island sits astride a critical juncture of sea lanes, air routes, and communication networks between Hawaii and Korea, the Philippines, and Japan. Leaders hope to transform their anchored aircraft carrier, as Guam has been called, into a new Hong Kong, a western Pacific financial center.

In the 21st Century, Guam will continue to play a strategic, geopolitical role in the vast Pacific Ocean as a key communications and support base for Commander in Chief Pacific. The island serves American satellites, space shuttles, war planes and ships, and all other creations of modern man that have followed in Magellan's wake.

The following remarks were made by Governor Carl Gutierrez in a radio address in April 2001. These excerpts sum up the Guamanians' continuing hope for the future.

Governor Carl Gutierrez, in a radio address in April 2001, said, "Guam has a lot going for it. Like the fact that we are among the top ten U. S. destinations for foreign visitors. That we are centrally located just three to five hours' flying time from most of the major cities in Asia and Australia, and our airport ranks 53rd in retail sales among all airports in the world. . . . There's no denying that we've been chosen as the Asia-Pacific hub for a new, state-of-the-art fiberoptic network that will circle the globe; and this news comes on top of the fact that more undersea fiberoptic cable already makes landfall here than anywhere else in the world. There's no arguing the fact that Japan's space agency is building a tracking station here because we have the infrastructure in place to support their mission and we are under the great United States' flag.

"Or that the Navy plans to base attack submarines here . . . its highest ranking officer, the Chief of Naval Operations, visited Guam and told me the island is still strategically important to the United States military and that more great things are being planned for Guam that will help raise the quality of our lives.

"This year, the Asia-Pacific Council of American Chambers of Commerce has chosen to hold its annual meeting in Guam. . . . Next week, the Pacific Asia Travel Association will honor the Guam Visitors Bureau at its annual meeting in Malaysia.

"... I met the vice president of a company that will base a fleet of private corporate jets here by June. I asked him, 'Why Guam?' and without hesitation he replied, 'Because it is the last vestige of American soil before reaching Asia. You are central to the part of the world where we see tremendous growth potential for the future.'

".... we must reach a consensus on how to address the problems facing us today and then put them in the past," Gutierrez concluded.

Good luck, Governor.

In the Foreword, I stated that most Americans know little or nothing about Guam. The residents of San Diego, California, are the exception.

In the early years after the Second World War, a significant number of islanders from American Samoa, Guam, and the Northern Mariana and Marshall Islands came to San Diego County while serving in the U.S. Navy and Marine Corps. After the war, many of these men and their families settled in the area.

In the early 1950s, the Guam Club was established. Today, there are more than 20,000 Guamanians in San Diego County, the largest number anywhere outside of Guam.

While enjoying American culture, Pacific Islanders were challenged by balancing acclimation with preserving their cultures. They want to pass their cultural values, history, and language to their children.

For the communities of about 2,600 descendants of indigenous Hawaiians and 20,000 Guamanians in San Diego, retaining their native languages has been difficult. While growing up in Guam schools, children weren't allowed to speak Guamanian; they had to speak English. Now, adults in their 30s and 40s don't learn their language, and they want their elders to teach them so they can share it with their children.

Since 1995, the Pacific Islander Festival Association has staged

Pacific Islander Day, which has become a San Diego institution. This is the only time of the year the Pacific Island community—Polynesians, Micronesians, and Melanesians–gets together. During the festival weekend, thousands of San Diegans learn firsthand, through music and dance, about the unique cultures of these Pacific Islanders.

Dear reader, I hope you have enjoyed this armchair trip to Micronesia as much as I've enjoyed relating those exciting years.

In my 2001 reverie, I picture myself sprawling like a gecko on the hot sand of Tarague Beach. When "night cuts day," in the words of a Chamorro poet, the brilliant sun transforms the blue heaven into a mackerel sky of dusky purples, burning reds, and glittering golds. The sun sets like a thunderbolt, and a bedazzling green flash explodes in the sky, then vanishes below the horizon.

While basking in this ethereal beauty, I conclude that although my life on Guam had not been one long fiesta, my good memories outweigh the others. The islanders and their lifestyle cling to me like tangan-tangan in the jungle.

As a long-time Navy civil servant, I was accustomed to listing lessons-learned upon completion of each project. Here are my lessons-learned from island living that I follow to this day.

—Remove shoes when entering my home;

—Store perishable food in the refrigerator, safe from ants, roaches, termites, and lizards;

—Keep cans of Spam® on the emergency shelf;

—Place candles and matches in every room, in case the electricity fails;

—Fill the car's gas tank when it reaches the half-full mark because who knows when the power may go off and gas pumps don't work;

—Keep lids down on toilet seats, in case snakes or other creatures crawl through the pipes;

—Douse finadeni on everything;

—Turn every social occasion into a fiesta; and
—Last, but not least, never forget that GUAM is a four-letter word. That word is GOOD.

-30-

APPENDIX

Information For Travelers

Guam is a duty-free port outside the U.S. Customs Zone and has quality merchandise from all over the world at prices usually below those in the country of origin.

Tourists from the United States can purchase up to $800 of non-U.S.-made goods, which are exempt from duty on returning home. The Antonio B. Won Pat International Air Terminal has a completely stocked duty-free shop. All major hotels have duty-free shops as well.

Entry to Guam

No passport or visa is required of U.S. citizens coming from the U.S. All others must conform to U.S. passport and visa requirements.

More than a decade ago, the U.S. federal government approved the Guam-only visa waiver program. Citizens of 36 countries are allowed entry to Guam without a visa for up to 15 days. Travel onward to other U.S. points is not allowed, except for citizens of Japan and the United Kingdom.

Customs checks are performed upon entry to Guam. Visitors

are allowed to bring into Guam, duty free, three cartons of cigarettes, three bottles of spirits, and small amounts of perfume for personal use.

The U. S. dollar is the currency of Guam and Micronesia.

Air Transportation

International airline carriers serve Guam's $50 million air terminal with connections to major cities. They are Continental Micronesia, Japan Air Lines, Air Nauru, Northwest Airlines, Japan Asia Airways, Korean Air, Thai Airways International, All Nippon Airways, and Philippine Airlines. Domestic airlines also serve the neighboring islands.

Guam's air terminal offers car rental agencies, a currency exchange facility, hotel telephones, and a duty-free shop, as well as a cocktail lounge, restaurant, and coffee shop. Nine food and beverage outlets sell a variety of name-brand food items. Seven locations throughout the terminal showcase local artwork.

The terminal is currently under renovation to accommodate projected passenger and cargo increases. Additions are being made to the present ground transportation facilities, aircraft parking aprons, and aircraft maintenance facilities.

Commercial Port

The Port Authority of Guam is situated within Apra Harbor, a natural lagoon enclosed by a submerged coral bank and a barrier reef on Guam's southwest coastline. The wide harbor entrance, which faces the Philippine Sea, has an average depth of 120 feet.

The commercial port and related facilities cover nearly 87 acres, containing four docking berths, a fuel pier, and the use of two additional berths for large tankers and passenger vessels. There are a 33-acre paved storage yard, 758 stalls for chassis-mounted containers, and a dry dock for ship repair.

Local Transportation

More than 25 tour agencies on Guam have tours with special options. Well-known car rental companies offer American and foreign cars at competitive rates. You can rent a moped, bicycle, or hire a taxi, too. Roads are well marked with numbered route signs, and markers point out scenic and historical sights.

Public Holidays

Public holidays include New Year's Day, Martin Luther King's Birthday, President's Day, Guam Discovery Day (first Monday in March), Good Friday, Easter Sunday, Memorial Day, July 4 Independence Day, Liberation Day (July 21), Labor Day, Columbus Day, Veteran's Day, Thanksgiving, Immaculate Conception (December 8), and Christmas.

Safety Tips

The Guam Visitors Bureau urges visitors to take precautions that they would normally take when visiting any city: don't carry too much cash in public; whenever possible, do not walk alone, and stay on busy, well lit streets. Use only designated crosswalks when crossing a street, and walk against the traffic. Never hitchhike or pick up hitchhikers.

Visitors are urged not to overexpose themselves to the tropical sun's rays, especially between 10 a.m. and 3 p.m., when the ultraviolet rays are strongest. Use a sunscreen and wear sunglasses and hats.

Do not swim in pools or at beaches where there are no lifeguards on duty and never swim alone. Stay close to shore and stay away from the reef, where unseen water currents can be life-threatening. In certain seasons, Guam's beaches attract jellyfish that can cause painful stings to the skin; don't enter the water if you see clear, jelly-like creatures along the shore.

Dorothy Horn's Publications

1994 Restaurants of Guam
Great Classic Spam Recipes of the World
Dorothy Horn's Christmas Treats
A Taste of Guam Calendar
Nibbles, Noshes & Numnums
Gecko Tracks Coloring Book
Stand-up Recipes For One To Eat Over the Sink
Guam's Filipino Recipes
Pacific Islands Club coloring book.

These may be ordered from Dorothy's Kitchen, Box 1554, Agaña, Guam 96910.

Guam Reunion

Guam Reunion, c/o Dee Bellows, 8145 Glen Canyon Court, Citrus Heights, CA 95610, telephone 916-722-5750. Next reunion: May 2002, Sun Harbor Budget Suites, Las Vegas, Nevada, 800-752-1501.

Ponape Pepper

Ponape gourmet pepper—black or white, ground or peppercorns—may be purchased from Island Traders, Box 704, Pohnpei, Federated States of Micronesia, 96941. Telephone 1-800-214-8035, FAX 691-320-2095.

Pacific Islander Festival

For information about the Eighth Annual Pacific Islander Festival in 2002, contact *www.pacificislanders.com* or call 619-699-8797.

For More Information

The Guam Visitors Bureau, 1220 Pale San Vitores Road, Tamuning, Guam 96911. Telephone, 671-646-5278/9. FAX 671-646-8861, website www.visitguam.org.

Guam Visitors Bureau, U.S. Representative, 516 Fifth Avenue, New York, N.Y. 10036. Telephone 212-391-2202 or 1-800-228-GUAM.

Marianas Visitors Authority, P. O. Box 861 Saipan, MP 96950. Telephone 670-664-3200, FAX 670-644-3237. Email *mva@saipan.com*.

Federated States of Micronesia, Department of Economic Affairs, FSM National Government Palikir, Pohnpei FSM 96911. Telephone 691-320-2646, FAX 691-320-5854, *www.visit-fsm.org*.

Marshall Islands Visitors Authority, P. O. Box 1727, Majuro, MH 96960. telephone 692-625-3206, FAX 692-625-3218, Email *tourism@ntamar.com*.

Palau Visitors Authority, Email *pva@palaunet.com*.